Senate Select Committee on Intelligence

Minority Report

**The U.S. Senate Intelligence Committee
Study of the CIA's Detention and Interrogation Program**

The GOP Rebuttal to the Torture Report

I0434372

with an introduction by
Rand Koch

Senate Select Committee on Intelligence

June 20, 2014

Revised for redaction December 5, 2014

Edited for this special edition
December 30, 2014

The GOP Rebuttal to the Torture Report

Editor's Introduction

This is the third book in what is commonly called the "Senate Torture Report." The full title is, the *Senate Intelligence Committee's Study of the Central Intelligence Agency's Detention and Interrogation Program — Minority Views.*

It's the one where the minority, Republican members explain what was wrong with the first, main book, written exclusively by the majority, Democrat members.

While the book itself is available elsewhere, this version is completely re-formatted, designed for easy reading, and coordinates easily with the ebook version. It also includes a few URLs to referenced source documents. As one would expect, page numbers for references within this book were properly adjusted.

I created this special edition because I believe it may prove the most important book of the three. Other than these minor additions and adjustments, *I did not change the contents of the report itself.*

Some critics of the CIA program oppose torture, as we all should, and in doing so they define torture as somewhere below what the CIA has been doing. The danger in broadening the definition of torture lies in forgetting the horrors that torture can be. It is reasonable to say that one believes waterboarding is torture even when limited to a certain number of pours over a certain number of seconds. It is harder to say that one single pour is already beyond the legal limit.

As if the critics didn't have enough to complain about, it is often said that mastermind Khalid Shaikh

Mohammed was waterboarded 183 times. But this means 183 *pours*, **not** 183 *sessions*, and there were strict limits on how many pours may be done per session.

There are already critics who say the Obama administration is guilty of torture because forced feeding is used for some detainees at Guantanamo who would otherwise starve themselves to death. This is to take torture unseriously while there are real victims, including children, having their eyes gouged out by America's enemies.

It is one thing to say we would not use torture to save a thousand American lives; it is quite another to say we would not go two steps below torture to save a thousand American lives.

The most prominent claim made by the first book is that enhanced interrogation was ineffective. Did it work?

Most of us who are interested in this report have heard of the interrogation tactic known as "Good Cop / Bad Cop," also known as "Mutt and Jeff."

One interrogator screams at the criminal, intimidating him as far as the law allows. A second interrogator comes in, treating him gently. He may even act like he's protecting him from the overly-aggressive "Bad Cop." This is an old trick. It is still legal for use in the Army Field Manual so long as the interrogator playing "Bad Cop" remains within the limits of the law.

I am not saying that this was all a matter of "Good Cop / Bad Cop." I am merely illustrating a point.

The point is this: Nobody would say that "Good Cop / Bad Cop" never works if it turns out that criminals only confess to the interrogators who play "Good Cop." To say that the "Bad Cop" had no role in the process would miss the point completely.

Indeed, former CIA National Clandestine Service Director Jose A. Rodriguez said they did not even ask questions during the interrogation phase that they did not already know the answers to. It was only after the terrorist was "broken" that the debriefing phase would begin, and they could then start using normal techniques again.

Of course, this isn't "Good Cop / Bad Cop." But these CIA interrogators were not investigating simple crimes either. They were working to save lives, and to stop further attacks which would have prevented the economy and society from functioning.

*

A few things one should know when reading this book:

Information that was not declassified is striked out, appearing like this " █████ ."

The number of characters describing blocked-out text is given only to convey what might be a general idea of the actual length. It should not be thought to represent the actual length of the text, or even necessarily a close approximation.

Nearly every paragraph in this document is preceded by a classification symbol. It is not important for most readers, but it is retained for historical purposes. A list of common classification codes follows this introduction.

Rand Koch

December 30, 2014

Classification symbols:

(FOUO)	For Official Use Only; sensitive, but unclassified; may be shared only with individuals with a need to know.
(U)	UNCLASSIFIED
(C)	CONFIDENTIAL
(S)	SECRET
(TS)	TOP SECRET
(S//NF)	SECRET // NOFORN; ("NO FOReign Nationals"); not for non-U.S. citizens, regardless of their clearance level (may also be used with TS designation)
(TS//█████//NF)	TOP SECRET // NOFORN with a codeword blacked out.

Abbreviations:

HPSCI	House Permanent Select Committee on Intelligence
ODNI	Office of the Director of National Intelligence
OLC	Office of Legal Counsel(U.S. Department of Justice)
RDI	Renditions, Detentions, and Interrogations
SSCI	Senate Select Committee on Intelligence

Δ

UNCLASSIFIED

(TOP SECRET// ███████████ //NOFORN)

Senate Select Committee on Intelligence

MINORITY VIEWS OF VICE CHAIRMAN CHAMBLISS JOINED BY SENATORS BURR, RISCH, COATS, RUBIO, AND COBURN *

June 20, 2014

[Revised for Redaction on December 5, 2014] †

* When these minority views were initially written in response to the original Study approved by the United States Senate Select Committee on Intelligence on December 13, 2012, the following members of the Committee signed on to them: Vice Chairman Chambliss joined by Senators Burr, Risch, Coats, Blunt, and Rubio.

† [[Please note that the double-bracketed text in this document is new explanatory text necessitated by substantive modifications to the Study's Executive Summary and Findings and Conclusions that were made *after* our June 20, 2014, Minority Views were submitted to the Central Intelligence Agency for the declassification review. We also note that these Minority Views are in response to, and at points predicated upon, the research and foundational work that underlie the Study's account of the CIA Detention and Interrogation Program. These Views should not be treated as an independent report based upon a separate investigation, but rather our evaluation and critique of the Study's problematic analysis, factual findings, and conclusions.]]

MINORITY VIEWS OF VICE CHAIRMAN CHAMBLISS JOINED BY SENATORS BURR, RISCH, COATS, RUBIO, AND COBURN [1]

(U) EXECUTIVE SUMMARY

(U) In March 2009, the Senate Select Committee on Intelligence ("SSCI" or "Committee") decided, by a vote of 14–1, to initiate a *Study of the Central Intelligence Agency's Detention and Interrogation Program*, (the Study).[2] On August 24, 2009, Attorney General Eric Holder decided to re-open the criminal inquiry related to the interrogation of certain detainees in the Central Intelligence Agency's (CIA) Detention and Interrogation Program ("the Program" or "the Detention and Interrogation Program").[3] Shortly thereafter, the minority withdrew from active participation in the Study when it determined that the Attorney General's decision would preclude a comprehensive review of the Program, since many of the relevant witnesses would likely decline to be interviewed by the Committee. Three years later, on August 30, 2012, Attorney General Holder closed the criminal investigation into the interrogation of certain detainees in the Detention and Interrogation Program.[4] At the end of the 112th Congress, on December 13, 2012, the Committee approved the adoption of the Study's three-volume report, executive summary, and findings and conclusions by a vote of 9–6.[5] On April 3, 2014, by a vote of 11–3, the Committee approved a motion to send updated versions of the Study's executive summary and findings and conclusions to the President for declassification review. [6]

(U) The latest version of the updated Study is a [[6,682]]-page interpretation of documents that, according to the CIA, has cost the American taxpayer more than 40 million dollars and diverted countless CIA analytic and support resources.[7] Contrary to the Terms of Reference, the Study does not offer any recommendations for improving intelligence interrogation practices, intelligence activities, or covert actions. Instead, it offers 20 conclusions, many of which attack the CIA's integrity and credibility in developing and implementing the Program. Absent the support of the documentary record, and on the basis of a flawed analytical methodology, these problematic claims and conclusions create the false impression that the CIA was actively misleading policy makers and impeding the counterterrorism efforts of other federal government agencies during the Program's operation.

(U) THE STUDY'S FLAWED PROCESS

(U) We begin with an examination of the procedural irregularities that negatively impacted the Study's problematic claims and conclusions. First, the Committee's decision not to interview key witnesses led to significant analytical and factual errors in the original and subsequent updated versions of the Study. Second, over the objection of the minority, the Committee did not provide a copy of the draft Study to the Intelligence Community for initial fact-checking prior to the vote to adopt the Study at the end of the 112th Congress. Third, Committee members and staff were not given sufficient time to review the Study prior to the scheduled vote on December 13, 2012. Fourth, the Committee largely ignored the CIA's response to the Study on June 27, 2013, which identified a number of factual and analytical errors in the Study. Fifth, during the summer and early fall of 2013, SSCI majority staff failed to take advantage of the nearly 60 hours of meetings with some of the CIA personnel who had led and participated in the CIA's study response. Instead of attempting to understand the factual and analytical errors that had been identified by the CIA, the majority staff spent a significant portion of the semeetings criticizing the CIA's study response and justifying the Study's flawed analytical methodology. Sixth, the production and release of the updated Study was marred by the alleged misconduct of majority staff and CIA employees in relation to a set of documents known as the "Panetta Internal Review." Finally, Committee members and staff were not given sufficient time to review the updated Executive Summary and Findings and Conclusions prior to the scheduled vote on April 4, 2014.

(U) With the exception of the decision not to interview relevant witnesses, most, if not all, of these procedural irregularities could have been avoided. As will be seen below, the updated Study still contains a significant number factual inaccuracies and invalid claims and conclusions. We believe that many of these problems could have been corrected if the Committee had simply adhered to our established procedural precedents for a report of this importance.

(U) THE STUDY'S PROBLEMATIC ANALYSIS

(U) We found a number of analytical deficiencies in the Study beginning with an inadequate discussion of the context that led to the implementation and operation of the CIA's Detention and Interrogation Program. Also, as an oversight body, this Committee reviews the Intelligence Community's analytic products with an expectation that they will follow certain analytic integrity standards. While these standards do not technically apply to this Committee's oversight products, the values behind these standards are useful in assessing our own analytic tradecraft. When applied to the Study, these standards were helpful in identifying some of the Study's general analytic deficiencies concerning objectivity, independence from political considerations, timeliness, the use of all available intelligence sources, and consistency with proper standards of analytic tradecraft.

(U) Inadequate Context

(U) The Study does very little to provide the context in which the CIA's Detention and Interrogation Program was initiated and operated. It is entirely silent on the surge in terrorist threat reporting that inundated the Intelligence Community following the September 11, 2001, terrorist attacks by al-Qa'ida. It also makes no mention of the pervasive, genuine apprehension about a possible second attack on the United States that gripped the CIA in 2002 and 2003. During our review of the documentary record, we could clearly discern a workforce traumatized by the thousands of lives lost as a result of the September 11, 2001, terrorist attacks, but also galvanized by the challenge of working to ensure such an attack never occurred again.

(U) Inadequate Objectivity

(U) With respect to the standard of objectivity, we were disappointed to find that the updated Study still contains evidence of strongly held biases. John Brennan emphasized this point prior to his confirmation as the Director of the CIA, when he told Vice Chairman Chambliss that, based on his reading of the originally approved Executive Summary and the Findings and Conclusions, the Study was "not objective" and was a "prosecutor's brief," "written with an eye toward finding problems." We agree with Director Brennan's assessments. We also agree with the criticism he relayed from Intelligence Community officials that it was written with a "bent on the part of the authors" with "political motivations."

(U) We found that those biases led to faulty analysis, serious inaccuracies, and misrepresentations of fact in the Study. For example, the Study states, "At no time during or after the aggressive interrogation phase did Abu Zubaydah provide the information that the CIA enhanced interrogation were premised upon, specifically, 'actionable intelligence about al-Qa'ida operatives in the United States and planned al-Qa'ida lethal attacks against U.S. citizens and U.S. interests.'"[8] Specifically, our review of the documentary record revealed that Abu Zubaydah provided actionable intelligence, after he was subjected to "aggressive" interrogation in April[9] and August[10] 2002, that helped lead to the capture of Ramzi bin al-Shibh and other al-Qa'ida associates during the Karachi safe house raids conducted on September 10-11, 2002. These captures effectively disrupted the al-Qa'ida plot to bomb certain named hotels in Karachi, Pakistan, that had been selected because they were frequented by American and German guests.

(U) The Study's lack of objectivity is also evidenced by the uneven treatment of key U.S. officials throughout the report, attacking the credibility and honesty of some, while making little mention of others. For example, former Director George Tenet led the CIA at the outset of the Program, during a period the Study contends was characterized by mismanagement. Tenet authorized the enhanced interrogation techniques, and if the Study is to be believed, headed an organization that withheld information from and misled policymakers in the executive branch and Congress. He is mentioned 62 times in the updated version of the Study's Executive Summary. By comparison, former Director Michael Hayden – who joined the CIA in 2006, after all but two detainees entered the Program and the most severe EITs were no longer in use – is mentioned over 200 times in the Executive Summary and disparaged numerous times. Notably, he was also the only Director to

6

brief the Program to all members of the congressional oversight committees.

(U) Indications of Political Considerations

(U) Ideally, oversight reports should not be distorted or altered with the intent of supporting or advocating a particular policy, political viewpoint, or specific audience."[11] We found indications of political considerations within the Study. For example, the Study uses out-of-context quotes from certain minority members to suggest incorrectly that they supported certain positions taken by the Study. The Study omits additional comments by these same members which contradict the out-of-context statements.

(U) Lack of Timeliness

(U) The analytic integrity standard of timeliness centers on the need to effectively inform key policy decisions. The same could be said for intelligence oversight reports. The updated version of the Study was released for declassification review on April 3, 2014 – more than five years after the Terms of Reference were approved. No version of the Study, updated or otherwise, has ever contained any recommendations. Moreover, there are no lessons learned, nor are there any suggestions of possible alternative measures. This absence of Committee recommendations is likely due to the fact that the key policy decisions about the CIA's Detention and Interrogation Program were decided by President Obama in 2009. Since it does little to effectively inform current policymakers, we found that the Study is not timely.

(U) Inadequate Use of Available Sources of Intelligence

(U) Despite the millions of records available for the Study's research, we found that important documents were not reviewed and some were never requested. We were surprised to learn that the e-mails of only 64 individuals were initially requested to support the review of a program that spanned eight years and included hundreds of government employees. Committee reviews of this magnitude typically involve interviewing the relevant witnesses. Here, these relevant witnesses were largely unavailable due to the Attorney General's decision to re-open a preliminary criminal review in connection with the interrogation of specific detainees at overseas locations. When DOJ closed this investigation in August 2013, however, the Committee had a window of opportunity to invite these relevant witnesses in for interviews, but apparently decided against that course of action. The lack of witness interviews should have been a clear warning flag to all Committee members about the difficulty of completing a truly "comprehensive" review on this subject.

(U) Poor Standards of Analytic Tradecraft

(U) We found numerous examples of poor analytic

tradecraft in the Study. There were instances where the Study did not accurately describe the quality and reliability of the sources of information supporting its analysis. For example, the Study states that a review by the CIA Inspector General (IG) "uncovered that additional unauthorized techniques were used against" a detainee, but the Inspector General report actually said it "heard allegations" of the use of unauthorized techniques and said, "[F]or all of the instances, the allegations were disputed or too ambiguous to reach any authoritative determination about the facts."[12] The Study rarely included caveats about uncertainties or confidence in its analytic judgments. Many of the Study's conclusions and underlying claims are offered as matters of unequivocal fact. As an example, the Study asserts "CIA officers conducted no research on successful interrogation strategies during the drafting of the [Memorandum of Notification], nor after it was issued."[13] Proving a negative is often very difficult, and in this particular case it is difficult to understand how such an absolute assertion can be made without interviewing the affected witnesses or even citing to one documentary source that might support such a claim.

(U) The Study also engaged in little alternative analysis of its claims and conclusions. In many respects, these minority views provide this necessary alternative analysis. For example, the Study is replete with uncited and absolute assertions like "there is no indication in CIA records that Abu Zubaydah provided information on bin al-Shibh's whereabouts."[14] Our review of the documentary record revealed that Abu Zubaydah did provide locational information about bin al-Shibh. As discussed below, Zubaydah made four separate photographic identifications of bin al-Shibh and placed him in Kandahar, Afghanistan, during the November to December 2001 timeframe and provided sufficient information for interrogators to conclude that bin al-Shibh was subsequently with Khalid Shaykh Mohammad (KSM) in Karachi, Pakistan.[15]

(U) Finally, we found instances where claims were supported more by rhetorical devices than sound logical reasoning. For example, in support of the Study's conclusion that the CIA's use of enhanced interrogation techniques were not effective, the Study stated:

> At least seven detainees were subjected to the CIA's enhanced interrogation techniques almost immediately after being rendered into CIA custody, *making it impossible to determine* whether the information they provided could have been obtained through non-coercive debriefing methods.[16]

This statement is a rhetorical attempt to persuade the reader that non-coercive techniques may have been equally or even more successful than the enhanced techniques. It is little more than an appeal to unknowable facts and is not based upon logical reasoning.[17]

(U) ERRONEOUS STUDY CONCLUSIONS

(U) Despite the fact that the CIA response and the summer staff meetings essentially validated our criticisms of the original Study, it appeal's that the updated version of the Study largely persists with many of its erroneous analytical and factual claims. We have used these past eleven weeks to update our own Minority Views and focus our attention on eight of the Study's most problematic conclusions.

(U) Conclusion 1 (The CIA's use of enhanced interrogation techniques was not effective)

(U) This updated conclusion asserts that the "CIA's use of enhanced interrogation techniques was not an effective means of acquiring intelligence or gaining cooperation from detainees.[18] The Study attempts to validate this conclusion by relying upon four faulty premises. The first faulty premise is that "seven of the 39 CIA detainees known to have been subjected to the CIA's enhanced interrogation techniques produced no intelligence while in CIA custody."[19] If true, that means that 82 percent of detainees subjected to enhanced interrogation techniques produced some intelligence while in CIA custody, which is better than the 57.5 percent effectiveness rate of detainees not subjected to enhanced interrogation techniques. Regardless, these statistics do not provide any real insight on the *qualitative* value of the intelligence information obtained. The true test of effectiveness is the value of *what* was obtained – not how much or how little was obtained.

(U) We have already discussed the second faulty premise, which involves a rhetorical appeal to ignorance based on the fact that at least seven detainees were subjected to enhanced interrogation techniques almost immediately after coming into the CIA's custody. Such speculation is not helpful in assessing whether the enhanced interrogation techniques were effective.

(U) The third faulty premise of this ineffective techniques conclusion focuses on the fact that "multiple" detainees subjected to enhanced interrogation techniques "fabricated information, resulting in faulty intelligence."[20] Our documentary review also found that "multiple" detainees who were not subjected to enhanced interrogation techniques also provided fabricated information to their interrogators. The only real inference that can be drawn from these facts is that detainees fabricated information regardless of whether they were subjected to enhanced interrogation.

(U) The final faulty premise used in support of this "effectiveness" conclusion was that "CIA officers regularly called into question whether the CIA's enhanced interrogation techniques were effective, assessing that the use of the techniques failed to elicit detainee cooperation or produce accurate intelligence."[21] While the *opinions* of these unidentified CIA officers may happen to coincide with the Study's first conclusion, there were at least three other CIA officials who held the opposite view – Directors Tenet, Goss, and Hayden.

(U) Conclusion 2 (CIA's Justification for EITs Rested on Inaccurate Effectiveness Claims)

(U) Conclusion 2 states, "[t]he CIA's justification for the use of its enhanced interrogation techniques rested on inaccurate claims of their effectiveness."[22] While our review of the documentary record did reveal some instances of inaccurate effectiveness claims by the CIA, we found that many of the Study's claims related to this conclusion were themselves inaccurate. We reviewed 17 of the 20 cases studies that the Study relies upon to support this flawed conclusion. We examined these case studies in logical groupings (e.g., related to information provided by Abu Zubaydah) using chronological order rather than the Study's confusing "primary" and "secondary" effectiveness representations. This approach helped us better understand how the intelligence resulting from these detainee interrogations was used by the CIA to disrupt terrorist plots and identify, capture, and sometimes prosecute other terrorists.

(U) The Study developed an analytical methodology to examine the effectiveness of the information obtained from the CIA's Detention and Interrogation Program that we found to be both confusing and deeply flawed. Usually, effectiveness is measured by establishing performance metrics that require the collection of pertinent data and the subsequent analysis of such data. For example, in the context of counterterrorism such metrics might include: (1) increased understanding of terrorist networks; (2) identification of terrorists and those providing material support; (3) terrorist captures; (4) terrorist interrogations; (5) disruption of terrorist operations and financing; (6) disruption of terrorist recruitment; (7) reduction in terrorist safehavens; (8) development of counterterrorism assets; (9) intelligence gathering of documents, computer equipment, communications devices, etc.; (10) improved information sharing; and (11) improved foreign liaison cooperation against terrorism. Such metrics could then be compared against the information provided by CIA detainees to assess the relative effectiveness of the Program.

(U) Instead of performance metrics, the Study's analytical methodology creates artificial categories that are used to *exclude* certain detainee information from being considered in an effectiveness assessment of the Program. For example, if the Study found that a detainee subjected to enhanced interrogation had provided similar information during an earlier non-enhanced interrogation, then such information could not be used for assessing the effectiveness of the program. This category appears to have been developed in an attempt to exclude much of the intelligence information provided by Abu Zubaydah after he was subjected to enhanced interrogation in August 2002, since some of the information Abu Zubaydah provided during those interrogations was similar to information he had provided prior to August. However, it turns out that this category is largely inapplicable to Abu Zubaydah's case, because he was subjected to enhanced interrogation by the CIA when he was released from the hospital on April 15, 2002.[23]

(U) Another category of information that the Study's flawed analytical methodology excludes is corroborative information. If a detainee subjected to enhanced interrogation provided information that was already available to the CIA or other elements of the Intelligence Community from another source, then the methodology dictates that such information cannot be considered to support a CIA effectiveness representation. This result occurs even in situations in which the detainee's information clarified or explained the significance of the prior information. Another exclusion category applies if the Study determined that there was no causal relationship between the information obtained from a detainee after the use of enhanced interrogation and the operational success claimed by the CIA. In these case studies, we often found documentary evidence that supported direct causal links between such detainee information and the operational success represented by the CIA. The final category excludes detainee information about terrorist plots when there was a subsequent assessment by intelligence and law enforcement personnel that such plots were infeasible or never operationalized.

(U) This flawed analytical methodology often forced the Study to use absolute language such as, "no connection," "no indication," "played no role," or "these representations were inaccurate." Our review of the documentary record often found valid counter-examples that disproved such absolute claims. We also found that when we invalidated the claims in the initial case studies, there was often a cascading effect that further undermined claims in the subsequent case studies. Here we summarize the claims for the case studies we examined and our alternate analysis of those claims.

(U) The Identification of Khalid Shaykh Mohammad as the Mastermind of the 9/11 Attacks and His "Mukhtar" Alias

(TS// ███████████ //NF) We combined our analysis of these two case studies because they share common facts and analytical issues. The Study claims that "[o]n at least two prominent occasions, the CIA represented, inaccurately, that Abu Zubaydah provided [information identifying KSM as the mastermind of 9/11] after the use of the CIA's enhanced interrogation techniques.[24] We found that neither of the occasions cited with respect to the "Mastermind of 9/11" information were "prominent." The first occasion was not even a CIA representation, but rather a mistake made by the Department of Justice in one of its legal opinions.[25] The second occasion involved a set of November 2007 documents and talking points for the CIA Director to use in a briefing with the President. Although these briefing materials did contain some erroneous information about KSM's interrogation, the Study fails to demonstrate whether this erroneous information was actually briefed to the President during that timeframe.[26]

(TS// ███████████ //NF) The Study also claims that "[i]n at least one instance in November 2007... the CIA asserted that Abu Zubaydah identified KSM as 'Mukhtar' after the use of the CIA's enhanced interrogation techniques.[27] However, this instance is no more "prominent" than the above "mastermind" occasion, because it was contained in the same November 2007 briefing materials used by the CIA Director to brief the President.[28] Again, the Study fails to demonstrate whether this erroneous information was actually briefed to the President during this timeframe.

~~(TS//~~ █████████████████████ ~~//NF)~~ The Study's third claim in relation to this case study is that "[t]here is no evidence to support the statement that Abu Zubaydah's information – obtained by FBI interrogators prior to the use of the CIA's enhanced interrogation techniques and while Abu Zubaydah was hospitalized – was uniquely important in the identification of KSM as the 'mastermind' of the 9/11 attacks."[29] We found considerable evidence that the information Abu Zubaydah provided identifying KSM as "Mukhtar" and the mastermind of 9/11 was significant to CIA analysts, operators, and FBI interrogators. Both the Congressional Joint Inquiry into the 9/11 Attacks and the 9/11 Commission discussed the importance of this information to the Intelligence Community in understanding KSM's role in the attacks and in the al-Qa'ida organization.

(U) The Thwarting of the Dirty Bomb / Tall Buildings Plot and the Capture of Jose Padilla

~~(TS//~~ █████████████████ ~~//NF)~~ The Study falsely claims that "[a review of CIA operational cables and other CIA records found that the use of the CIA's *enhanced interrogation techniques played no role* in the identification of 'Jose Padilla' or the thwarting of the Dirty Bomb or Tall Buildings plotting. CIA records indicate that: ... (3) Abu

Zubaydah provided this information to FBI officers who were using rapport-building techniques, in April 2002, more than three months prior to the CIA's 'use of DOJ-approved enhanced interrogation techniques,'..."[30] However, CIA records clearly indicate that during the time period when FBI agents and CIA officers were working together in rotating, round-the-clock shifts, some of the interrogation techniques used on Abu Zubaydah included *nudity*,[31] *liquid diet*,[32] *sensory deprivation*,[33] and *extended sleep deprivation*.[34] Specifically, sleep deprivation played a significant role in Abu Zubaydah's identification of Jose Padilla as an al-Qa'ida operative tasked to carry out an attack against the United States. Abu Zubaydah provided this information to FBI agents during an interrogation session that began late at night on April 20, 2002, and ended on April 21, 2002. Between April 15, 2002 and April 21, 2002, *Abu Zubaydah was deprived of sleep for a total of 126.5 hours (5.27 days) over a 136 hour (5.6 day) period – while only being permitted several brief sleep breaks between April 19, 2002 and April 21, 2002, which totaled 9.5 hours.* Thus, all information provided by Abu Zubaydah subsequent to his return from the hospital on April 15, 2002, was obtained during or after the use of enhanced interrogation techniques and cannot be excluded from supporting the CIA's effectiveness representations under the Study's flawed analytical methodology. Over the course of his detention, Abu Zubaydah provided 766 sole source disseminated intelligence reports.[35]

(U) The Capture of Ramzi bin al-Shibh

(TS// ████████████████ //NF) The Study claims, "[a] review of CIA records found *no connection* between Abu Zubaydah's reporting on Ramzi bin al-Shibh and Ramzi bin al-Shibh's capture.... While CIA records indicate that Abu Zubaydah provided information on Ramzi bin al-Shibh, there is *no indication* that Abu Zubaydah provided information on bin al-Shibh's whereabouts. Further, while Abu Zubaydah provided information on bin al-Shibh while being subjected to the CIA's enhanced interrogation techniques, he provided similar information to FBI interrogators prior to the initiation of the CIA's enhanced interrogation techniques. [36]

(TS// ████████████████ //NF) CIA records demonstrate that Abu Zubaydah was subjected to enhanced interrogation techniques during two separate periods in April 2002 and August 2002. During these timeframes, Abu Zubaydah made several photographic identifications of Ramzi bin al-Shibh and provided information that bin al-Shibh had been in Kandahar at the end of 2001, but was then working with KSM in Karachi, Pakistan. More important, Abu Zubaydah provided information about how he would go about locating Hassan Ghul and other al-Qa'ida associates in Karachi. This information caused ██████████████ Pakistani authorities to intensify their efforts and helped lead them to capture Ramzi bin al-Shibh and other al-Qa'ida associates during the Karachi safe house raids conducted on September 10-11, 2002.

(U) The Capture of Khalid Shaykh Mohammad

<del>(TS//</del> █████████████████ <del>//NF)</del> The Study claims "there are no CIA records to support the assertion that Abu Zubaydah, Ramzi bin al-Shibh, or any other CIA detainee played any role in 'the planning and execution of the operation that captured Khalid Sheikh Mohammed.'"[37] However, information obtained from CIA detainee Abu Zubaydah was essential to furthering the CIA's understanding of KSM's role in the September 11, 2001, terrorist attacks and helped lead to the capture of Ramzi bin al-Shibh. The ██████████████████████ interrogations of bin al-Shibh and DETAINEE R provided key insights about KSM ███████████████████. Information produced through detainee interrogation was pivotal to the retention of a key CIA asset whose cooperation led directly to the capture of KSM.

(U) The Disruption of the Karachi Hotels Bombing Plot

<del>(TS//</del> ███████████████ <del>//NF)</del> The Study claims, "[T]he CIA's enhanced interrogation techniques – to include the waterboard – played no role in the disruption of the Karachi Plot(s)."[38] However, CIA documents show that key intelligence collected through the CIA's Detention and Interrogation Program, including information obtained after the use of enhanced interrogation techniques, played a major role in disrupting the Karachi hotels bombing plot. Specifically, Abu Zubaydah provided crucial information

that helped lead to the successful ████████ raids of the al-Qa'ida safe houses on September 11, 2002 – the same raids that yielded the "perfume letter" and disrupted the Karachi hotels plot. Specifically, the raids were the direct result of information provided by Abu Zubaydah on August 20, 2002, during his second period of enhanced interrogation.

(U) The Heathrow and Canary Wharf Plots

(TS// ████████████████ //NF) The Study asserts that "contrary to CIA representations, information acquired during or after the use of the CIA's enhanced interrogation techniques played no role in 'alert[ing]' the CIA to the threat to – or the 'disrupting' the plotting against – Heathrow Airport and Canary Wharf."[39] We found that the CIA interrogation program played a key role in disrupting the Heathrow and Canary Wharf plotting. Specifically, the Study itself twice concedes these plots were "fully disrupted" with the detentions of Ramzi bin al-Shibh, KSM, Ammar al-Baluchi, and Khallad bin Attash.[40] The Study then incorrectly asserts, "There are no CIA records to indicate that any of the detainees were captured as a result of CIA detainee reporting.[41] Information obtained from the CIA interrogation program played a key role in the capture of al-Shibh and KSM.[42] Also, Ramzi bin al-Shibh provided information about Ammar al-Baluchi and Abu Zubaydah provided information about Khallad bin Attash prior to their arrests.[43] The same detainee information that helped lead to the capture of these terrorists also played a key role in fully disrupting the Heathrow Airport and

Canary Wharf plots.

(U) The Capture of Hambali

~~(TS//~~ ▮▮▮▮▮▮▮▮▮▮▮▮▮▮▮ ~~//NF)~~ The Study claims that "[a] review of CIA operational cables and other records found that information obtained from KSM during or after the use of the CIA's enhanced interrogation techniques played no role in the capture of Hambali."[44] However, CIA documents show that the interrogation of KSM and al-Qa'ida operative Zubair, during and after the use of enhanced interrogation techniques on both individuals, played a key role in the capture of Hambali. Specifically, CIA documents indicate it was the combination of reporting from KSM and Majid Khan that led to the efforts to find Hambali through Zubair. A CIA summary of Hambali's capture timeline states, while "numerous sources had placed Hambali in various Southeast Asian countries, it was captured al-Qa'ida leader KSM who put ▮▮▮▮▮▮▮▮ ▮▮▮▮▮▮▮▮▮▮▮▮▮▮▮▮▮▮▮▮▮▮▮▮▮▮▮▮▮▮▮▮ on Hambali's trail" – contradicting the Study's claim that the KSM interrogation played "no role."[45]

(U) The Thwarting of the Second Wave Plots and Discovery of the Al-Ghuraba Group

~~(TS//~~ ▮▮▮▮▮▮▮▮▮▮▮▮▮▮▮ ~~//NF)~~ The Study claims that, "[a] review of CIA operational cables and other documents found that the CIA's enhanced interrogation techniques played no role in the 'discovery' or thwarting of either 'Second Wave' plot. Likewise, records indicate that the CIA's enhanced interrogation techniques played no role in the 'discovery' of a 17-member 'cell tasked with executing the 'Second Wave.'"[46] However, we found that the CIA interrogation program played a key role in disrupting the "Second Wave" plot and led to the capture of the 17-member al-Ghuraba group. Specifically, the Study ignores that KSM, who had also been subjected to the CIA's enhanced interrogation techniques, provided information months earlier on this same group of JI students and their location in Karachi – information that helped lead to the capture of Gunawan himself. According to CIA information, while the CIA was already aware of Gunawan, "KSM's identification of his role as Hambali's potential successor prioritized his capture. Information from multiple detainees, including KSM, narrowed down [Gunawan's] location and enabled his capture in September 2003."[47] This information was excluded from the Study. Pakistani authorities arrested the members of the al-Ghuraba group during raids on ███████████████████████████. A cable describing the arrests said █████ captured this cell based on the debriefings of captured senior al-Qa'ida operatives, who stated that some members of this cell were to be part of senior al-Qa[']ida leader Khalid Shaykh Muhammad (KSM)['s] [']second wave['] operation to attack the United States using the same modus operandi as was used in the September 11, 2001 attacks."[48]

(U) Critical Intelligence Alerting the CIA to Jaffar al-Tayyar

~~(TS//~~ █████████████████████ ~~//NF)~~ The Study asserts that,

> CIA representations [about detainee reporting on Jaffar al-Tayyar] also omitted key contextual facts, including that... (2) CIA detainee Abu Zubaydah provided a description and information on a KSM associate named Jaffar al-Tayyar to FBI Special Agents in May 2002, prior to being subjected to the CIA's enhanced interrogation techniques... and (5) CIA records indicate that KSM did not know al-Tayyar's true name and that it was Jose Padilla – in military custody and being questioned by the FBI – who provided al-Tayyar's true name as Adnan el-Shukrijumah."[49]

~~(TS//~~ █████████████████████ ~~//NF)~~ On May 20, 2002, while in CIA custody, Abu Zubaydah provided information on an associate of KSM by the name of Abu Jaffar al-Thayer. Abu Zubaydah provided a detailed description of Abu Jaffar al-Thayer, including that he spoke English well and may have studied in the United States.[50] The Study incorrectly claims that this May 20, 2002, interrogation took place prior to the initiation of the CIA's enhanced interrogation techniques.[51] Abu Zubaydah had already been subjected to an extended period of sleep deprivation and other enhanced interrogation techniques during his interrogation between April 15, 2002 and April 21, 2002, about one month *prior* to his May 20 interrogation.[52]

~~(TS//~~ █████████████████████ ~~//NF)~~ The Study also cites as a key contextual fact omitted from CIA representations that KSM did not know al-Tayyar's true name, and it was Jose Padilla, in military custody and being questioned by the FBI, who provided al-Tayyar's true name as Adnan el-Shukrijumah.[53] However, this omission was rendered moot because, as the Study itself notes a few pages later,[54] the "FBI began participating in the military debriefings [of Padilla] in March 2003, *after KSM reported Padilla might know the true name of a US-bound al-Qa'ida operative known at the time only as Jaffar al-Tayyar*. Padilla confirmed Jaffar's true name as Adnan El Shukrijumah."[55]

(U) The Arrest and Prosecution of Saleh al-Marri

(TS// ▓▓▓▓▓▓▓▓▓▓▓▓▓▓ //NF) The Study correctly asserts, "The CIA represented to the CIA Office of Inspector General that 'as a result of the lawful use of EITs,' KSM 'provided information that helped lead to the arrests of terrorists including... Saleh Almari, a sleeper operative in New York.'"[56] As the Study makes clear, al-Marri was not arrested based on information from KSM, and could not have been, because al-Marri was arrested in December 2001, before the detention of KSM in March 2003.[57]

(TS// ▓▓▓▓▓▓▓▓▓▓▓▓▓ //NF) In its response to the Study, the CIA concedes that the agency erred in describing detainee reporting as contributing to al-Marri's arrest. However, the agency stresses that KSM did provide valuable intelligence on al-Marri – intelligence that played a significant role in al-Marri's prosecution.[58] It was KSM who identified a photograph of al-Marri and described him as an al-Qa'ida sleeper operative sent to the United States shortly before 9/11. KSM said he planned for al-Marri, who "had the perfect built-in cover for travel to the United States as a student pursuing his advanced degree in computer studies at a university near New York, to serve as al-Qa'ida's point of contact to settle other operatives in the United States for follow-on attacks after 9/11.[59] KSM also said that al-Marri trained at the al-Faruq camp, had poisons training, and had offered himself as a martyr to bin Ladin. [60]

(TS// ▓▓▓▓▓▓▓▓▓▓▓▓▓▓▓▓▓ //NF) Prior to the information from KSM, al-Marri was charged with credit card fraud and false statements. After the information from KSM, al-Marri was designated as an enemy combatant. In 2009, after being transferred to federal court, al-Marri pled guilty to one count of conspiracy to provide material support to al-Qa'ida. In his plea, he admitted that he attended terrorist training camps and met with KSM to offer his services al-Qa'ida, who told him to travel to the United States before 9/11 and await instructions – *all information initially provided by KSM.*

(U) The Arrest and Prosecution of Iyman Faris

(U) The Study claims, "[o]ver a period of years, the CIA provided the 'identification,' 'arrest,' 'capture,' 'investigation,' and 'prosecution' of Iyman Faris as evidence for the effectiveness of the CIA's enhanced interrogation techniques. These representations were inaccurate."[61] The Study correctly points out that CIA statements implying that detainee information led to the "identification" or "investigation" of Iyman Faris were inaccurate. However, CIA, FBI, and Department of Justice documents show that information obtained from KSM after he was waterboarded led directly to Faris's arrest and was key in his prosecution.

(TS// ███████████████ //NF) On March 17 and 18, 2003, the CIA questioned KSM about Majid Khan's family and KSM stated that another Khan relative, whom he identified from a picture of Faris, was a "truck driver in Ohio."[62] On March 18, 2003, KSM told interrogators he tasked the truck driver to procure specialized machine tools that would be useful to al-Qaida in loosening the nuts and bolts of suspension bridges in the United States. KSM said he was informed by an intermediary that Faris could not find the tools.[63] This revelation would turn out to be a key piece of incriminating evidence against Iyman Faris. The Study excluded information found in CIA documents which shows that, immediately after obtaining information from KSM and Majid Khan regarding Faris, the CTA queried the FBI for "additional details" on Faris, "including a readout on his current activities and plans for FBI continued investigation."[64] The cable specifically noted that "KSM seems to have accurately identified" Faris from a photograph as the "truck driver in Ohio."[65]

(TS// ███████████████ //NF) On March 20, 2003, the FBI picked up Faris for questioning and conducted a consent search of his apartment, seizing his laptop. When our staff asked the FBI why Faris was picked up, they cited the cables from CIA.[66] The FBI investigators went into this interview armed with the information revealed by KSM and Majid Khan, which enabled them to explore Faris's ties with

KSM and al-Qa'ida plotting in the United States.[67] On May 1, 2003, Faris pled guilty to "casing a New York City bridge for al Qaeda, and researching and providing information to al Qaeda regarding the tools necessary for possible attacks on U.S. targets," *the exact terrorist activities described by KSM.* Ultimately, the CIA's representation concerning the identification and initial investigation of Faris is much less important than the details that led to his arrest and prosecution.

(U) The Arrest and Prosecution of Uzhair Paracha and the Arrest of Saifullah Paracha

(TS// ███████████████ //NF) The Study asserts, "[t]he CIA represented that information obtained through the use of the CIA's enhanced interrogation techniques produced otherwise unavailable intelligence that led to the identification and/or arrest of Uzhair Paracha and his father Saifullah Paracha (aka, Sayf al-Rahman Paracha). These CIA representations included inaccurate information and omitted significant material information, specifically a body [of] intelligence reporting – acquired prior to CIA detainee reporting – that linked the Parachas to al-Qa'ida-related terrorist activities."[68]

(TS// ███████████████ //NF) We found, however, that information obtained from KSM during his enhanced interrogation on March 25, 2003, about alleged explosives smuggling into the United States, attacks on U.S. gas stations, and related material support to al-Qa'ida, motivated the FBI to track down and arrest Uzhair Paracha in New York a few days later on March 31, 2003.[69] The Intelligence Community continued its pursuit of Saifullah, who was later arrested ████████████████████████ ████████████████ on July 6, 2003. Among other charges, Uzhair was successfully convicted on November 23, 2005, of providing material support to al-Qa'ida and sentenced to 30 years in prison. KSM's description of Uzhair's involvement in the gas station plots and his claim that Uzhair may have provided other logistical support for Majid's entry into the United States was consistent with the press release's description of some of the evidence used during Uzhair's trial.[70]

(U) Tactical Intelligence on Shkai, Pakistan

(U) This case study is no longer as problematic as the version contained in the appendix to the original Findings and Conclusions section of the Study approved by the Committee during the 112th Congress. That appendix falsely accused the CIA of providing an inaccurate representation about the tactical intelligence acquired on Shkai, Pakistan, during the interrogations of Hassan Ghul after the use of enhanced interrogation techniques.[71] Fortunately, that appendix has been dropped from the Study's updated Findings and Conclusions and there is no claim in the updated version of the Study that the representation concerning Shkai, Pakistan, was inaccurate.

(U) Thwarting of the Camp Lemonier Plotting

(TS// ███████████████████████ //NF) The Study claims, "[t]he CIA represented that intelligence derived from the use of CIA's enhanced interrogation techniques thwarted plotting against the U.S. military base, Camp Lemonier, in Djibouti. These representations were inaccurate."[72] We found, however that representations about the thwarting of an attack against Camp Lemonier in Djibouti, specifically President Bush's 2006 comments that "Terrorists held in CIA custody have also provided information that helped stop a planned strike on U.S. Marines at Camp Lemonier in Djibouti," were accurate and have been mischaracterized by the Study.[73] Specifically, contrary to the Study's assertions, the President did not attribute the thwarting of this plot exclusively to the use of enhanced interrogation techniques, but information from "[t]errorists held in CIA custody." In addition, the President never stated that the plot was disrupted exclusively because of information from detainees in CIA custody. The President was clear that information from detainees "helped" to stop the planned strike. This idea that detainee reporting builds on and contextualizes previous and subsequent reporting is repeated a few lines later in the speech, when the President makes clear, "[t]he information we get from these detainees is corroborated by intelligence... that we've received from other sources, and together this intelligence has helped us connect the dots and stop attacks before they occur."[74]

(U) CIA Detainees Subjected to EITs Validated CIA Sources

~~(TS//~~ ███████████████████ ~~//NF)~~ The Study claims, "the CIA also represented that its enhanced interrogation techniques were necessary to validate CIA sources. The claim was based on one CIA detainee – Janat Gul – contradicting the reporting of one CIA asset."[75] Contrary to the Study's claim, the representations cited by the Study do not assert that enhanced interrogation techniques helped to validate sources. Rather, the representations only make reference to "detainee information" or detainee "reporting." Also contrary to the Study's claim, we found evidence in the documentary record where the CIA representations about Janat Gul also contained additional examples of source validation. Moreover, the three items of information that the Study asserts should have been included in the Janat Gul asset validation representations were not "critical" and their inclusion does not alter the fact that Gul's persistent contradiction of the asset's claims did help the CIA "validate" that particular asset.

(U) The Identification of Bin Ladin's Courier

~~(TS//~~ ███████████████████ ~~//NF)~~ The Study asserts, "the 'tipoff' on Abu Ahmad al-Kuwaiti in 2002 did not come from the interrogation of CIA detainees and was obtained prior to any CIA detainee reporting."[76] However, CIA documents show that detainee information served as the "tip-off" and played a significant role in leading CIA analysts to the courier Abu Ahmad al-Kuwaiti. While there was other information in CIA databases about al-Kuwaiti, this information was not recognized as important by analysts until after detainees provided information on him. Specifically, a CIA paper in November 2007 noted that "over twenty mid to high-value detainees have discussed Abu Ahmad's ties to senior al-Qa'ida leaders, including his role in delivering messages from Bin Ladin and his close association with former al-Qa'ida third-in-command Abu Faraj al-Libi."[77] The report highlighted specific reporting from two detainees, Hassan Ghul and Ammar al-Baluchi, who both identified Abu Faraj al-Libi's role in communicating to bin Ladin through Abu Ahmad. It was this and similar reporting from other detainees that helped analysts realize Abu Faraj's categorical denials that he even knew anyone named Abu Ahmad al-Kuwaiti, "almost certainly were an attempt to protect Abu Ahmed," thus showing his importance.[78]

(TS// ███████████ //NF) The Study also asserts, "the most accurate information on Abu Ahmad al-Kuwaiti obtained from a CIA detainee [Hassan Ghul] was provided by a CIA detainee who had not yet been subjected to the CIA's enhanced interrogation techniques."[79] We found, however, that Detainees who provided useful and accurate information on Abu Ahmad al-Kuwaiti and bin Ladin had undergone enhanced interrogation prior to providing the information. Specifically, Ammar al-Baluchi, who appears to be the first detainee to mention Abu Ahmad al-Kuwaiti's role as a bin Ladin courier and a possible connection with Abu Faraj al-Libi, provided this information at a CIA blacksite during a period of enhanced interrogation.[80]

(TS// ██████████████████ //NF) Additional CIA-fact checking explained that Ghul offered more details about Abu Ahmad's role after being transferred from COBALT and receiving enhanced interrogation. Specifically, the CIA stated:

> After undergoing enhanced techniques, Gul stated that Abu Ahmad specifically passed a letter from Bin Ladin to Abu Faraj in late 2003 and that Abu Ahmad had "disappeared" from Karachi, Pakistan in 2002. This information was not only more concrete and less speculative, it also corroborated information from Ammar that Khalid Shaykh Muhammad (KSM) was lying when he claimed Abu Ahmad left al-Qa'ida in 2002.[81]

Ghul stated that while he had "no proof," he believed that Abu Faraj was in contact with Abu Ahmad and that Abu Ahmad might act as an intermediary contact between Abu Faraj and Bin Ladin. Ghul said that this belief "made sense" since Abu Ahmad had disappeared and Ghul had heard that Abu Ahmad was in contact with Abu Faraj.[82] Months later, Ghul also told his interrogators that he knew Abu Ahmad was close to Bin Ladin, which was another reason he suggested that Abu Ahmad had direct contact with Bin Ladin as one of his couriers.[83]

(TS// ██████████████████ //NF) The role of other detainees who had undergone enhanced interrogation, but were believed to be untruthful about knowing Abu Ahmad al-Kuwaiti, was described by CIA analysts as being very significant in their understanding of the courier as well. CIA documents make clear that when detainees like Abu Zubaydah, KSM, and Abu Faraj al-Libi – who had undergone enhanced interrogation and were otherwise cooperative – denied knowing Abu Ahmad Kuwaiti or suggested that he had "retired," it was a clear sign to CIA analysts that these detainees had something to hide, and it further confirmed other detainee information that had tipped them off about the true importance of Abu Ahmad al-Kuwaiti.[84]

(U) Conclusion 6 (CIA Impeded Congressional Oversight)

(TS// ███████████████ //NF) Conclusion 6 states: "[t]he CIA has actively avoided or impeded congressionai oversight of the program."[85] In reality, the overall pattern of engagement with the Congress shows that the CIA attempted to keep the Congress informed of its activities. From 2002 to 2008, the CIA provided more than 35 briefings to SSCI members and staff, more than 30 similar briefings to HPSCI members and staff, and more than 20 congressional notifications.[86] Because the Study did not interview the participants in these restricted briefings, it is impossible to document how much information the CIA provided to Committee leadership during those briefings. Often, the Study's own examples contradict the assertion that the CIA tried to avoid its overseers' scrutiny. For example, the Study notes that the CIA reacted to Vice Chairman Rockefeller's suspicion about the agency's honesty by planning a detailed briefing on the Program for him.[87]

(TS// ███████████ //NF) The Study claims, "[t]he CIA did not brief the Senate Intelligence Committee leadership on the CIA's enhanced interrogation techniques until September 2002, after the techniques had been approved and used."[88] We found that the CIA provided information to the Committee in hearings, briefings, and notifications beginning shortly after the signing of the Memorandum of Notification (MON) on September 17, 2001. The Study's own review of the CIA's representations to Congress cites CIA hearing testimony from November 7, 2001, discussing the uncertainty in the boundaries on interrogation techniques.[89] The Study also cites additional discussions between staff and CIA lawyers in February 2002.[90] The Study seems to fault the CIA for not briefing the Committee leadership until after the enhanced interrogation techniques had been approved and used. However, the use of DOJ-approved enhanced interrogation techniques began during the congressional recess period in August, an important fact that the Study conveniently omitted.[91] The CIA briefed HPSCI leadership on September 4, 2002. SSCI leadership received the same briefing on September 27, 2002.[92]

(TS// ███████████ //NF) The Study also asserts, "[t]he CIA subsequently resisted efforts by then-Vice Chairman John D. Rockefeller, IV, to investigate the program, including by refusing in 2006 to provide requested documents."[93] However, we determined that the CIA provided access to the documents requested. On

January 5, 2006, the Director of National Intelligence's Chief of Staff wrote a letter to Vice Chairman Rockefeller which denied an earlier request for full Committee access to over 100 documents related to the Inspector General's May 2004 Special Review.[94] However, this denial of "full Committee access," did not mean that the documents were not made available to the CIA's congressional overseers. In fact, the Chief of Staff's letter stated, "Consistent with the provisions of the National Security Act of 1947, the White House has directed that specific information related to aspects of the detention and interrogation program be provided only to the SSCI leadership and staff directors."[95] The letter concluded by advising Vice Chairman Rockefeller that the documents "remain available for review by SSCI leadership and staff directors at any time through arrangements with CIA's Office of Congressional Affairs."[96]

(TS// █████████████████ //NF) In support of this erroneous conclusion that the CIA impeded congressional oversight, the Study notes that the "CIA restricted access to information about the program from members of the Committee beyond the Chairman and Vice Chairman until September 6, 2006."[97] Although we agree that the full Committee should have been briefed much earlier, the CIA's limitation of access to sensitive covert action information is a long-standing practice codified in Section 503 of the National Security Act of 1947, as amended.

(TS// █████████████████ //NF) The Study notes that the CIA briefed a number of additional Senators who were not on the Select Committee on Intelligence.[98] The National Security Act permits the President to provide senators with information about covert action programs at his discretion, without regard to Committee membership. Moreover, providing a briefing to inform key senators working on legislation relevant to the CIA's program is inconsistent with the narrative that the CIA sought to avoid congressional sciutiny.

(U) Conclusion 7 (CIA Impeded White House Oversight)

(U) Conclusion 7 states, "[t]he CIA impeded effective White House oversight and decision-making."[99] It is important to place this serious allegation within its proper context – the CIA's Detention and Interrogation Program was conducted as a covert action.[100] Covert action is the sole responsibility of the White House, a principle enshrined in law since the National Security Act of 1947. [101] The President, working with his National Security Staff, approves and oversees all coveit action programs. The congressional intelligence committees also conduct ongoing oversight of all covert actions and receive quarterly covert action briefings. Given this extensive covert action oversight regime, this conclusion seems to imply falsely that the CIA was operating a rogue intelligence operation designed to "impede" the White House. We reject this unfounded implication.

(TS// ████████████████ //NF) The Study asserts, "[a]ccording to CIA records, no CIA officer, up to and including CIA Directors George Tenet and Porter Goss, briefed the President on the specific CIA enhanced interro-

37

gation techniques before April 2006. By that time, 38 of the 39 detainees identified as having been subjected to the CIA's enhanced interrogation techniques had already been subjected to the techniques."[102] We found that the CIA records are contradictory and incomplete regarding when the President was briefed, but President Bush himself says he was briefed in 2002, before any techniques were used."[103]

(TS// ███████████████ //NF) The Study claims that, "[t]he information provided connecting the CIA's detention and interrogation program directly to [the "Dirty Bomb" Plot / Tall Buildings Plot, the Karachi Plots, Heathrow and Canary Wharf Plot, and the Identification/Capture of Iyman Faris] was, to a great extent, inaccurate.[104] We found, however, the information provided to the White House attributing the arrests of these terrorists and the thwarting of these plots to the CIA's Detention and Interrogation Program was accurate.[105]

(U) Conclusion 8 (CIA Impeded National Security Missions of Executive Branch Agencies)

(U) Conclusion 8 states, "[t]he CIA's operation and management of the program complicated, and in some cases impeded, the national security missions of other Executive Branch agencies."[106] As noted in the CIA response to the Study, "the National Security Council established the parameters for when and how CIA could engage on the program with other Executive Branch agencies."[107] The CIA was not responsible nor did it have control over the sharing ordissemination of information to other executive branch agencies or members of the Principals Committee itself. That responsibly rested solely with the White House.

~~(TS//~~ ███████████████ ~~//NF)~~ The Study claims, "[t]he CIA blocked State Department leadership from access to information crucial to foreign policy decision-making and diplomatic activities.[108] However, the Study does not provide any evidence that the CIA deliberately impeded, obstructed or blocked the State Department from obtaining information about the Program inconsistent with directions from the White House or the National Security Council. CIA officers were in close and constant contact with their State Department counterparts where detention facilities were located and among senior leadership to include the Secretary of State and the Deputy Secretary of State. For example, leading to the establishment of a facility in Country ██████ the Study notes that the chief of station (COS) was coordinating activities with the ambassador. Because the Program was highly compart-mented, the ambassador was directed by the National Security Council not to discuss with his immediate superior at headquarters due to the highly compartmented nature of the covert action. Instead, the COS, sent feedback from the ambassador through CIA channels, to the NSC, whereby the Deputy Secretary of State with the knowledge of the Secretary, would discuss any issues or concerns with the ambassador in country.[109] While the process was less direct, the security precautions to protect sensitive information did not impede the national security mission of the State Department.

(TS// ███████████ //NF) The Study also claims, "[t]he CIA denied specific requests from FBI Director Robert Mueller, III, for FBI access to CIA detainees that the FBI believed was necessary to understand CIA detainee reporting on threats to the U.S. Homeland."[110] While the FBI's participation in the interrogation of detainees was self-proscribed, the Bureau was still able to submit requirements to the CIA and received reports on interrogations. Recognizing the need for FBI access to detainees, both agencies finalized a memorandum of understanding in the fall of 2003 that detailed how FBI ███████████████████████████████████ ███████████████████████████ agents would be provided access to detainees ███████████████ ███████████████████████████ [111]

(TS// ███████████ //NF) The Study asserts, "[t]he ODNI was provided with inaccurate and incomplete information about the program, preventing the ODNI from effectively carrying out its statutory responsibility to serve as the principal advisor to the President on intelligence matters."[112] We do not agree with this assertion. The updated Study treats this assertion differently than it did in the version that was adopted by the Committee during the 112th Congress. In the original Study, the assertion sought to dispute claims regarding the use of enhanced interrogation techniques and disruption of several plots. However, the updated Study drops the direct reference to coercive measures and instead focuses on the Detention and Interrogation Program in general.[113] The

2006 press release from the Office of Director of National Intelligence[114] does not reference the use of enhanced interrogation techniques, but states unequivocally: "The detention of terrorists disrupts – at least temporarily – the plots they were involved in." To assert that the detention and interrogation of terrorists did not yield intelligence of value is simply not credible.

(U) Conclusion 5 (CIA Provided Inaccurate Information to the Department of Justice)

(U) Conclusion 5 states, "[t]he CIA repeatedly provided inaccurate information to the Department of Justice, impeding a proper legal analysis of the CIA's detention and Interrogation Program."[115] Our analysis of the claims used in support of this conclusion revealed that many were themselves inaccurate or otherwise without merit.

(TS// ███████████████████ //NF) The Study falsely claims that "CIA attorneys stated that 'a novel application of using the necessity defense' could be used 'to avoid prosecution of U.S. officials who tortured to obtain information that saved many lives.'"[116] We found that the draft CIA Office of General Counsel (OGC) legal appendix cited by the report contained a cursory discussion of the necessity defense that *did not* support the use of such defense in the context of the CIA's Detention and Interrogation Program.[117] Specifically, the claim here altered the meaning of the quoted text in draft legal appendix by separating portions of the text and inserting its own factually misleading text, which was not supported by the legal analysis, to achieve the following result: *"CIA attorneys stated that* a novel application of the necessity defense *could be used* to avoid prosecution of U.S. officials who tortured to obtain information that saved lives."[118] Fortunately, this erroneously doctored quotation only appears once in the Study – in this Conclusion.

(TS// ███████████████ //NF) Also in support of this conclusion, the Study makes a number of claims related to the accuracy of the information provided by the CIA about Abu Zubaydah to OLC. First, the Study asserts that the OLC "relied on inaccurate CIA representations about Abu Zubaydah's status in al-Qa'ida and the interrogation team's certain[ty] that Abu Zubaydah was withholding information about planned terrorist attacks."[119] We found that the information relied upon by the Study to criticize the CIA's representations about Abu Zubaydah withholding information about planned terrorists attacks neglected to include important statements from within that same intelligence cable, which supported those representations by the CIA. Specifically, the Study cites an email from the CIA's interrogation team that included the sentence: "[o]ur assumption is the objective of this operation [the interrogation of Abu Zubaydah] is to achieve a high degree of confidence that [Abu Zubaydah] is not holding back actionable information concerning threats to the United States beyond that which [Abu Zubaydah] has already provided."[120] However, this carefully chosen text omits critical statements from later in the same cable: "[t]here is information and analysis to indicate that subject has information on terrorist threats to the United States" and "[h]e is an incredibly strong willed individual which is why he has resisted this long."[121]

~~(TS//~~ ███████████████████████ //NF)~~ Second, the Study asserts the CIA assessment that Abu Zubaydah was the "third or fourth man" in al-Qa'ida was "based on single-source reporting that was recanted prior to the August 1, 2002, OLC memorandum."[122] The CIA was in possession of multiple threads of intelligence supporting Abu Zubaydah's prominent role in al-Qa'ida.[123] ██████████

██
██
██
██
██

████████ However, the level of detail that ███████████████████ had previously provided about Abu Zubaydah undermined his later attempts to retract his earlier admissions about his involvement in future terrorist attacks ████████████ and his denials about meeting with Abu Zubaydah.[124] Moreover, Abu Zubaydah himself admitted to at least one meeting with ████████████ which undermines ████████████ denials about such meetings.[125]

~~(TS//~~ ████████████████ //NF)~~ Third, the Study incredibly claims that *"[t]he CIA later concluded that Abu Zubaydah was not a member of al-Qa'ida."* We found that the one document cited by the Study did not support this unbelievable and factually incorrect assertion. Specifically, a text box in this cited intelligence product makes the following assertions:

> A common misperception in outside articles is that Khaldan camp was run by al-Qa'ida. Pre-9/11 September 2001 reporting miscast Abu Zubaydah as a "senior al-Qa'ida lieutenant," which led to the inference that the Khaldan camp he was administering was tied to Usama Bin Ladin....

> Al-Qa'ida rejected Abu Zubaydah's request in 1993 to join the group and that Khaldan was not overseen by Bin Ladin's organization.[127]

The Study fails to state that the interrogation of this supposed "non-member" resulted in 766 sole-source disseminated intelligence reports by the Study's own count. [128] Ironically, this intelligence product was written based on "information from detainees and captured documents" – including from Abu Zubaydah.

(TS// ▮▮▮▮▮▮▮▮▮▮▮▮ //NF) In further support of this conclusion, the Study correctly asserts that the CIA applied its enhanced interrogation techniques to numerous other CIA detainees without seeking additional formal legal advice from the OLC."[130] However, the CIA appropriately applied the legal principles of the August 1, 2002, OLC memorandum to other CIA detainees. Specifically, the fact that the CIA felt comfortable enough with OLC's August 1, 2002, legal opinion to apply the same legal principles to other detainees does not constitute an impediment to DOJ's legal analysis of the Program. In fact, the Attorney General later expressed the view that "the legal principles reflected in DOJ's specific original advice could appropriately be extended to allow use of the same approved techniques (under the same conditions and subject to the same safeguards) to other individuals besides the subject of DOJ's specific original advice."[131]

~~(TS//~~ ███████████████ ~~//NF)~~ The Study asserts that the CIA made inaccurate representations to DOJ that Janat Gul and Ahmed Khalfan Ghailani were high-value al Qaeda operatives with knowledge of a pre-election plot against the United States when seeking legal guidance on whether the use of four additional interrogation techniques might violate U.S. law or treaty obligations.[132] Contrary to the Study's claim, the CIA believed the representations to be true at the time it made them to the OLC. The CIA did not learn that some of these representations had been fabricated by a sensitive CIA source until months *after* OLC had approved the use of enhanced interrogation techniques against Janat Gul and Ahmed Khalfan Ghailani. Also, the Study claims that "the threat of a terrorist attack to precede the November 2004 U.S. election was found to be based on a CIA source whose information was questioned by senior CTC officials at the time. The same CIA source admitted to fabricating the information after ███████████████ in ███████ October 2004."[133] However, the email relied upon by the Study does not support the proposition that senior CTC officials questioned the veracity of the sensitive CIA source. While the source did admit to fabricating information about a meeting that never occurred, the Study does not acknowledge that the Chief of Base believed that the source was "generally truthful" about his discussions on the pre-election threat, despite the source's ███████ ███████████████████████ on that issue.

~~(TS//~~ ███████████████ ~~//NF)~~ The Study also

45

repeats its other claims that the CIA's "representations of 'effectiveness' were almost entirely inaccurate and mirrored other inaccurate information provided to the White House, Congress, and the CIA inspector general."[134] Based upon our examination of the "effectiveness" case studies, we assess that the CIA's Detention and Interrogation Program, to include the use of enhanced interrogation techniques, was effective and yielded valuable intelligence. The Study's exaggerated and absolute claims about inaccurate "effectiveness" representations by the CIA have been largely discredited by these minority views and the CIA's June 27, 2013, response to the Study. For the most part, we found that the CIA acknowledged those representations that were made in error or could have benefited from the inclusion of additional clarification.

(U) Conclusion 9 (CIA Impeded Oversight by CIA Office of Inspector General)

(U) Conclusion 9 states, "[t]he CIA impeded oversight by the CIA's Office of Inspector General."[135] However, we found that the Study itself is replete with examples that lead to the opposite conclusion – that the CIA did not significantly impede oversight by the CIA Office of the Inspector General (OIG). The law requires the CIA Inspector General to certify that "the Inspector General has had full and direct access to all information relevant to the performance of his function."[136] Yet, during the timeframe of the Program, the Inspector General certified in every one of its semiannual reports that it had "full and direct access to all CIA information relevant to the performance of its oversight duties."[137] The law also requires the Inspector General to immediately report to the congressional intelligence committees if the Inspector General is "unable to obtain significant documentary information in the course of an investigation, inspection or audit....[138] Again, we are not aware of any such report being made to the SSCI during the relevant time period. We do know, however, that John Helgerson, the CIA Inspector General, testified before SSCI prior to the commencement of the SSCI's review of the CIA Detention and Interrogation Program in February 2007 and did not complain of access to Agency information.[139] Instead, he said that, during 2006, the IG took a comprehensive look at the operations of the CIA's Counterterrorism Center and conducted a separate comprehensive audit of detention facilities. General Helgerson also testified,

> [W]e look carefully at *all* cases of alleged abuse of detainees. The first paper of this kind that came to the Committee was in October 2003, not long after these programs had begun, when we looked at allegations of unauthorized interrogation techniques used at one of our facilities. It proved that indeed unauthorized techniques had been used. I'm happy to say that the processes worked properly. An Accountability Board was held. The individuals were in fact disciplined. The system worked as it should.

> On this subject, Mr. Chairman, I cannot but underscore that we also look at a fair number of cases where, at the end of the day, we find that we cannot find that there was substance to the allegation that came to our attention. We, of course, make careful

47

> record of these investigations because we think it
> important that you and others know that we investigate
> all allegations, some of which are borne out, some of
> which are not.[140]

(U) Another possible indicator of impeded oversight would be evidence that the CIA OIG was blocked from conducting or completing its desired reviews of the Program. The Study itself acknowledges the existence of at least 29 OIG investigations on detainee-related issues, including 23 that were open or had been completed in 2005. [141] We would also expect to see indications in completed OIG reports that the investigation was hampered by limited access to documents, personnel, or site locations necessary for completing such investigations. Again, according to the OIG's own reports, we found evidence that the OIG had extensive access to documents, personnel, and locations. For example, in its May 2004 Special Review of the RDl program, the CIA OIG reported that it was provided more than 38,000 pages of documents and conducted more than 100 interviews, including with the DCI, the Deputy Director of the CIA, the Executive Director, the General Counsel, and the Deputy Director of Operations. The OIG made site visits to two interrogation facilities ███████████████ ██████████████████████████reviewed 92 videotapes of the interrogation of Abu Zubaydah. The CIA IG's 2006 Audit is another good example of extensive access to documents, personnel, and locations. During this audit, the OIG not only conducted interviews of current and former officials responsible for CIA-controlled detention facilities, but it also reviewed operational cable traffic in extremely restricted access databases, reports, other Agency documents, policies, standard operating procedures, and guidelines pertaining to the detention program. The OIG also had access to the facilities and officials responsible for managing and operating three detention sites. The OIG was able to review documentation on site, observe detainees through closed-circuit television or one-way mirrors, and the IG even observed the transfer of a detainee aboard a transport aircraft. They even reviewed the medical and operational files maintained on each detainee in those locations.[142]

(U) Conclusion 10 (The CIA Released Classified Information on EITs to the Media)

(U) Conclusion 10 asserts, "[t]he CIA coordinated the release of classified information to the media, including inaccurate information concerning the effectiveness of the CIA's enhanced interrogation techniques."[143] This conclusion insinuates that there was something improper about the manner in which the CIA managed the process by which information about the Detention and Interrogation Program was disclosed to the media. We found the National Security Council Policy Coordinating Committee determined that the CIA would have "the lead" on the "Public Diplomacy issue regarding detainees."[144]

(U) The Study also repeats one of its main faulty claims – that the CIA released inaccurate information about the Program's effectiveness. Our examination of the record revealed that the CIA's disclosures were authorized and that the CIA's representations about the Program were largely accurate. Specifically, we found that the Study's flawed analytical methodology cannot negate the reality that the CIA's Detention and Interrogation Program set up an effective cycle of events whereby al-Qa'ida terrorists were removed from the battlefield, which had a disruptive effect on their current terrorist activities and often permitted the Intelligence Community to collect additional intelligence, which, in turn, often led back to the capture of more terrorists. We also found, with a few limited exceptions, that the CIA generally did a good job in explaining the Program's accomplishments to policymakers.

(U) CONCLUSION

The CIA called the detention program a "crucial pillar of US counterterrorism efforts, aiding intelligence and law enforcement operations to capture additional terrorists, helping to thwart terrorist plots, and advancing our analysis of the al-Qa'ida target.[145] We agree. We have no doubt that the CIA's detention program saved lives and played a vital role in weakening al-Qa'ida while the Program was in operation. When asked about the value of detainee information and whether he missed the intelligence from it, one senior CIA operator ██████████ ████████████████████ told members, "I miss it every day."[146] We understand why.

Δ

Endnotes

[1] The following members of the Committee signed onto the minority views drafted in response to the original Study approved by the United States Senate Select Committee on Intelligence on December 13, 2012: Vice Chairman Chambliss joined by Senators Burr, Risch, Coats, Blunt, and Rubio.
[[Please note that the double-bracketed text in this document is new explanatory text necessitated by substantive modifications to the Study's Executive Summary and Findings and Conclusions that were made *after* our June 20, 2014, Minority Views were submitted to the Central Intelligence Agency for the declassification review. We also note that these Minority Views are in response to, and at points predicated upon, the research and foundational work that underlie the Study's account of the CIA Detention and Interrogation Program. These Views should not be treated as an independent report based upon a separate investigation, but rather ou revaluation and critique of the Study's problematic analysis, factual findings, and conclusions.]]

[2] SSCI Transcript, Business Meeting to Discuss and Revote on the Terms of Reference for the Committee's Study of the CIA's Detention and Interrogation Program, March 5, 2009, p. 10 (DTS 2009-1916).

[3] DOJ, *Attorney General Eric Holder, Regarding a Preliminary Review into the Interrogation of Certain Detainees*, August 24, 2009, p. 1.
[http://www.justice.gov/opa/speech/attorney-general-eric-holder-regarding-preliminary-review-interrogation-cer-tain-detainees]

[4] *See* DOJ, *Statement of Attorney General Eric Holder on*

Closure of investigation into the Interrogation of Certain Detainees, August 30, 2012. p. 1.
[http://www.justice.gov/opa/pr/statement-attorney-general-eric-holder-closure-investigation-interrogation-certain-detainees]

[5] SSCI Transcript, *Business Meeting to Consider the Report on the CIA Detention and Interrogation Program*, p. 74 (DTS 2013-0452).

[6] SSCI Transcript, *Hearing to Vote on Declassification of the SSCI Study of the CIA's Detention and Interrogation Program*, April 3, 2014, pp. 8-9 (DTS 2014-1137).

[7] CIA, Letter from V. Sue Bromley, Associate Deputy Director, November 6, 2012, p. 1 (DTS 2012-4143).

[8] SSCI Study, Volume I, March 31, 2014, p. 146.

[9] *See* SSCI Minority Views of Vice Chairman Chambliss joined by Senators Burr, Risch, Coats, Rubio, and Coburn, June 20, 2014, p. 150.

[10] *See* CIA, ▨▨ 10586, August 4, 2002. pp 2-5.

[11] Intelligence Community Directive Number 203, Analytic Standards (effective June 21, 2007), p. 2.

[12] *Compare* SSCI Study, Volume I, March 31, 2014, p. 229 *with* CIA Office of Inspector General, *Special Review: Counterterrorism Detention and Interrogation Activities (September 2001 – October 2003)*, May 7, 2004, p. 41 (DTS 2004-2710).
[http://media.washingtonpost.com/wp-srv/nation/documents/cia_oig_report.pdf]
[[This tradecraft error was partially corrected in the November 26, 2014, version of the Executive Summary by editing the offending sentence to read, "The Office of Inspector General later *described*

additional *allegations* of unauthorized techniques used against...." (emphasis added). *Compare* SSCI Study, Executive Summary, April 3, 2014, p. 67 *with* SSCI Study, Executive Summary, December 3, 2014, p. 70.]]

[13] SSCI Study, Volume I, March 31, 2014, p. 20.

[14] SSCI Study, Executive Summary, December 3, 2014, p. 318.

[15] *See* SSCI Minority Views of Vice Chairman Chambliss joined by Senators Burr, Risch, Coats, Rubio, and Coburn, June 20, 2014, p. 159-160.

[16] SSCI Study, Findings and Conclusions, April 3, 2014, p. 2 (emphasis added). [[This false reasoning was tempered in the December 3, 2014, version of the Executive Summary by editing the sentence to read, "CIA detainees who were subjected to the CIA's enhanced interrogation techniques were usually subjected to the techniques immediately after being rendered to CIA custody. Other detainees provided significant accurate intelligence prior to, or without having been subjected to these techniques." *Compare* SSCI Study, Findings and Conclusions, April 3, 2014. p. 2 *with* SSCI Study, Findings and Conclusions, December 3, 2014, p. 2.]]

[17] For a more detailed analysis of this unsupported claim, *see infra*, SSCI Minority Views of Vice Chairman Chambliss joined by Senators Burr, Risch, Coats, Rubio, and Coburn, December 5, 2014, p. 122.

[18] SSCI Study, Findings and Conclusions, December 3, 2014, p. 2. The first and second conclusions in the updated Findings and Conclusion had been combined in Conclusion 9 of the original Study.

[19] SSCI Study, Findings and Conclusions, December 3, 2014, p. 2. The assertion of "produced no

intelligence" as used by the Study reflects that the interrogations of these detainees resulted in no intelligence reports.

[20] SSCI Study, Findings and Conclusions, December 3, 2014, p. 2.

[21] SSCI Study, Findings and Conclusions, December 3, 2014, p. 2.

[22] SSCJ Study, Findings and Conclusions, December 3, 2014, p. 2.

[23] *See infra*, SSCI Minority Views of Vice Chairman Chambliss joined by Senators Burr, Risch, Coats, Rubio, and Coburn, December 5, 2014. pp. 150-155.

[24] SSCI Study, Executive Summary, December 3, 2014, p. 312.

[25] *See* SSCI Study, Executive Summary, December 3, 2014, p. 313, n.1748.

[26] *See* DCIA Talking Points: Waterboard, 06 November 2007, pp. 1-3. This document was sent to DCIA on November 6 in preparation for a meeting with the President.

[27] SSCI Study, Executive Summary, December 3, 2014, p. 315.

[28] *See* DCIA Talking Points: Waterboard, 06 November 2007, pp. 1-3.

[29] SSCI Study, Executive Summary. December 3, 2014, p. 313.

[30] SSCI Study, Executive Summary, December 3, 2014, pp. 229-31 (emphasis added).

[31] SSCI Transcript, *Staff Interview of FBI Special Agent Ali Soufan*, April 28, 2008, p. 22. (DTS 2008-2411).

[32] *See* CIA, ████████ 10090, April 21, 2002, p. 5.

[33] *See* CIA, ████████ 10116, April 25, 2002, pp. 3-4;
CIA, ████████ 10016, April 12, 2002, pp. 4-5.

[34] *See* CIA, ████████ 10094, April 21, 2002, p. 3;
CIA, ████████ 10071, April 19, 2002, p. 2; CIA,
████████ 10091, April 21, 2002, p. 2. Dietary manipu-
lation, nudity, and sleep deprivation (more than 48
hours) were also subsequently authorized as enhanced
interrogation techniques by the Department of Justice.
See Memorandum for John A. Rizzo, Senior Deputy
General Counsel, Central Intelligence Agency, from
Steven G. Bradbury, Principal Deputy Assistant
Attorney General, Office of Legal Counsel,
Department of Justice, May 30, 2005, *Re: Application of
United States Obligations under Article 16 of the Convention
Against Torture to Certain Techniques that May be Used in
the Interrogation of High value Al Qaeda Detainees* (DTS
2009-1810. Tab-11).
[http://www.justice.gov/sites/default/files/olc/legacy/201
3/10/21/memo-bradbury2005.pdf]

[35] SSCI Study, Volume III, March 31, 2014, pp. 282-
283.

[36] SSCI Study, Executive Summary, December 3,
2014, p. 318 (emphasis added).

[37] SSCI Study, Executive Summary, December 3,
2014, p. 327.

[38] SSCI Study, Executive Summary, December 3,
2014, p. 242.

[39] SSCI Study, Executive Summary, December 3,
2014, pp. 297-298.

[40] *See* SSCI Study, Executive Summary, December 3,
2014. pp.295 and 299.

[41] SSCI Study, Executive Summary December 3, 2014, p. 299.

[42] *See* SSCI Minority Views of Vice Chairman Chambliss joined by Senators Burr, Risch, Coats, Rubio, and Coburn, December 5, 2014. pp. 159-166.

[43] *See* SSCI Minority Views of Vice Chairman Chambliss joined by Senators Burr, Risch, Coats, Rubio, and Coburn, December 5, 2014, pp. ███ and 184.

[44] SSCI Study, Executive Summary, December 3, 2014, p. 305.

[45] CIA, *Hambali Capture/Detention Timeline*, no date, p. 6.

[46] SSCI Study, Executive Summary, December 3, 2014, p. 251. This claim has been modified from the version that appeared in the report that was approved by the Committee at the end of the 112th Congress. For example, it no longer claims that the CIA's interrogation program, excluding the use of enhanced interrogation techniques, did not play a role in the thwarting of the al-Ghuraba Group. It also substitutes the words "discovery *or* thwarting" in place of the original "identification *and* disruption." (emphasis added).

[47] CIA, *Detainee Reporting Pivotal for the War Against Al-Qa'ida*, June 1, 2005, p. 2 (DTS 2009-1387) [http://documents.nytimes.com/c-i-a-reports-on-interrogation-methods#p=245]

[48] CIA, CIA CABLE 52981, ████████████████ ███████

[49] SSCI Study, Executive Summary, December 3, 2014, pp. 358-359.

[50] *See* FBI draft report of the interrogation of Abu

Zubaydah, May 20, 2002, 5:25 p.m. to 8:40 p.m., p. 3.

[51] *See* SSCI Study, Executive Summary, December 3, 2014, p. 362.

[52] *See infra.* SSCI Minority Views of Vice Chairman Chambliss joined by Senators Buit, Risch, Coats, Rubio. and Coburn, December 5, 2014, pp. 150-155.

[53] *See* SSCI Study, Executive Summary, December 3, 2014. p. 359.

[54] *See* SSCI Study, Executive Summary, December 3. 2014, p. 365 (emphasis added).

[55] *See* CIA *Briefing Notes on the Value of Detainee Reporting*, April 15, 2005, p. 3 (emphasis added); *See also* CIA, ALEC ███████ March 21, 2003, p. 6 ("Our service has developed new information, based on leads from detained al-Qa'ida operations chief Khalid Shaykh Muhammad (KSM), that al-Qa'ida operative Jafar al-Tayyar's true name is Adnan Shukri Jumah and he could be involved in an imminent suicide attack in the United States").

[56] SSCI Study, Executive Summary, December 3, 2014, p. 366.

[57] SSCI Study, Executive Summary, December 3, 2014, p. 366.

[58] *See* CIA Study Response, *Case Studies (TAB C)*, June 27, 2013, p. 35

[59] CIA, WASHINGTON DC ████████████ ███████

[60] *See* CIA, CIA WASHINGTON DC ████████ ███████

[61] SSCI Study, Executive Summary, December 3, 2014, p. 276-277.

[62] CIA, CIA CABLE 10886, March 18, 2003, pp. 5-6.

[63] CIA, CIA CABLE 10886, March 18, 2003, pp. 5-6.

[64] CIA, ██████████████████████████████
███████████████████████ *Information from KSM*
on Majid Khan.

[65] CIA, ██████████████████████████████
███████████████████████ *Information from KSM*
on Majid Khan.

[66] Phone call from the FBI responding to minority staff questions from a document review, January 25, 2013.

[67] *See* CIA Study Response, *Case Studies (TAB C),* June 27. 2013, p. 13; FBI WASH 040537Z, April 4, 2003, p. 2.

[68] SSCI Study, Executive Summary, December 3, 2014. p. 352.

[69] CIA, DIRECTOR

[70] *See* DOJ, United States Attorney, Southern District of New York, *Pakistani Man Convicted of Providing Material Support to Al Qaeda Sentenced to 30 Years in Federal Prison,* July 20, 2006, p. 2. [http://www.justice.gov/usao/nys/pressreleases/July06/parachasentencing-pr.pdf]

[71] SSCI Study, December 13, 2012, Findings and Conclusions, *Appendix: Details on CIA's Effectiveness Representations-Conclusion #9,* p. 92.

[72] SSCI Study, Executive Summary, December 3, 2014, p. 336.

[73] President George W. Bush, *Trying Detainees; Address on the Creation of Military Commissions,* Washington, D.C., September 6, 2006.

[http://georgewbush-whitehouse.archives.gov/news/-releases/2006/09/20060906-3.html]

[74] President George W. Bush, *Trying Detainees; Address on the Creation of Military Commissions*, Washington, D.C., September 6, 2006. [http://georgewbush-whitehouse.archives.gov/news/-releases/2006/09/20060906-3.html]

[75] SSCI Study, Executive Summary, December 3, 2014, p. 342.

[76] SSCI Study, Executive Summary, December 3, 2014, p. 389.

[77] CIA Intelligence Assessment, *Al-Qa'ida Watch, Probable Identification of Suspected Bin Ladin Facilitator Abu Ahmad al-Kuwaiti*, November 23, 2007, p. 2.

[78] CIA Intelligence Assessment, *Al-Qa'ida Watch, Probable Identification of Suspected Bin Ladin Facilitator Abu Ahmad al-Kuwaiti*, November 23, 2007, p. 2.

[79] SSCI Study, Executive Summary, December 3, 2014, p. 379.

[80] *See* CIA, WASHINGTON DC ████████████ ████████████████████ Ammar al-Baluchi attempted to recant his earlier description of Abu Ahmad as a Bin Ladin courier. CIA. DIRECTOR ████████████████████.

[81] CIA Study Response, *Case Studies (TAB C)*, June 27, 2013, p. 38 (citing CIA, ██████ ████████████.

[82] CIA, ██████████████████████

[83] CIA, DIRECTOR ████████

[84] CIA, DIRECTOR ███████████████ ██████████ CIA Center for the Study of Intelligence, *Lessons from the Hunt for Usama Bin Ladin*, dated September 2012, pp. 9-10 (DTS 2012-3826); CIA Intelligence Assessment, *Al-Qa'ida Watch, Probable Identification of Suspected Bin Ladin Facilitator Abu Ahmad al-Kuwaiti*, November 23, 2007, p. 2.

[85] SSCI Study, Findings and Conclusions, December 3, 2014, p. 5.

[86] CIA Study Response, *Conclusions (TAB B)*. June 27, 2013, p. 35

[87] *See* SSCI Study, Executive Summary, December 3, 2014, p. 441.

[88] SSCI Study, Findings and Conclusions, December 3, 2014, p. 5.

[89] SSCI Study, Executive Summary, December 3, 2014, p. 437 n.2447. *See also* SSCI Transcript, *Briefing on Covert Action*, November 7, 2001, p. 56 (DTS 2002-0611).

[90] *See* SSCI Study, Executive Summary, December 3, 2014, p. 437; Email from: Christopher Ford, SSCI Staff, to: ██████ Cleared SSCI staff; subject: Meeting yesterday with CIA lawyers on ██████████████- ██████ date: February 26,2002 (DTS 2002-0925).

[91] *See* CIA Study Response, *Conclusions (TAB B)*, June 27, 2013, p. 36.

[92] CIA Study Response, *Conclusions (TAB B)*, June 27, 2013, p. 36.

[93] SSCI Study, Findings and Conclusions, December 3, 2014, pp. 5-6.

[94] SSCI Study, Executive Summary, December 3,

2014, p. 442.

[95] Letter from David Shedd to Andy Johnson, January 5, 2006 (DTS 2006-0373).

[96] Letter from David Shedd to Andy Johnson, January 5, 2006 (DTS 2006-0373).

[97] SSCI Study, Findings and Conclusions, December 3, 2014, p. 6.

[98] *See* SSCI Study, Executive Summary, December 3. 2014, p. 443.

[99] SSCI Study, Findings and Conclusions, December 3, 2014, p. 6.

[100] *See* SSCI Study, Executive Summary, December 3, 2014, p. 11. "On September 17, 2001, six days after the terrorist attacks of September 11, 2001, President George W. Bush signed a covert action MON to authorize the Director of Central Intelligence (DCI) to *'undertake operations designed to capture and detain* persons who pose a continuing, serious threat of violence or death to U.S. persons and interests or who are planning terrorist activities.'" (emphasis added).

[101] In 1974, the Hughes-Ryan amendment to the Foreign Assistance Act of 1961 created the requirement for presidential "Findings" for covert action. The Intelligence Oversight Acts of 1980 and 1988 amended the Finding process, and the Intelligence Oversight Act of 1991 replaced Hughes-Ryan with the current Finding process. *See* William Daugherty, *Executive Secrets, Covert Action and the Presidency*, The University Press of Kentucky 2004 pp. 92-98. [http://www.amazon.com/dp/B0078XFPO8]

[102] SSCI Study, Findings and Conclusions, December 3, 2014, p. 6.

[103] *See* George W. Bush, *Decision Points*, Broadway Paperbacks, New York, 2010, p. 169. [http://www.amazon.com/dp/B003F3PK5Y/]

[104] SSCI Study, April 1, 2014, Volume II, p. 446.

[105] *See* SSCI Minority Views of Vice Chairman Chambliss joined by Senators Burr, Risch, Coats, Rubio, and Coburn, June 20, 2014, *The Thwarting of the Dirty Bomb / Tall Buildings Plot and the Capture of Jose Padilla*, pp. 150-155; *The Thwarting of the Karachi Plots*, pp. 181-185; *The Heathrow and Canary Wharf Plots*, pp. 188-192;, and *The Arrest and Prosecution of Iyman Faris*, pp. 215-221.

[106] SSCI Study, Findings and Conclusions, December 3. 2014, p. 7.

[107] CIA Study Response, *Conclusions (TAB B)*, June 27, 2013, p. 11.

[108] SSCI Study, Findings and Conclusions, December 3, 2014, p. 7.

[109] CIA CABLE ████████████████████
████ CIA CABLE ███████████████████
███████ CIA CABLE ████████████████
██████████████.

[110] SSCI Study, Findings and Conclusions, December 3, 2014, p. 7.

[111] SSCI Study, Volume I, March 31, 2014, p. 413.

[112] SSCI Study, Findings and Conclusions, December 3, 2014, p. 8.

[113] SSCI Study, Findings and Conclusions, December 3, 2014, p. 8.

[114] ODNI Press Release, September 6, 2006, "Information on the High Value Terrorist Detainee

Program."
[http://www.dni.gov/files/documents/Newsroom/Press
%20Releases/2006%20Press%20Releases/TheHighVal-
ueDetaineeProgram.pdf]

[115] SSCI Study, Findings and Conclusions,
December 3, 2014, p. 4.

[116] SSCI Study, Findings and Conclusions,
December 3, 2014, p. 5.

[117] *See* CIA Office of General Counsel draft *Legal
Appendix: Paragraph 5 – Hostile Interrogations: Legal
Considerations for CIA Officers*, November 26, 2001,
pp. 5-6 (CIA, Draft Appendix on Necessity Defense).
This document is attached as Appendix IV to the SSCI
Minority Views of Vice Chairman Chambliss joined by
Senators Burr, Risch, Coats, Rubio, and Coburn, June
20, 2014. p. 363.

[118] SSCI Study, Findings and Conclusions,
December 3. 2014, p. 5 (Erroneous text indicated by
italics).

[119] SSCI Study, Findings and Conclusions,
December 3, 2014, p. 5.

[120] CIA, [REDACTED] 73208, July 23, 2003, p. 3;
Email from: CIA staff officer; to: [REDACTED],
[REDACTED],   ; subject:
Addendum from GREEN, [REDACTED] 73208
(231043Z JUL 02); date: July 23, 2004, at 07:56:49 PM.
See also email from: [REDACTED]; to: [REDACTED];
subject: Re: Grayson SWIGERT and Hammond
DUNBAR date: August 8, 21, 2002, at 10:21 PM.

[121] CIA, [REDACTED] 73208, July 23, 2003, p. 3;
Email from: CIA staff officer; to: [REDACTED],
[REDACTED],   ; subject:
Addendum from GREEN, [REDACTED] 73208

(231043Z JUL 02); date: July 23, 2004, at 07:56 PM. *See also* email from: [REDACTED]; to: [REDACTED]; subject: Re: Grayson SWIGERT and Hammond DUNBAR date: August 8, 21, 2002, at 10:21 PM.

[122] SSCI Study, Executive Summary, December 3, 2014, p. 410 (emphasis added).

[123] *See* CIA Study Response, Conclusions (TAB B), June 27, 2013, p. 32.

[124] *See* SSCI Minority Views of Vice Chairman Chambliss joined by Senators Burr, Risch, Coats, Rubio, and Coburn, June 20, 2014, p. 91.

[125] CIA, ALEC ███████████████ CIA, ALEC ███████████ ██████████████ Abu Zubaydah and accounts differ as to the location of this meeting(s).

[126] SSCI Study, Executive Summary, December 3, 2014, p. 410 (emphasis added).

[127] CIA, *Countering Misconceptions About Training Camps in Afghanistan, 1990-2001*, August 16, 2006, p. 2 (emphasis added). This document is attached as Appendix I to the SSCI Minority Views of Vice Chairman Chambliss joined by Senators Burr, Risch, Coats, Rubio, and Coburn, June 20. 2014, p. 336.

[128] *See* SSCI Study, Volume III, March 31, 2014, pp. 282-283.

[129] CIA, *Countering Misconceptions About Training Camps in Afghanistan, 1990-2001*, August 16, 2006, p. I (DTS 2006-3254).

[130] SSCI Study, Executive Summary, December 3, 2014, p. 411.

[131] *See* Memorandum from Jack Goldsmith III,

Assistant Attorney General, Office of Legal Counsel, Department of Justice, to John Helgerson, Inspector General, Central Intelligence Agency, June 18, 2004, Addendum p. 2 (DTS 2004-2730).

[132] *See* SSCI Study, Executive Summary, December 3, 2014, pp. 416-418.

[133] *See* SSCI Study, Executive Summary, December 3, 2014, p. 417.

[134] SSCI Study, Executive Summary, December 3, 2014, p. 426.

[135] SSCI Study, Findings and Conclusions, December 3, 2014, p. 8.

[136] 50 U.S.C. 3517(d)(I)(D).

[137] *See* CIA OIG, *Semi-Annual Report to the Director, Central Intelligence Agency*, July-Dec. 2006, p. 5 (DTS 2007-0669); CIA OIG, *Semi-Annual Report to the Director, Central Intelligence Agency*, Jan.-June 2006, p. 5 (DTS 2006-3195); CIA OIG, *Semi-Annual Report to the Director, Central Intelligence Agency*, July-Dec. 2005, p. 5 (DTS 2006-0678); CIA OIG, *Semi-Annual Report to the Director, Central Intelligence Agency*, Jan.-June 2005, p. 5 (DTS 2005-3140); CIA OIG, *Semi-Annual Report to the Director of Central Intelligence*, January-June 2004, p. 5 (DTS 2004-3307); and CIA OIG, *Semi-Annual Report to the Director of Central Intelligence*, Jan.-June 2003, p. 5 (DTS 2003-3327); CIA Study Response, *Comments (TAB A)*, Jun 27, 2013, pp. 4-6; and 10; and CIA Study Response, *Conclusions (TAB B)*, June 27, 2013, pp. 7-9.

[138] 50 U.S.C. 3517(d)(3)(E).

[139] *See* SSCI Transcript, *Hearing on the Central Intelligence Agency Rendition Program*, February 14, 2007, p. 24 (DTS 2007-1337).

[140] SSCI Transcript, *Hearing on the Central Intelligence Agency Rendition Program*, February 14, 2007, p. 25 (DTS 2007-1337).

[141] SSCI Study, Volume I, April 1, 2014, p. 899 n.6257. The CIA asserts that the "OIG conducted nearly 60 investigations" related to the CIA's Detention and Interrogation Program and that the OIG found the initial allegations in 50 of these investigations to be unsubstantiated or did not make findings warranting an accountability review. Of the remaining 10 investigations, one resulted in a felony conviction, one resulted in the termination of a contractor and the revocation of his security clearances, and six led to Agency accountability reviews. CIA Study Response, *Conclusions (TAB B)*, June 27, 2013, p. 7.

[142] "CIA-controlled Detention Facilities Operated Under the 17 September 2001 Memorandum of Notification," July 14, 2006, APPENDIX A, page 1-2, DTS 2006-2793.

[143] SSCI Study, Findings and Conclusions, December 3, 2014, p. 8.

[144] Email from: ████████████████████ to: CIA attorney; subject: Brokaw interview: Take one; date: April 15, 2005 at 1:00 PM.

[145] *Detainee Reporting Pivotal for the War Against al-Qa'ida*, June 1, 2005, p. i. [http://documents.nytimes.com/c-i-a-reports-on-interrogation-methods#p=245]

[146] ████████████ Chambliss, ████████████ ████ conversation between SSCI members and CIA officers. ████████████████

MINORITY VIEWS OF VICE CHAIRMAN CHAMBLISS JOINED BY SENATORS BURR, RISCH, COATS, RUBIO, AND COBURN [1]

(U) INTRODUCTION

(U) In January 2009, as one of his first official acts, President Obama issued three Executive orders relating to the detention and interrogation of terror suspects, one of which ended the Central Intelligence Agency's (CIA) Detention and Interrogation Program ("the Program" or "the Detention and Interrogation Program"). At the same time, there were ongoing calls from critics of the Program for the appointment of a special committee or independent commission to review the Program and "hold accountable" those involved. Against this backdrop, in March 2009, the Senate Select Committee on Intelligence ("SSCI" or "Committee") decided, by a vote of 14–1, to initiate a Study of the Central Intelligence Agency's Detention and Interrogation Program, hereinafter "the Study," and adopt Terms of Reference.[2] While most minority members supported the Study in the hope that a fair, objective, and apolitical look at the Program could put calls for an "aggressive"[3] and burdensome Commission to rest and might result in thoughtful and helpful recommendations for detention and interrogation policy going forward,

Senator Chambliss was the sole Committee member to vote against the Committee conducting this review.[4] He believed then, as today, that vital Committee and Intelligence Community resources would be squandered and the Committee's ability to conduct effective intelligence oversight would be jeopardized by looking in the rear-view mirror and debating matters that were, in practice, already settled by Congress, the executive branch, and the Supreme Court.

(U) Indeed, by the time the Study began, Congress had passed two separate acts directly related to detention and interrogation issues, specifically the Detainee Treatment Act of 2005 (DTA) and the Military Commissions Act of 2006 (MCA). The executive branch had terminated the CIA's program, ordered the closure of the Guantanamo Bay, Cuba, detention facility within one year, directed a review of detention and interrogation policies, and required that – except for the use of authorized, non-coercive interrogation techniques by federal law enforcement agencies – future interrogations be conducted in accordance with the U.S. Army Field Manual on Interrogation. The Supreme Court had decided *Rasul v. Bush*, 542 U.S. 466 (2004), *Hamdi v. Rumsfeld*, 542 U.S. 507 (2004), *Hamdan v. Rumsfeld*, 548 U.S. 557 (2006), and *Boumediene v. Bush*, 553 U.S. 723 (2008), which established that detainees were entitled to habeas corpus review and identified certain deficiencies in both the DTA and MCA.

(U) Nonetheless, a majority of Committee members agreed to review the Program, and after its inception, the Study proceeded in a bipartisan manner until August 24,

2009, when Attorney General Eric Holder announced that the Department of Justice (DOJ) had re-opened a preliminary review into whether federal criminal laws were violated in connection with the interrogation of specific detainees at overseas locations.[5] Once the Attorney General made this announcement, the minority correctly predicted that the criminal investigation would frustrate the Committee's efforts to conduct a thorough and effective review of the Program. Absent a grant of immunity, key CIA witnesses would likely follow the inevitable and understandable advice of counsel and decline to participate in any Committee interviews or hearings. This situation would make it very difficult for the Committee to comply with one of the key requirements in the Terms of Reference adopted for the Study, which specifically called for interviews of witnesses and testimony at hearings.

(U) Without interviews, the Study was essentially limited to a cold document review with more questions likely raised than answered. Although in a prior, related review of the destruction of CIA's interrogation video tapes, the Committee had wisely suspended its own review rather than forego interviews or potentially jeopardize a criminal investigation, inexplicably, this precedent was not followed in the case of the Study. When Chairman Feinstein decided to continue the Study despite these impediments to a full and accurate review, then-Vice Chairman Bond informed her that he had directed the minority staff to withdraw from further active participation.

(U) On August 30, 2012, Attorney General Holder announced the closure of the criminal investigation into the

69

interrogation of certain detainees in the Detention and Interrogation Program.[6] This provided the Committee a window of opportunity to invite relevant witnesses in for interviews, but that course of action was not pursued.

Δ

Endnotes

[1] When these minority views were initially written in response to the original Study approved by the United States Senate Select Committee on Intelligence on December 13, 2012, the following members of the Committee signed on to them: Vice Chairman Chambliss joined by Senators Burr, Risch, Coats, Blunt, and Rubio.
[[Please note that the double-bracketed text in this document is new explanatory text necessitated by substantive modifications to the Study's Executive Summary and Findings and Conclusions that were made *after* our June 20, 2014, Minority Views were submitted to the Central Intelligence Agency for the declassification review. We also note that these Minority Views are in response to, and at points predicated upon, the research and foundational work that underlie the Study's account of the CIA Detention and Interrogation Program. These Views should not be treated as an independent report based upon a separate investigation, but rather our evaluation and critique of the Study's problematic analysis, factual findings, and conclusions.]]

[2] SSCI Transcript, *Business Meeting to Discuss and Revote on the Terms of Reference for the Committee's Study of the CIA's Detention and Interrogation Program*, March 5, 2009, pp. 10-11 (DTS 2009-1916).

[3] *See e.g.* SSCI Transcript, *Business Meeting to Discuss the Committee's Investigation of the CIA's Detention and Interrogation Program*, February 11, 2009, p. 69 (DTS 2009-1420) (description by Majority member of potential commission on this matter).

[4] SSCI Transcript, *Business Meeting to Discuss and Revote on the Terms of Reference for the Committee's Study of the CIA's Detention and Interrogation Program*, March 5, 2009, p. 10 (DTS 2009-1916).

[5] DOJ, *Attorney General Eric Holder Regarding a Preliminary Review into the Interrogation of Certain Detainees*, August 24, 2009, p. 1.
[http://www.justice.gov/opa/speech/attorney-general-eric-holder-regarding-preliminary-review-interrogation-certain-detainees]

[6] *See* DOJ, *Statement of Attorney General Eric Holder on Closure of investigation into the Interrogation of Certain Detainees*, August 30, 2012, p. 1.
[http://www.justice.gov/opa/pr/statement-attorney-general-eric-holder-closure-investigation-interrogation-certain-detainees]

(U) THE STUDY'S FLAWED PROCESS

~~(S)~~ Now, five years later, the minority's prediction has come to pass. With the decision not to conduct interviews, the latest version of the Study is a [[6,682]]-page interpretation of documents that, according to the CIA, has cost the American taxpayer more than 40 million dollars and diverted countless CIA analytic and support resources. [7] After expending tens of thousands of Committee and CIA staff working hours, this Study does not even offer a *single recommendation* for improving our intelligence interrogation practices – even though the Terms of Reference expressly contemplated both findings and recommendations.[8] Rather, the Study purports to serve intelligence oversight interests by proffering 20 questionable and inflammatory conclusions attacking the CIA's integrity and credibility in developing and implementing the Program. To us, this Study appears to be more of an exercise of partisan politics than effective congressional oversight of the Intelligence Community.

(U) It is important to understand that the Executive Summary and the Findings and Conclusions which the Committee recently sent to the executive branch for a declassification review are not the same documents that were approved by the Committee during the 112th Congress or even at the April 3, 2014, declassification review business meeting. The original Executive Summary

72

had 282 pages; the updated business meeting version had 479 pages; and the updated version transmitted to President Obama had 488 pages. Conversely, the original Findings and Conclusions shrank down from 95 pages to 31-page updated business meeting version, only to shrink further to the 20-page updated version that was transmitted to the President. The 20 conclusions originally approved by the Committee during the 112th Congress are not the same as the 20 conclusions sent for declassification review. For example, two of the original conclusions – Conclusions 2 and 11 – were dropped and two other conclusions – Conclusions 9 and 19 – were split in a manner that kept the total number of conclusions at 20. Although some remnants of Conclusions 2 and 11 can still be found in the Study, we believe that these conclusions were properly dropped as headline conclusions. While there have been numerous and repeated calls for the declassification of the Study since it was adopted on December 13, 2012,[9] these individuals and groups did not understand that they were calling for the release of a report that was still being re-written more than 15 months after it was first approved by the Committee.

Δ

Endnotes

[7] CIA, Letter from V. Sue Bromley, Associate Deputy Director, November 6, 2012, p. 1 (DTS 2012-4143).

[8] *See* SSCI Review of the Central Intelligence Agency's Detention and Interrogation Program (SSCI

Study), December 13, 2013 (SSCI Study), Volume I,
pp. 1214-1215.

[9] On December 12, 2012, 26 retired generals and
admirals urged the Committee to adopt the Study and
make it public with as few redactions as possible. In
early January 2013, Senators Feinstein, Levin, and
McCain criticized the movie *Zero Dark Thirty* for its
portrayal of the decade-long hunt for Usama Bin
Ladin, because they believed it suggested that
information obtained by torturing al-Qa'ida detainees
aided in locating him. On November 26, 2013, the
American Civil Liberties Union filed a lawsuit under
the Freedom of Information Act to compel the CIA to
release the SSCI Study and the CIA's June 27, 2013,
response. On December 13, 2013, the Center for
Victims of Torture released a statement supporting the
release of the Study signed by 58 retired generals and
admirals, national security experts, foreign policy
experts, and religious leaders.

(U) Failure to Interview Witnesses

(U) Although the Study asserts that it "is the most comprehensive review ever conducted of the CIA's Detention and Interrogation Program,"[10] it began to experience serious problems when the Attorney General decided to re-open the criminal inquiry into the Program in 2009. The Attorney General's decision resulted in the Committee's inability to interview key witnesses during the pendency of that inquiry and led to significant analytical and factual errors in the original and subsequently updated versions of the Study, apoint we made in our original minority views and one that was strongly echoed in the CIA response.

(U) In a *Washington Post* opinion piece published on April 10, 2014, the current and former Chairmen of the Senate Select Committee on Intelligence admitted that:

> Although the committee was not able to conduct new interviews, it had access to and used transcripts from more than 100 interviews conducted by the CIA inspector general and other agency offices while the program was ongoing and shortly after it ended. Many of these transcripts were from interviews of the same people the committee would have talked to, with answers to the same questions that would have been asked. This included top managers, lawyers, counter-terrorism personnel, analysts, interrogators and others at the CIA.[11]

While these statements are true and might lead someone to infer that these interview transcripts may have been adequate substitutes for conducting new interviews of these key personnel, the Study itself appears to reach the opposite conclusion:

> There are no indications in CIA records that any of the past reviews attempted to independently validate the intelligence claims related to the CIA's use of its enhanced interrogation techniques that were presented by CIA personnel in interviews and documents. As such, no previous review confirmed whether the specific intelligence cited by the CIA was acquired from a CIA detainee during or after being subjected to the CIA's enhanced interrogation techniques or if the intelligence acquired was otherwise unknown to the United States government ("otherwise unavailable"), and therefore uniquely valuable.[12]

We suppose that this critique is leveled against the CIA IG Special Report, at least in part, because the special report concluded that:

> The detention of terrorists has prevented them from engaging in further terrorist activity, and their interrogation has provided intelligence that has enabled the identification and apprehension of terrorists, warned of terrorist plots planned for the United States and around the world, and supported articles frequently used in the finished intelligence publications for senior policymakers and war fighters. In this regard, there is no doubt that the Program has been effective. Measuring the effectiveness of EITs, however, is more subjective process and not without some concern.

The CIA OIG Special Report also noted that George Tenet, the Director of Central Intelligence (DCI), said he believed, "the use of EITs has proven to be extremely valuable in obtaining enormous amounts of critical threat information from detainees who had otherwise believed they were safe from any harm in the hands of Americans."[14]

(U) The Study cannot have it both ways. Either the CIA IG Special Review interview transcripts were adequate substitutes for new interviews or they were not. Conclusion 9 of the Study states that the "CIA impeded oversight by the CIA's Office of Inspector General."[15] Specifically, the Study alleges that "[d]uring the OIG reviews, CIA personnel provided OIG with inaccurate information on the operation and management of the CIA's Detention and Interrogation Program, as well as on the effectiveness of the CIA's enhanced interrogation techniques."[16] This conclusion seems to establish that the prior interview transcripts were inadequate substitutes for new interviews. While we do not agree with Conclusion 9, or any of the other conclusions examined in these views, it seems pretty clear that the lack of new interviews has prevented the Committee from conducting the comprehensive review that was envisioned in the original Terms of Reference. Unlike the Study, we are willing to acknowledge that our own analysis in these views was similarly hampered by the inability to interview key personnel who might be able to shed light on any documentary inconsistencies or inaccurate interpretations. Regardless, we remain convinced that the minority's non-partisan decision to withdraw from further active participation in the Study was the correct decision.

Δ

Endnotes

[10] SSCI Study, Executive Summary, December 3, 2014, p. 9. It would be more precise to assert that the SSCI Study is the most comprehensive *documentary* review ever conducted of the CIA's Detention and Interrogation Program.

[11] Senator Dianne Feinstein and Senator Jay Rockefeller, *The Senate report on the CIA's interrogation program should be made public*, April 10, 2014. [http://www.washingtonpost.com/opinions/the-senate-report-on-the-cias-interrogation-program-should-be-made-public/2014/04/10/eeeb237a-c0c3-11e3-bcec-b71ee10e9bc3_story.html]

[12] SSCI Study, Executive Summary, December 3, 2014, p. 179.

[13] CIA, Office of Inspector General, Special Review: Counterterrorism Detention and Interrogation Activities. (September 2001 – October 2003), May 7, 2004, p. 85 (DTS 2004-2710) (emphasis added). [http://media.washingtonpost.com/wp-srv/nation/documents/cia_oig_report.pdf]

[14] CIA Office of Inspector General, Special Review: Counterterrorism Detention and Interrogation Activities (September 2001– October 2003), May 7, 2004, p. 88-89 (DTS 2004-2710). [http://media.washingtonpost.com/wp-srv/nation/documents/cia_oig_report.pdf]

[15] SSCI Study, Findings and Conclusions, December 3, 2014, p. 8.

[16] SSCI Study, Findings and Conclusions, December 3, 2014, p. 8.

(U) Insufficient Member Review of the Approved Study

(U) Our concerns about the quality of the Study's analysis drove our efforts, before and during the Committee's business meeting on December 13, 2012, to implore the majority to give members sufficient opportunity to review the Study and submit it for review and comment by the Intelligence Community prior to a Vote. Unfortunately, members were only given a little over three weeks to review the 2,148 pages released in the last tranche of the draft Study prior to the vote for adoption at the scheduled business meeting. This material provided the first look at the majority's analysis of the effectiveness of the interrogation program and became the core of the report adopted by the Committee. This last tranche contained nearly all of the most consequential analysis and – with the 282-page Executive Summary and the 95-pages of Findings and Conclusions provided to members for the first time just *three days* prior to the business meeting – comprised 40 percent of the adopted Study. The *day before* the December 13, 2012, business meeting, the Committee members received another "final version" of the report that made extensive changes to Study text, including the conclusions. [17] This unreasonably short time-period to review thousands of pages of text essentially precluded the possibility of formulating and offering amendments to the Study – had such an opportunity even been afforded to our Committee members.

(U) Aside from the sheer volume of the material, underlying the request for more time was the fact that almost all of the source material used to write the Study was located 40 minutes from Capitol Hill and thus not readily accessible to members and staff during the busiest month of the 112th Congress, when the Committee was simultaneously working on the Study, the Intelligence Authorization Act for Fiscal Year 2013, Foreign Intelligence Surveillance Act reauthorization, and its review of the Benghazi attacks. Nevertheless, the Chairman denied the Vice Chairman's request both prior to, and during, the Committee's business meeting for more time to review the draft Study.

Δ

Endnote

[17] *See* SSCI Transcript, Business Meeting to Consider the Report on the CIA Detention and Interrogation Program December 13, 2012, p. 25 (DTS 2013-0452).

(U) Insufficient Initial Fact Checking

(U) The 2,148-page tranche release, which specifically addressed the intelligence acquired from the Program and the CIA's representations regarding the effectiveness of the Program, also made serious allegations attacking the honesty and integrity of the CIA as an institution and of many of its senior and junior officers. In preparing this part of the Study, the majority selected 20 cases in which they claim the CIA inaccurately described information acquired from the interrogation program. This is ironic, since we found the Study itself consistently mischaracterized CIA's analysis. In each of these 20 cases, the Study absolutely and categorically dismissed any correlation previously drawn by the CIA between the Detention and Interrogation Program and the capture of terrorists, thwarting of terrorist plots, or the collection of significant intelligence. There is no ambiguity in the Study's indictment: in every one of these cases, the CIA and its officers lied – to Congress, to the White House, to the Department of Justice, and ultimately to the American people.

(U) We believe that the serious nature of these original conclusions required, as the Committee has done in the past with reports of such magnitude, submitting the Study to the Intelligence Community for review and comment before the vote. This deviation not only hampered the Committee's efforts to approve a factually accurate report, but it deprived the Intelligence Community of its traditional opportunity to provide important feedback to the

Committee prior to the approval of the Study. Moreover, the near absence of any timely interviews of relevant Intelligence Community witnesses during the course of this Study was a warning flag that should have signaled the increased need for initial fact-checking prior to the Study's adoption.

(U) The Committee has a long-standing practice of sending reports to the executive branch for review dating back to the Church Committee reports in 1975.[18] More recently, in 2004, the Committee provided the draft report on the *U.S. Intelligence Community's Prewar Intelligence Assessments on Iraq* to the Intelligence Community for fact-checking. The Committee wanted to ensure that a report of that magnitude, which purported to tell the Intelligence Community why years of analysis on Iraq's weapons of mass destruction programs was wrong, needed to be unquestionably accurate and not subject to challenge by the Intelligence Community. Only after the Intelligence Community provided its feedback and after the Committee held a hearing with the Director of Central Intelligence to give him the chance to comment on the record, did the Committee vote on the report. Thus, both the Committee and the Intelligence Community had a full and fair opportunity to review and check the report before a vote and before members provided additional or minority views. Also, unlike this Study, the Committee had conducted over 200 interviews with Intelligence Community witnesses who, over the course of a year, provided the investigative staff with information, insight, and clarification that could not be found in the documents alone.

(U) Unfortunately, in spite of a specific request at the December 2012 business meeting to follow these precedents, the majority refused to do so. Adhering to our established precedent for a report of this importance would have sent a clear signal to the entire Intelligence Community that the Committee's primary goal was to provide an accurate accounting of the Detention and Interrogation Program. Had the CIA been allowed to do so, the Study could have been modified, if necessary, or if not, members would at least have had the benefit of understanding the CIA's perspective prior to casting their votes. Yet, because the Committee approved the Study as final, before the Study had been sent to the Intelligence Community for review, the CIA was placed in the unenviable position – not of fact-checking – but of critiquing the Study of its own oversight Committee. In doing so, the Committee significantly undermined and diminished its own credibility,

Δ

Endnote

[18] *See* Loch K. Johnson, *A Season of Inquiry: The Senate Intelligence Investigation*, University Press of Kentucky, Lexington. 1985, p. 108.
[http://www.amazon.com/dp/0813153018]

(U) The CIA Response

(U) On June 27, 2013, the CIA provided a 130-page response to the original Study approved during the 112th Congress. The CIA also provided a two-page response to our initial minority views.[19] The purpose of the CIA response was to focus "on the Agency's conduct of the RDI program, in the interest of promoting historical accuracy and identifying lessons learned for the future, with the ultimate goal of improving the Agency's execution of other covert action programs."[20] The CIA noted, however, that a comprehensive review of the Study's almost 6,000 pages was an impossible task given the time allotted. They chose to concentrate their efforts on the Study's 20 conclusions and that part of the Study that assessed the value of the information derived from the CIA's RDI activities. When the CIA was able to review certain portions of the Study in detail, it found that the Study's accuracy "was encumbered as much by the authors' interpretation, selection, and contextualization of the facts as it was by errors in their recitation of the facts, making it difficult to address its flaws with specific technical correction."[21]

(U) Consistent with our own observations, the CIA response found that, while the Study has all the appearances of an authoritative history of the CIA's Detention and Interrogation Program and contains an impressive amount of detail, it fails in significant and consequential ways to correctly portray and analyze that detail. The CIA attributed these failures to two basic limitations on the authors: (1) a methodology that relied exclusively on a review of documents with no opportunity to interview participants; and (2) an apparent lack of familiarity with some of the ways the CIA analyzes and uses intelligence.[22]

(U) Unlike the Study, the CIA response actually offered eight specific recommendations for improving future covert actions: (1) improve management's ability to manage risk by submitting more covert action programs to the special review process currently used ███████████████████ ███████████████(2) better plan covert actions by explicitly addressing at the outset the implications of leaks, an exit strategy, lines of authority, and resources; (3) revamp the way in which CIA assesses the effectiveness of covert actions; (4) ensure that all necessary information is factored into the selection process for officers being considered for the most sensitive assignments; (5) create a mechanism for periodically revalidating Office of Legal Counsel guidance on which the Agency continues to rely; (6) broaden the scope of accountability reviews; (7) improve recordkeeping for interactions with the media; and (8) improve record-keeping for interactions with Congress.[23] We believe the CIA should implement these recommendations.

Δ

Endnotes

[19] We modified these minority views based upon the CIA's input.

[20] CIA Study Response, Comments (TAB A), June

27, 2013, p. 1.

[21] CIA Study Response, Comments (TAB A), June 27, 2013, pp. 1-2.

[22] CIA Study Response. Comments (TAB A), June 27, 2013, p. 2.

[23] CIA Study Response, Comments (TAB A), June 27, 2013, pp. 17-18.

(U) The Summer Meetings

(U) During the summer and early fall of 2013, SSCI staff spent about sixty hours with CIA personnel who had led and participated in the preparation of the CIA's response to the Study. The purpose of these meetings was to discuss factual discrepancies and areas of disagreement between the SSCI Study and the CIA Study Response. These exchanges would have been much more productive if they had occurred *before* the Study was approved by the Committee in December 2012.

(U) The majority staff did not start these sessions with discussions about the substance of the Study or the CIA's response. Rather, they began by spending an inordinate amount of time questioning the CIA personnel about the process by which the CIA had prepared its response to the Study. Eventually, the discussions turned to more substantive issues. Prior to each session, the majority staff typically determined the order in which the Study conclusions would be discussed. Although the CIA and minority staff expressed repeated interest in discussing some of the more problematic conclusions and underlying "effectiveness" case studies, the majority staff proceeded with discussions of the least controversial portions of the Study.

(U) Our staff reported to us that the general tenor of these sessions was "unpleasant." Instead of giving the CIA an opportunity to help improve the Study by explaining the errors and factual inaccuracies identified in their response, the majority staff spent the vast majority of these sessions in "transmit" rather than "receive" mode. When the discussions finally turned to the "effectiveness" case studies, the majority staff spent a significant portion of the remaining time explaining its "methodology" and reading large portions of the report into the record. The CIA initially made arrangements to have certain key analysts participate in these discussions to help the Committee understand the meaning of certain parts of the historical documentary record. Unfortunately, these analysts were often kept waiting outside of the meeting room while the majority staff plowed through its set agenda with the senior CIA personnel. Some of those waiting analysts never received an opportunity to participate. Seeing the writing on the wall, the lead CIA personnel eventually stopped bringing the pertinent analysts along, which did not seem to concern the majority staff. The most problematic case studies were summarily discussed in just a few hours during the very last session.

(U) Given the unproductive manner in which these meetings were conducted, the Committee missed a significant opportunity to improve its Study through a better understanding of the CIA's analytical and operational practices that produced the documentary record upon which the Study was based. We commend the CIA personnel who patiently and professionally participated in these unproductive sessions and thank them for their dedicated service to our Nation.

(U) The Clash Over the Panetta Review

(U) On January 15, 2014, Chairman Feinstein and Vice Chairman Chambliss met with the Director of the Central Intelligence Agency (CIA), John Brennan, at his urgent request. At this meeting, Director Brennan disclosed that the CIA conducted a "search"[24] of a CIA computer network used by the Committee. The CIA established this network at a CIA facility in 2009 pursuant to written agreements between the Committee and then-Director Leon Panetta. It is the understanding of the Committee that the CIA conducted the "Panetta Internal Review" for the purpose of summarizing for CIA leadership the contents of documents likely to be reviewed by the Committee during its review.

(U) As evidenced by repeated unauthorized disclosures in the news media, the production and release of the Study has been manned by the alleged misconduct of CIA employees and majority staff as it pertains to the so-called "Panetta Internal Review." Regardless of differences of opinion and policy, the relationship between the CIA and this Committee should not have escalated to this level of embarrassment and provocation. It is one of the most delicate oversight relationships in the Federal government and must be treated as such at all times. It would be a shame if this incident tarnished the reputation of the Committee or the CIA to such a degree that the normally constructive cooperation between the CIA and the Committee is scarred beyond repair.

(U) Typically, matters such as these are handled discreetly through the accommodation process and would involve internal investigations or joint inquiries. These options were not available in this situation. Presently, the Department of Justice, the CIA Inspector General, and the U.S. Senate Sergeant at Arms are conducting ongoing investigation into these matters. Nonetheless, for the purpose of these Views, it is worth noting the following observations:

> (U) First, Committee majority staff knowingly removed the Panetta Internal Review, a highly classified, privileged CIA document, from a CIA facility without authorization and in clear violation of the existing agreed-upon procedures by the Committee and the CIA.

> (U) Second, although the Committee certainly needs to understand the facts and circumstances of whether the CIA acted inappropriately when it allegedly "searched" a Committee shared drive on certain CIA computers, this issue is separate and distinct from the

earlier incident involving the unauthorized removal of the Panetta Internal Review document from the CIA facility. The subsequent "search" does not excuse or justify the earlier staff behavior or vice versa.

(U) Third, the Panetta Internal Review document that was brought back to Committee spaces was not handled in accordance with Committee protocols. Committee Rule 9.4 states, "Each member of the Committee shall at all times have access to all papers and other material received from any source." It appears that the existence, handling, and the majority's possession of this privileged document were not disclosed to the minority for months, and might never have been revealed but for the public disclosures about the document which led to the January meeting with Director Brennan.

(U) Finally, given the CIA's repeated assertions of privilege concerning the document since the January meeting with Director Brennan, at no time has a minority member or staff handled the document or reviewed its contents.

Δ

Endnote

[24] The 2009 written agreement permitted CIA access to the network for technical support, but at the time of this writing, the forensic details of the CIA "search" are unknown.

(U) The Declassification Review Business Meeting

(U) The majority's practice of providing insufficient time for member review of the report's contents was repeated just prior to the Committee's April 3, 2014, business meeting to consider whether to send the report to the executive branch for a declassification review. On April 1, 2014, updated versions of the Study's three volume report, totaling 6,178 pages, were made available on a Committee shared drive. The majority staff did not release its third updated versions of the Executive Summary and Findings and Conclusions *until the day before the business meeting*. Finally, *four days after the business meeting*, the Chairman transmitted to President Obama one last revised version of the updated Executive Summary and Findings and Conclusions.[25]

Δ

Endnote

[25] The citations to the updated Executive Summary and Findings and Conclusions in these minority views have been revised to match up with the versions that were transmitted to the President. The citations to the updated three-volume report are keyed to the versions that were placed on the Committee's shared drive.

(U) THE STUDY'S PROBLEMATIC ANALYSIS

(U) As previously discussed, the flawed process used for the approval of the original Study and this updated version resulted in numerous factual errors. These factual errors were further compounded by the Study's numerous analytical shortfalls, which ultimately led to an unacceptable number of incorrect claims and invalid conclusions. This section will generally highlight many of the analytical shortcomings we found in the Study. The next section will then specifically examine some of the Study's most problematic conclusions, including our analysis of the factual premises, claims, and flawed analytical methodology upon which many of these faulty conclusions were based.

(U) When this Committee reviews the Intelligence Community's analytic products, it does so with the expectation of adherence to certain analytic integrity standards.[26] These standards "act as guidelines and goals for analysts and managers throughout the Intelligence Community who strive for excellence in their analytic work practices and products."[27] Although these specific analytic standards do not technically apply to this Committee's oversight reporting, the aspirational analytical values they represent are applicable to the Committee's analytical expectations for its own oversight work product. The examples offered in this section illustrate some of the Study's general analytic deficiencies concerning objectivity, independence from political considerations, timeliness, the use of all available intelligence sources, and consistency with proper standards of analytic tradecraft. These examples also serve as a useful backdrop for our specific analysis and critique of some of the Study's erroneous conclusions and claims.[28]

Δ

Endnotes

[26] In 2004, the SSCI was instrumental in including in the Intelligence Reform and Terrorism Prevention Act. P.L. 108-458, a provision mandating that the Director of National Intelligence "ensure the most accurate analysis" by implementing policies and procedure "to encourage sound analytic tradecraft."

[27] Intelligence Community Directive Number 203, Analytic Standards (effective June 21, 2007), p. 1.

[28] *See* Intelligence Community Directive Number 203, Analytic Standards (effective June 21, 2007), p. 2.

(U) Inadequate Context

(TS// ▮▮▮▮▮▮▮▮▮▮▮▮▮▮▮▮▮ //NF) We begin, however, with a review of the context in which the CIA Program was initiated and operated. Although there is no specific, Intelligence Community analytic standard addressing context, it is important in any analysis or report to provide appropriate context so that the reader is able to understand why events transpired as they did. The Study does very little to provide such context – it is entirely silent on the surge in terrorist threat reporting that inundated the Intelligence Community following the September 11, 2001, terrorist attacks by al-Qa'ida, and it makes no mention of the pervasive, genuine apprehension about a possible second attack on the United States that gripped the CIA in 2002 and 2003. Rather, the Study begins by coldly describing the September 17, 2001, covert action Memorandum of Notification (MON) signed by the President authorizing the CIA to detain "persons who pose a continuing, serious threat of violence or death to U.S. persons and interests or who are planning terrorist activities," as if the attacks that had killed nearly 3,000 Americans just six days prior, were incidental to the extraordinary authorities granted under the MON, and all other events described in the Study.[29] They were not. In our collective view, to depict judgments and decisions arising from the administration of this program as having been made in a vacuum, or somehow in isolation of these events, is both unrealistic and unfair.

(U) During our review of the materials provided by the CIA for the Study, we could clearly discern a workforce traumatized by an intelligence failure that had left thousands of Americans dead, but also galvanized by the challenge of working on the frontline to ensure such an attack never occurred again. In the early years of this effort, there were constant threats of new attacks, and endless leads to track down. CIA and other Intelligence Community personnel worked relentlessly, day in and day out, to follow up on every one.

(U) There is no doubt that the CIA Program – executed hastily in the aftermath of the worst terrorist attack in our Nation's history – had flaws. The CIA has admitted as much in its June 27, 2013, response to the Study. However, the Study's conclusion that the use of enhanced interrogation techniques was ineffective does not comport with a massive documentary record that clearly demonstrates a series of significant counterterrorism operational successes. That same documentary record also undercuts the Study's flawed conclusions that the CIA "impeded" congressional and executive branch oversight of the Program, as well as the counterterrorism and diplomatic missions of other federal entities. Our review of the record revealed this conclusion – one the Study twists itself in knots to avoid – that the CIA Program was a vital source of critical intelligence that led to the detention of multiple terrorists and helped keep America safe.

(U) Whether the CIA should operate a clandestine detention program and whether it is in America's interests to interrogate suspected terrorists using methods beyond those in the U.S. Army Field Manual are valid questions worthy of serious debate. Unfortunately, the utility of Study's considerable work product in such a debate is seriously undermined by its disregard of the Program's historical context and its reliance upon an unrealistic analytical methodology, which appears to have been designed to exclude from consideration any inconvenient facts not fitting within the Study's preconceived view that such enhanced methods produced nothing of intelligence value. Although there are a number of findings in the Study with which we agree, our own review of the documentary record compelled us to focus our discussion in these minority views on these inconvenient facts that invalidate much of the revisionist history that is being advocated by many of the Study's findings and conclusions.

Δ

Endnotes

[29] *See* SSCI Study, Executive Summary, December 3, 2014, p. 11.

(U) Inadequate Objectivity

~~(TS//~~ ███████████████████ ~~//NF)~~ The standard of objectivity requires that analysts perform their analytic functions from an unbiased perspective – analysis "should be free of emotional content, give due regard to alternative perspectives, and acknowledge developments that necessitate adjustments to analytic judgments."[30]

~~(TS//~~ ███████████████ ~~//NF)~~ We were disappointed to find the updated version of the Study still contains evidence of strongly held biases by the authors – a point emphasized by John Brennan prior to his confirmation as the Director of the CIA, when he told Vice Chairman Chambliss that, based on his reading of the originally approved Executive Summary and the Findings and Conclusions, the Study was "not objective" and was a "prosecutor's brief," "written with an eye toward finding problems." We still agree with Director Brennan's assessments. We also agree with the criticism he relayed from Intelligence Community officials that it was written with a "bent on the part of the authors" with "political motivations." We similarly found these problems, but more importantly, we found that those biases were not only present, but they resulted in faulty analysis, serious inaccuracies, and misrepresentations of fact in the Study.

~~(TS//~~ ███████████████ ~~//NF)~~ For example, there were instances when detainees told their interrogators that they had provided everything they knew or denied that they were terrorists, and the Study seems to take them at their word. In June 2002, Abu Zubaydah told his interrogators, "What I have, I give it all... I have no more."[31]   The Study seems to have bought into this lie when it subsequently concluded, "At no time during or after the aggressive interrogation phase did Abu Zubaydah provide the information that the CIA enhanced [interrogations] were premised upon, specifically, 'actionable intelligence about al-Qa'ida operatives in the United States and planned al-Qa'ida lethal attacks against U.S. citizens and U.S. interests.'"[32]

<del>(TS//</del>███████████████<del>//NF)</del> In fact, Abu Zubaydah did provide actionable intelligence that helped disrupt planned al-Qa'ida lethal attacks against U.S. citizens and interests following his June 2002 denials of having more information. Although our review of the documentary record revealed that Abu Zubaydah's first period of "aggressive" interrogation actually began on April 15, 2002, [33] he certainly provided valuable intelligence *after* his second period of aggressive interrogation began on August 4, 2002. For example, on August 20, 2002,[35] Abu Zubaydah provided information about how he would go about locating Hassan Ghul and other al-Qa'ida associates in Karachi. This information caused ████████████████ Pakistani authorities to intensify their efforts and helped lead them to capture Ramzi bin al-Shibh and other al-Qa'ida associates during the Karachi safe house raids conducted on September 10-11, 2002."[36]   These arrests effectively disrupted a then ongoing plot to bomb certain named hotels in Karachi, Pakistan.[37]   In April 2002, Khalid Shaykh Mohammad (KSM) confirmed the hotels plot had been

directed against U.S. citizens and interests when he told his interrogators that the hotels had been selected because they were frequented by American and German guests.[38]

~~(TS//~~ ███████████████████ ~~//NF)~~ The Study's lack of objectivity is further illustrated in the acceptance as factual those CIA documents that support its findings and conclusions, and the dismissal of documents contradictory to its findings and conclusions as being "inaccurate" or "misrepresentations." For example, the Study cites to a finished intelligence product published in 2006 as support for its stunning claim that the "CIA later concluded that Abu Zubaydah was not a member of al-Qa'ida."[39] In fact, the product states: "Al-Qa'ida rejected Abu Zubaydah's request *in 1993* to join the group and that Khaldan was not overseen by Bin Ladin's organization."[40] The Study fails to state that the interrogation of this supposed "non-member" resulted in 766 sole-source disseminated intelligence reports by the Study's own count.[41] Ironically, this intelligence product was written based on "information from detainees and captured documents" – including from Abu Zubaydah.[42]

~~(TS//~~ ███████████████████ ~~//NF)~~ Another indication of the Study's lack of objectivity is its tendency to state its conclusions in such a manner as to be technically accurate, but factually misleading. For example, in the Executive Summary, the Study authors state,

> a review of CIA records found no connection between Abu Zubaydah's reporting on Ramzi bin al-Shibh and Ramzi bin al-Shibh's capture. CIA records indicate that

> Ramzi bin al-Shibh was captured unexpectedly – on
> September 11, 2002, when Pakistani authorities, were
> conducting raids targeting Hassan Ghul in
> Pakistan."[43]

The implication is that none of the information Zubaydah provided pursuant after enhanced interrogation led to al-Shibh's capture. What is ignored here is the exact expression of Zubaydah's role in al-Shibh's apprehension, captured in a CIA internal communication, where it is made clear, "[Zubaydah's] knowledge of al-Qa'ida lower-level facilitators, modus operandi and safehouses, which he shared with us as a result of EITs... played a key role in the ultimate capture of Ramzi Bin al-Shibh."[44] Zubaydah's reporting on how to locate terrorists in Pakistan, by trying to find another terrorist, is what led to bin al-Shibh's arrest."[45]

(TS// ████████████████ //NF) The Study's uneven treatment of key U.S. officials throughout the report, attacking the credibility and honesty of some, while making little mention of others, also lacked objectivity. For example, former Director George Tenet led the CIA at the outset of the Program, during a period the Study contends was characterized by mismanagement. Tenet authorized the enhanced interrogation techniques, and if the Study is to be believed, headed an organization that withheld information from and misled policymakers in the executive branch and Congress. He is mentioned 62 times in the updated version of the Study's Executive Summary. By comparison, former Director Michael Hayden joined the CIA in 2006, after all but two detainees entered the Program and the most severe EITs were no longer in use. He was also the only Director to brief the Program to all members of the congressional oversight committees. Yet, Director Hayden is mentioned 172 times in the Executive Summary, where he is disparaged numerous times. For example, in Conclusion 18, which alleges the CIA marginalized criticisms and objections concerning the Detention and Interrogation Program, the Executive Summary states: "CIA Director Hayden testified to the Committee that 'numerous false allegations of physical and threatened abuse and faulty legal assumptions and analysis in the [ICRC] report undermine its overall credibility.'"[46] The Study also states:

> After multiple Senators had been critical of the program and written letters expressing concerns to CIA Director Michael Hayden, Director Hayden nonetheless told a meeting of foreign ambassadors to the United States that every Committee member was 'fully briefed,' and that '[t]his is not CIA's program. This is not the President's program. This is America's program.'[47]

Beyond the imbalance with which some officials are treated in the Study, we are particularly concerned that such treatment will send the perverse message to future CIA Directors and the CIA that they will face less criticism if they keep information limited to only a few members.

Δ

Endnotes

[30] Intelligence Community Directive Number 203, Analytic Standards (effective June 21, 2007), p. 2.

[31] SSCI Study, Volume I, March 31, 2014, p. 113:

CIA, ███████ 10487, June 18, 2002, p. 4.

[32] SSCI Study, Volume I, March 31, 2014, p. 146.

[33] *See infra*, p. 150.

[34] *See* CIA, ███████ 10586, August 4, 2002, pp. 2-5.

[35] *See* Captures Resulting From Detainee Information: Four Case Studies, November 26, 2003, p. 2; CIA ALEC ███████ August 29, 2002, pp. 2-7.

[36] *See infra*, pp. 152-166.

[37] *See infra*, pp. 181-183.

[38] *See* [REDACTED] 34513, March 5, 2003, p. 2.

[39] SSCI Study, Executive Summary, December 3, 2014, p. 410 n.2301.

[40] CIA, *Countering Misconceptions About Training Camps in Afghanistan, 1990-2001*, August 16. 2006, p. 2 (DTS 2006-3254) (emphasis added). This document is attached as Appendix I, *see infra*, p. I-1.

[41] *See* SSCI Study, Volume III, March 31, 2014. pp. 282-283.

[42] CIA, Countering Misconceptions About Training Camps in Afghanistan, 1990-2001, August 16, 2006, p. i (DTS 2006-3254).

[43] SSCI Study, Executive Summary, December 3, 2014, p. 318.

[44] CIA Memo from Pavitt to CIA IG on Draft Special Review, February 27, 2004, pp. 13-14. For a more detailed examination of this issue, *see infra*, pp. 160-172.

[45] *See* CIA, ALEC ███████████ August 29, 2002, pp. 2-3; CIA, ALEC ██████████ September 11, 2002, p. 2.

[46] SSCI Study, Findings and Conclusions, December 3, 2014, p. 15.

[47] SSCI Study, Executive Summary, December 3, 2014, p. 448.

(U) Indications of Political Considerations

(U) The analysis and products of the Intelligence Community are supposed to remain independent of political consideration, leaving policy and political determinations to the policymakers and politicians. It follows that, Intelligence Community analysts "should provide objective assessments informed by available information that are not distorted or altered with the intent of supporting or advocating a particular policy, political viewpoint, or audience."[48] Although some might think that this analytic standard would have little applicability to Congress, which is an inherently political body, in the context of congressional oversight of the Intelligence Community, our Committee was designed to function in a bipartisan manner. Thus, this analytical standard is useful in assessing whether a particular Committee oversight report was crafted in a bipartisan manner or suffers from indications of political considerations.

(TS// ███████████████ //NF) Far from being free of political consideration, the Study uses quotes from minority members out of context to suggest they supported positions in the Study, that they in fact did not, and entirely omits contradictory comments. For example, the Study selectively quotes from a February 11, 2009, meeting organized around the discussion of a report prepared by majority staff, evaluating the detention and interrogation of two detainees. The Study indicates that "a Committee staff presented the report, and quotes Chairman Feinstein saying the review represented, "the most comprehensive statement on the treatment of these two detainees."[49] What the Study fails to note, however, is that Vice Chairman Bond clarified the draft was "the work of two majority staff members," and that neither he, "nor any minority staff was informed of the work going into the memo over the course of the last year." He also noted that the minority had offered some input, but had not been able to review the document thoroughly, or fact check it, and therefore did not view the report as a bipartisan document. Moreover, he noted that the minority staff had just received the remarks the majority staff had prepared, several points of which were subsequently disputed by minority staff during the meeting.

(TS// ▮▮▮▮▮▮▮▮▮▮▮▮▮▮ //NF) The Study also claims that a minority member's comments during the meeting, "expressed support for expanding the Committee investigation to learn more about the program."[51] In fact, the member was explaining to two majority members, who were already talking about declassifying a report they had just seen, why he would like to know a lot more "before I pass judgment" on the CIA officers described in the document. Suggesting doubt about the allegations in the document, he commented, "It's hard to believe, and I can't help but think that there isn't more here."[52]

Δ

Endnotes

[48] Intelligence Community Directive Number 203,

Analytic Standards (effective June 21, 2007), p. 2.

[49] SSCI Study, Volume I, March 31, 2014, p. 1211.

[50] *See* SSCI Transcript, Business Meeting to Discuss the Committee's Investigation of the CIA's Detention and Interrogation Program, February 11, 2009, pp. 6-7 and 33-34 (DTS 2009-1420).

[51] SSCI Study, Volume I, March 31, 2014, p. 1213.

[52] SSCI Transcript, Business Meeting to Discuss the Committee's Investigation of the CIA's Detention and Interrogation Program, February 11, 2009, pp. 48-51 (DTS 2009-1420).

(U) Lack of Timeliness

(U) The analytic integrity standard of timeliness is predicated on maximizing the impact and utility of intelligence, and it encourages the Intelligence Community to produce relevant analysis that effectively informs key policy decisions.[53] The "effectively informs" aspect of this notion means that intelligence products which are published too near to a decision point, let alone after it, are of diminishing or negligible value. This same susceptibility holds true for intelligence oversight reports.

(TS// ███████████ //NF) On January 22, 2009, President Obama issued Executive Order 13491, which required the CIA to "close as expeditiously as possible any detention facilities that it currently operates and... not operate any such detention facility in the future." The Executive Order prohibited any U.S. government employee from using interrogation techniques other than those in the Army Field Manual 2-22.3 on Human Intelligence Collector Operations.[54] The Terms of Reference for the Study were approved by the Committee on March 5, 2009.[55] However, the original Study was adopted by the Committee on December 13, 2012 – approximately three years and nine months after the approval of the Terms of Reference.[56] On April 3, 2014 – *more than five years after* the Terms of Reference were approved – the Committee sent updated versions of the previously approved Executive Summary and Findings and Conclusions to the executive branch for a declassification review.

(TS//███████████████//NF) This Study purports to represent "the most comprehensive review ever conducted of the CIA's Detention and Interrogation Program."[57] Certainly, there is some utility in the exercise of studying an intelligence program so expansive and intricate, that the document production phase alone lasted more than three years, and produced more than six million pages of material.[58] Normally, a review of this magnitude might be expected to yield valuable lessons learned and best practices, which might then be applied to future intelligence programs. However, no version of the Study has ever contained any recommendations.[59] Moreover, there are no lessons learned, nor are there any suggestions of possible alternative measures. This absence of Committee recommendations is likely due to the fact that the key policy decisions about the CIA's Detention and Interrogation Program were decided years ago by President Obama in 2009. Despite its massive size, the Study does little to effectively inform current policymakers, but rather makes a number of inaccurate historical judgments about the CIA's Program. For these reasons, we conclude that the Study is not timely.

Δ

Endnotes

[53] *See* Intelligence Community Directive Number 203, Analytic Standards (effective June 21, 2007), p. 2.

[54] Executive Order 13491, "Ensuring Lawful

Interrogation," January 22, 2009, Section 3(b), p. 2. [http://www.whitehouse.gov/the_press_office/EnsuringLa wfulInterrogations/]

[55] *See* SSCI Transcript, Business Meeting to Discuss and Revote on the Terms of Reference for the Committee's Study of the CIA's Detention and Interrogation Program, March 5, 2009, p. 11 (DTS 2009-1916).

[56] *See* SSCI Transcript, Business Meeting to Consider the Report on the CIA Detention and Interrogation Program, December 13, 2012, p. 74 (DTS 2013-0452).

[57] SSCI Study, Executive Summary, December 3, 2004, p. 9. A more accurate statement would have been, "the most comprehensive documentary review ever conducted of the CIA's Detention and Interrogation Program."

[58] SSCI Study, Executive Summary, December 3, 2004, p. 9.

[59] At least the CIA's June 27, 2013, response to the Study identified eight recommendations derived from the lessons it had learned related to the Detention and Interrogation Program. *See* CIA Study Response, Comments (Tab A), June 27, 2013, pp. 16-17.

(U) Inadequate Use of Available Sources of Intelligence

(U) Despite the millions of records available for the Study's research, we found that important documents were not reviewed and some were never requested. We were surprised to learn that the e-mails of only 64 individuals were requested to support the review of a program that spanned eight years and included hundreds of government employees. Committee reviews of this magnitude typically involve interviewing the relevant witnesses. Here, these relevant witnesses were largely unavailable due to the Attorney General's decision to re-open a preliminaiy criminal review in connection with the interrogation of specific detainees at overseas locations. When DOJ closed this investigation in August 2013, however, the Committee had a window of opportunity to invite these relevant witnesses in for interviews, but apparently decided against that course of action. The lack of witness interviews should have been a clear warning flag to all Committee members about the difficulty of completing a truly "comprehensive" review on this subject.

(U) Exhibits Poor Standards of Analytic Tradecraft

(U) Compounding its disconcerting analytic integrity challenges, the Study's content is littered with examples of poor analytic tradecraft, across several critical measures of proficiency for authoring intelligence products. Here we provide some examples of the Study's poor analytic tradecraft.

(U) Inadequately Describes the Quality and Reliability of Sources

~~(TS//~~ ███████████████ ~~//NF)~~ Analysis that adheres to Intelligence Community tradecraft standards properly describes the quality and reliability of sources. Analysis that misrepresents or misinterprets the quality of source material compromises the integrity of the resulting analysis. At points, the Study relies upon "draft talking points" documents as being authoritative.[60] Doing so raises questions about the credibility of the assessment being drawn based on such a source, because draft talking points are prepared by staff for a senior leader and it is often difficult to ascertain, absent interviews, whether all, some, or none of the information contained in talking points was even used by the senior leader.

~~(TS//~~ ███████████████ ~~//NF)~~ We found frequent examples if citations that pointed to documents that did not discuss the material in question, were taken out of context, or did not accurately reflect the contents of the cited source documents – in some cases changing the meaning entirely. For example, the Study states that a review by the CIA Inspector General (IG) "uncovered that additional unauthorized techniques were used against" a detainee, but the Inspector General report actually said it "heard allegations" of the use of unauthorized techniques and said, "For all of the instances, the allegations were disputed or too ambiguous to reach any authoritative determination about the facts."[61] In another case, the Study states: "By early October 2002, the CIA completed a search of the names identified in the 'perfume letter' in its databases and found most of the individuals who 'had assigned roles in support of the operation' were arrested by Pakistani authorities during the raids.[62] This inaccurate paraphrase is different from the actual language of the quote, which states, "it appears that most of the detainees jested on [September 11, 2002], had assigned roles in support of the operation outlined in the 'perfume' letter."[63] After explaining that a detainee had already admitted that "purchasing perfumes" likely referred to purchasing or making poisons, the cable states that, "[O]ur concern over this letter is heightened because of the identities of the individuals involved in the operation it outlines."[64] The Study's inaccurate paraphrase appears to minimize the remaining threat, while the cable itself indicates heightened concern. In hindsight, it appears that while the September 11, 2002, safe house raids helped to derail the Karachi hotels plot, the threat evolved into a planned attack on the U.S. consulate in Karachi by Ammar al-Baluchi and Khallad bin Attash, who were not captured during the September 2002 safe house raids.[65]

(U) Inadequate Caveats About Uncertainties or Confidence in Analytic Judgments

~~(TS//~~ ██████████████ ~~//NF)~~ Proper tradecraft requires that the strength of an analytic judgment should be expressed when appropriate, through confidence level statements and the identification of uncertainty. This is an important check on analytical judgments that provides a key safeguard for policy makers. Many of the Study's conclusions and underlying claims are offered as matters of unequivocal fact. As an example, the Study asserts "CIA officers conducted no research on successful interrogation strategies during the drafting of the MON, nor after it was issued."[66] Proving a negative is often very difficult, and in this particular case it is difficult to understand how such an absolute assertion can be made without interviewing the affected witnesses or even citing to one documentary source that might support such a claim.

(U) Inadequate Incorporation of Alternative Analysis Where Appropriate

~~(TS//~~ ██████████████ ~~//NF)~~ Analysts are generally encouraged to incorporate alternative analysis into their production where they can. Sometimes this exercise helps identify weaknesses in the analysis or highlights intelligence collection gaps. The Study is replete with uncited and potentially unknowable assertions like "there is no indication in CIA records that Abi Zubaydah provided information on bin al-Shibh's whereabouts"[67] or

██

███████ never visited the site."[68] Alternate analysis would certainly have been helpful in disproving the first claim and may have been helpful in the determination of whether the second assertion could really be established by records alone. With respect to the first claim, Abu Zubaydah did provide locational information about bin al-Shibh. As discussed below, Zubaydah made four separate photographic identifications of bin al-Shibh and placed him in Kandahar, Afghanistan, during the November to December 2001 timeframe and provided sufficient information for interrogators to conclude that bin al-Shibh was subsequently with KSM in Karachi, Pakistan.[69] With respect to the absolute claim that ██████████████ ████████████████████████████ never visited a particular site, alternative analysis may have demonstrated a need for additional information beyond that contained in the documentary record. That alternative analysis may have counseled in favor of modifying the assertion to something like, "It appears that no ███████████████████████ █████████████ visited the site during that timeframe" or dropping the assertion in its entirety.

(U) Based on Flawed Logical Argumentation

~~(TS//~~ ███████████████ ~~//NF)~~ Proper tradecraft entails understanding of the information and reasoning underlying analytic judgments. Key points should be made effectively and supported by information and coherent reasoning. Substandard analysis presents unsupported assertions that appear contrary to the evidence cited or in violation of common sense. We found instances where claims were supported more by rhetorical devices than sound logical reasoning. For example, in support of the Study's conclusion that the CIA's use of enhanced interrogation techniques was not effective, the Study stated:

> At least seven detainees were subjected to the CIA's enhanced interrogation techniques almost immediately after being rendered into CIA custody, *making it impossible to determine* whether the information they provided could have been obtained through non-coercive debriefing methods."[70]

This statement is a rhetorical attempt to persuade the reader that non-coercive techniques may have been equally or even more successful than the enhanced techniques. It is little more than an appeal to unknowable facts and is not based upon logical reasoning.[71]

~~(TS//~~ ███████████████ ~~//NF)~~ We also found instances where the Study undermined its own claims by citing to documents that contradicted those claims. For example, while discussing testimony given by then CIA Director Hayden on the Program, the Study states,

115

"Hayden's testimony included *the representation that Abu Zubaydah had a religious basis for cooperating* after the use of the CIA's enhanced interrogation techniques... Research Note: *CIA records do not support this representation related to Abu Zubaydah....*[72] The Study also asserted, "Abu Zubaydah explained that he informed trainees at the training camp that "'no brother' should be expected to hold out for an extended time," and that captured individuals will provide information in detention. For that reason, the captured individuals, he explained, should "expect that the organization will make adjustments to protect people and plans when someone with knowledge is captured."[73] However, in the same intelligence report cited for the above proposition, Abu Zubaydah revealed, that as his conditions in CIA detention worsened,

> [H]e became increasingly concerned for his long-term wellbeing. *He said that this process eventually became an 'unbearable weight' that Allah would no longer require him to carry. Under these conditions, Allah would have mercy and forgive him* ('As Jesus forgave Peter for denying him three times') *for revealing to the Americans what he knew about al Qa'ida and the brothers.*[74]

This one admission by Abu Zubaydah, unexplainably omitted from the Study, completely contradicts the flawed logic of the Study's claim that religion played no role in his cooperation with the Americans. The criticism of Director Hayden here is unwarranted.

Δ

Endnotes

[60] SSCI Study, Executive Summary, December 3, 2014, pp. 143 and 196.

[61] *Compare* SSCI Study, Volume I, March 31, 2014, p. 229, *with* CIA Office of Inspector General, Special Review: Counterterrorism Detention and Interrogation Activities (September 2001 – October 2003), May 7, 2004, p. 41 (DTS 2004-2710). [http://media.washingtonpost.com/wp-srv/nation/documents/cia_oig_report.pdf] [[This tradecraft error was partially corrected in the November 26, 2014, version of the Executive Summary by editing the offending sentence to read, "The Office of Inspector General later described additional allegations of unauthorized techniques used against...." (emphasis added). *Compare* SSCI Study, Executive Summary, April 3, 2014, p. 67 with SSCI Study, Executive Summary, December 3, 2014, p. 70.]]

[62] SSCI Study, Executive Summary, December 3, 2014, p. 242. The Study cites to CIA, ALEC 188560, October 3, 2002, but the quoted language actually appears in CIA, ALEC 188565,October 3, 2002, p. 2.

[63] CIA, ALEC ▮▮▮▮▮▮▮▮ October 3, 2002, p. 2.

[64] CIA, ALEC ▮▮▮▮▮▮▮▮ October 3, 2002, pp. 2-3.

[65] CIA, CIA CABLE 45028,▮▮▮▮▮▮▮▮▮▮▮▮ CIA, [CIA CABLE] 38405, May 17, 2003, p. 4-7. *See infra*, pp. 181-183.

[66] SSCI Study, Volume I, March 31, 2014, p. 20.

[67] SSCI Study, Executive Summary, December 3, 2014, p. 317.

[68] SSCI Study, Volume I, March 31, 2014, p. 227.

[69] *See infra*, p. 160.

[70] SSCI Study, Findings and Conclusions, April 3, 2014, p. 2 (emphasis added). [[This false reasoning was tempered in the December 3, 2014, version of the Executive Summary by editing the sentence to read, "CIA detainees who were subjected to the CIA's enhanced interrogation techniques were usually subjected to the techniques immediately after being rendered to CIA custody. Other detainees provided significant accurate intelligence prior to, or without having been subjected to these techniques." *Compare* SSCI Study, Findings and Conclusions, April 3, 2014, p. 2 *with* SSCI Study, Findings and Conclusions, December 3. 2014, p. 2. |]

[71] For a more detailed analysis of this unsupported claim, *see infra*, p. 122.

[72] SSCI Study, Volume I, March 31, 2014, p. 1130 (emphasis added).

[73] SSCI Study, Executive Summary, December 3, 2014, p. 469 (citing CIA, 10496, February 16, 2003, p. 2).

[74] CIA, ████████ 10496, February 16, 2003, p. 3 (emphasis added).

(U) ERRONEOUS STUDY CONCLUSIONS

(U) We were only given 60 days to prepare our initial minority views in response to the more than 6,000-page Study, which was approved by the Committee at the end of the 112th Congress. In those initial views, we successfully endeavored to describe the major fallacies and problematic findings that we had time to identify in the Study. Despite the fact that the CIA response and the summer staff meetings essentially validated our criticisms of the original Study, it appears that the updated version of the Study largely persists with many of its erroneous analytical and factual claims. We have used these past eleven weeks to update our own minority views and focus our attention on eight of the Study's most problematic conclusions.[75]

(U) Conclusion 1 (The CIA's use of enhanced interrogation techniques was not effective)

(U) The first of these updated conclusions asserts that the "CIA's use of enhanced interrogation techniques was not an effective means of acquiring intelligence or gaining cooperation from detainees."[76] The Study attempts to validate this apparently absolute conclusion by relying upon a number of faulty premises.

(U) The first faulty premise is that "seven of the 39 CIA

119

detainees known to have been subjected to the CIA's enhanced interrogation techniques produced no intelligence while in CIA custody."[77] This 18 percent "failure rate" statistic may encourage some readers to jump to the hasty judgment that enhanced interrogation techniques were not an effective means of acquiring intelligence, because they failed to produce intelligence from every detainee against whom they were used. Such a judgment seems unreasonable, given that, in most human endeavors, 100 percent success rates are pretty rare, especially in complex processes like the ones involved here. If the Study's statistic is true, then it is just as true that 32 of the 39 detainees subjected to enhanced interrogation techniques did produce some intelligence while in CIA custody. That is an "effectiveness" rate of 82 percent for obtaining intelligence from detainees who were subjected to enhanced interrogation techniques. While an 82 percent effectiveness rate in obtaining some information sounds pretty good, this claim suffers from the same analytical defect as the Study's 18 percent failure rate, in that it does not provide any real insight about the *qualitative* value of the intelligence information obtained. The true test of effectiveness is the value of *what* was obtained – not how much or how little was obtained.

(U) As long as we are considering quantitative assessments of whether detainee interrogations led to the creation of intelligence reports, it might be useful to look at the "failure" and "effectiveness" rates for those detainees who were not subjected to enhanced interrogation. Using some of the Study's own numbers, a total of 119 detainees were in the CIA's Detention and Interrogation Program. Of these detainees, the interrogations of 41 of them resulted in no disseminated intelligence reports.[78] If true, we can deduce that 80 detainees were not subjected to enhanced interrogation and that the interrogations of 34 of these same detainees resulted in no disseminated intelligence reports. [79] Turning to the failure rate first, 34 of 80 CIA detainees who were not subjected to enhanced interrogation techniques produced no intelligence while in CIA custody. That is a 42.5 percent failure rate, more than double the 18 percent failure rate for the detainees subjected to enhanced interrogation techniques. Conversely, 46 of 80 detainees who were not subjected to enhanced interrogation techniques produced some intelligence while in CIA custody. That is a 57.5 percent effectiveness rate, which is also considerably lower than the 82 percent effectiveness rate for the detainees subjected to enhanced interrogation.

(U) Unlike the above measures, there are some quantitative statistics in the Study that are useful in comparing the relative "productivity" of certain detainees. The Study estimates that a total of 5,874 sole source disseminated intelligence reports were produced from the interrogation of 78 of the 119 detainees. Of these, 4266 reports (72.6 percent) were produced from the interrogation of 32 of the 39 detainees subjected to enhanced interrogation.[80] Thus, 1608 reports (27.4 percent) were produced from the interrogation of 46 of the 90 detainees not subjected to enhanced interrogation.[81] The Study also credits Abu Zubaydah and KSM with 1597 (27.1 percent) of the total number of disseminated reports.[82] While these

121

statistics cannot be used to assess the qualitative value of the specific intelligence in these disseminated reports, they do seem to provide insight into the CIA's perceived value of the information being produced by the detainees who were subjected to enhanced interrogation, especially Abu Zubaydah and KSM. Given that the vast majority of these intelligence reports came from detainees selected for enhanced interrogations, these statistics seem to indicate that the CIA was proficient at identifying those detainees who might possess information worthy of dissemination.

(U) The second faulty premise states:

> At least seven detainees were subjected to the CIA's enhanced interrogation techniques almost immediately after being rendered to CIA custody, *making it impossible to determine* whether the information they provided could have been obtained through non-coercive debriefing methods. By contrast, other detainees provided significant accurate intelligence prior to, or without having been, subjected to these techniques.[83]

(U) This premise is problematic for at least two reasons. First, the premise itself admits that it is based upon ignorance – we will never know whether less coercive techniques would have provided the same amount of intelligence from these seven detainees as was obtained by using enhanced interrogation, it is troubling that the very first conclusion in this Study is based, at least in part, upon an appeal to unknowable facts. Second, this appeal to ignorance is linked to an observation that other detainees provided "significant accurate intelligence" without having been subjected to enhanced interrogation, in an apparent effort to persuade us that the use of less coercive techniques might have also resulted in "significant accurate intelligence." While this second observation is factually correct, it is misleading. We know from our earlier examination of the "productivity" statistics that the group of detainees who were not subjected to enhanced interrogation only provided 27.4 percent of the disseminated intelligence reporting, which undercuts the very inference raised by this empty premise.

(U) The third faulty premise of this ineffective means conclusion focuses on the fact that "multiple" detainees subjected to enhanced interrogation techniques "fabricated information, resulting in faulty intelligence."[84] Like the first faulty premise, this premise only tells one side of the story. It implies that only detainees subjected to enhanced interrogation provided fabricated information. Not surprisingly, our review of the documentary record revealed that "multiple" detainees whose non-enhanced interrogations resulted in at least one sole source intelligence report also provided fabricated information to their interrogators.[85] Fabrication is simply not a good measure of "effectiveness," because detainees are often strongly motivated to protect the identities of their terrorist colleagues and the details of their terrorist operations. We train our own military personnel to resist against providing sensitive information to their captors during the inevitable interrogation process. We understand that such resistance may occasionally lead our personnel to provide fabricated information to their interrogators. This is an ancient and well-recognized occupational hazard of war.

(U) Another problematic aspect of this third faulty premise is that it ignores the fact that fabricated information can sometimes turn out to be highly significant. One of the best examples of this concept can be found in our discussion about how the courier who led us to Bin Ladin's hideout was finally located.[86] Specifically, many of the senior al-Qa'ida detainees lied to protect the identity and importance of Abu Ahmad al-Kuwaiti. Abu Zubaydah and Abu Faraj al-Libi both lied when they claimed that they did not know anyone named Abu Ahmad al-Kuwaiti. KSM fabricated a story that Ahmad had retired from al-Qa'ida. When compared against other detainee information, these fabrications were clear signals to CIA analysts that these three detainees were trying very hard to keep Ahmad hidden.[87]

(U) The final faulty premise used in support of this "effectiveness" conclusion was that "CIA officers regularly called into question whether the CIA's enhanced interrogation techniques were effective, assessing that the use of the techniques failed to elicit detainee cooperation or produce accurate intelligence."[88] While the *opinions* of these unidentified CIA officers may happen to coincide with the Study's first conclusion, there were at least three other CIA officials who held the opposite view – Directors Tenet, Goss, and Hayden. DCI Tenet stated that he "firmly believes that the interrogation program, and specifically the use of EITs, has saved many lives." Tenet added that the use of the CIA's enhanced interrogation techniques was "extremely valuable" in obtaining "enormous amounts of critical threat information," and he did not believe that the information could have been gained any other way.[89] Director Goss told our Committee members that

> This program has brought us incredible information. It's a program that could continue to bring us incredible information. It's a program that could continue to operate in a very professional way. It's a program that I think if you saw how it's operated you would agree that you would be proud that it's done right and well, with proper safeguards."[90]

CIA Director Hayden also told our Committee that the CIA's interrogation Program existed "for one purpose – intelligence," and that the Program "is about preventing future attacks.... In that purpose, preventing attacks, disabling al-Qa'ida, this is the most successful program being conducted by American intelligence today."[91]

(U) In our opinion, the reasons cited by the Study to support this conclusion that the CIA's use of enhanced interrogation techniques was not an effective means of acquiring intelligence or gaining cooperation from detainees are largely invalid. The faulty premises upon which the conclusion is based are more rhetorical than analytical. Our review of the facts contained in the documentary record has led us to the opposite conclusion – that the CIA's Detention and Interrogation Program, including the use of enhanced interrogation, was an effective means of gathering significant intelligence information and cooperation from a majority of these CIA detainees. Our conclusion, however, should not be read as an endorsement of any of these particular enhanced interrogation techniques.

Δ

Endnotes

[75] We will address these eight conclusions in the following order: (1) Conclusion 1; (2) Conclusion 2; (3) Conclusion 6; (4) Conclusion 7; (5) Conclusion 8; (6) Conclusion 5; (7) Conclusion 9; and (8) Conclusion 10.

[76] SSCI Study, Findings and Conclusions, December 3, 2014, p. 2. The first and second conclusions in the updated Findings and Conclusion had been combined in Conclusion 9 of the original Study.

[77] SSCI Study, Findings and Conclusions, December 3, 2014, p. 2. The assertion of "produced no intelligence" as used by the Study reflects that the interrogations of these detainees resulted in no intelligence reports.

[78] *See* SSCI Study, Volume II, April 1, 2014, pp. 420-421.

[79] Subtracting the 39 detainees subjected to enhanced interrogation from 119 total detainees equals 80 detainees not subjected to enhanced interrogation. We know that seven of the detainees subjected to enhanced interrogation resulted in no intelligence reports. Subtracting these seven from the 41 total detainees whose interrogation did not result in disseminated intelligence reports leaves 34 detainees whose information did not result in disseminated intelligence products, even though they were not subjected to enhanced interrogation.

[80] *See* SSCI Study, Volume 11, April 1, 2014, p. 421.

[81] Subtracting the 4,266 reports produced from the interrogation of detainees subjected to enhanced

interrogation from the 5,874 total number of reports equals 1,608 reports (27.4 percent) produced from the interrogation of detainees not subjected to enhanced interrogation.

[82] *See* SSCI Study, Volume II. April 1, 2014, p. 421.

[83] SSCI Study, Findings and Conclusions, April 3,2014, p. 2 (emphasis added). [[This false reasoning was tempered in the December 3. 2014, version of the Executive Summary by editing the sentence to read, "CIA detainees who were subjected to the CIA's enhanced interrogation techniques were usually subjected to the techniques immediately after being rendered to CIA custody. Other detainees provided significant accurate intelligence prior to, or without having been subjected to these techniques." *Compare* SSCI Study, Findings and Conclusions, April 3, 2014. p. 2 *with* SSCI Study, Findings and Conclusions, December 3, 2014, p. 2.]]

[84] SSCI Study, Findings and Conclusions, December 3, 2014, p. 2.

[85] Our review examined the first 15 of the 46 detainees whose non-coercive interrogations had resulted in at least one sole-source intelligence report. *See* SSCI Study, Executive Summary, December 3, 2014, p. 462. We found documentary evidence supporting the proposition that 11 of these 15 detainees provided deceptive or fabricated information to their interrogators. The 11 deceptive detainees were: Zakariya (CIA, [CIA CABLE] 22576, ▄▄▄▄▄▄▄ ; CIA, CABLE ▄▄▄▄▄▄ CIA, CIA CABLE ▄▄▄▄▄▄▄▄▄▄ Jamal Eldin Boudraa, (CIA, [CIA CABLE] 22576 ▄▄▄▄ - CIA [CIA CABLE] 21520, ▄▄▄▄▄▄▄▄▄▄ Bashir Nasir Ali

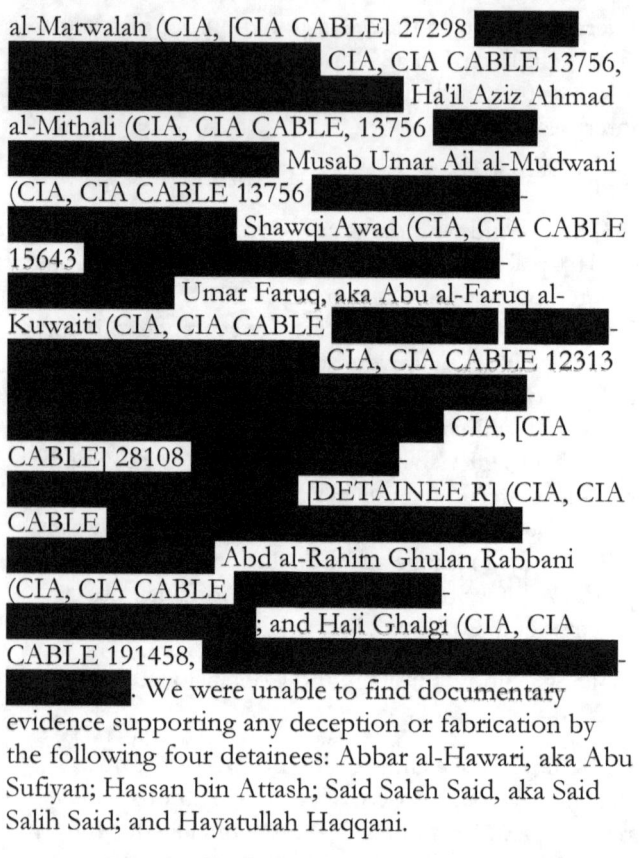

al-Marwalah (CIA, [CIA CABLE] 27298 ▮▮▮ - ▮▮▮ CIA, CIA CABLE 13756, ▮▮▮ Ha'il Aziz Ahmad al-Mithali (CIA, CIA CABLE, 13756 ▮▮▮ - ▮▮▮ Musab Umar Ail al-Mudwani (CIA, CIA CABLE 13756 ▮▮▮ - ▮▮▮ Shawqi Awad (CIA, CIA CABLE 15643 ▮▮▮ - ▮▮▮ Umar Faruq, aka Abu al-Faruq al-Kuwaiti (CIA, CIA CABLE ▮▮▮ ▮▮▮ - ▮▮▮ CIA, CIA CABLE 12313 ▮▮▮ - ▮▮▮ CIA, [CIA CABLE] 28108 ▮▮▮ - ▮▮▮ [DETAINEE R] (CIA, CIA CABLE ▮▮▮ - ▮▮▮ Abd al-Rahim Ghulan Rabbani (CIA, CIA CABLE ▮▮▮ - ▮▮▮ ; and Haji Ghalgi (CIA, CIA CABLE 191458, ▮▮▮ - ▮▮▮. We were unable to find documentary evidence supporting any deception or fabrication by the following four detainees: Abbar al-Hawari, aka Abu Sufiyan; Hassan bin Attash; Said Saleh Said, aka Said Salih Said; and Hayatullah Haqqani.

[86] *See infra*, pp. 253-259.

[87] *See* CIA. DIRECTOR ▮▮▮ - ▮▮▮ CIA Center for the Study of Intelligence, Lessons from the Hunt for Usama Bin Ladin, dated September 2012, pp. 9-10 (DTS 2012-3826); CIA Intelligence Assessment, Al-Qa'ida Watch, Probable Identification of Suspected Bin Ladin Facilitator Abu Ahmad al-Kuwaiti, November 23, 2007, p. 2.

[87] *See* SSCI Study, Executive Summary, December 3,

2014, p. 378-379.

[88] SSCI Study, Findings and Conclusions, December 3, 2014, p. 2.

[89] Interview of George Tenet, by [REDACTED], [REDACTED], Office of the Inspector General, 8 September, 2003.

[90] SSCI Transcript, Briefing by the Director of the Central Intelligence Agency Regarding CIA's Counter-terrorism Operations and Detention, Interrogation, and Rendition Program, March 15, 2006, p. 8 (DTS 2006-1308).

[91] SSCI Transcript, Hearing on the Central Intelligence Agency Detention and Interrogation Program, April 12, 2007, pp. 16-17 (DTS 2007-3158).

(U) Conclusion 2 (CIA's Justification for EITs Rested on Inaccurate Effectiveness Claims)

(U) Conclusion 2 states, "[t]he CIA's justification for the use of its enhanced interrogation techniques rested on inaccurate claims of their effectiveness."[92] The Study continues to rely upon 20 separate case studies to support this erroneous conclusion. In our original minority views, we only had time to identify the significant flaws in seven of these case studies. Prior to our receipt of the June 27, 2013, CIA response, we identified significant problems with four more of the case studies. Ultimately, the CIAresponse validated our critique of the original seven case studies and identified additional issues with the remaining case studies. We have decided to address 17 of these ease studies in our examination of this conclusion.[93] Although one may have individual views on the relative effectiveness of the enhanced interrogation techniques; it is important for the public to understand that these flawed ease studies are insufficient to establish that the CIA's justification for the use of enhanced interrogation techniques rested upon inaccurate claims of their effectiveness.

(U) The Study's Flawed Analytical Methodology

(U) In general, the Study essentially refuses to admit that CIA detainees, especially CIA detainees subjected to enhanced interrogation techniques, provided intelligence information which helped the United States government and its allies neutralize numerous terrorist threats. On its face, this position does not make much sense, given the vast amount of information gained from these interrogations, the thousands of intelligence reports that were generated as a result of them, the capture of additional terrorists, and the disruption of the plots those captured terrorists were planning.

(U) We reviewed 17 of the 20 cases studies that the Study relies upon to support this flawed conclusion. We examined these case studies in logical groupings (e.g., related to information provided by Abu Zubaydah) using chronological orderrather than the Study's confusing "primary" and "secondary" effectiveness representations. This approach helped us better understand how the intelligence resulting from these detainee interrogations was used by the CIA to disrupt terrorist plots and identify, capture, and sometimes prosecute other terrorists.

(U) The Study developed an analytical methodology to examine the effectiveness of the information obtained from the CIA's Detention and Interrogation Program that we found to be both confusing and deeply flawed. Usually, effectiveness is measured by establishing performance metrics that require the collection of pertinent data and the subsequent analysis of such data. For example, in the context of counterterrorism such metrics might include: (1) increased understanding of terrorist networks; (2) identification of terrorists and those providing material support; (3) terrorist captures; (4) terrorist interrogations; (5) disruption of terrorist operations and financing; (6)

disruption of terrorist recruitment; (7) reduction in terrorist safehavens; (8) development of counterterrorism assets; (9) intelligence gathering of documents, computer equipment, communications devices, etc.; (10) improved information sharing; and (11) improved foreign liaison cooperation against terrorism. Such metrics could then be compared against the information provided by CIA detainees to assess the relative effectiveness of the Program.

(U) Instead of performance metrics, the Study's analytical methodology creates artificial categories that are used to *exclude* certain detainee information from being considered in an effectiveness assessment of the Program. For example, if the Study found that a detainee subjected to enhanced interrogation had provided similar information during an earlier non-enhanced interrogation, then such information could not be used for assessing the effectiveness of the program. This category appears to have been developed in an attempt to exclude much of the intelligence information provided by Abu Zubaydah after he was subjected to enhanced interrogation in August 2002, since some of the information Abu Zubaydah provided during those interrogations was similar to information he had provided prior to August. However, it turns out that this category is largely inapplicable to Abu Zubaydah's case, because he was subjected to enhanced interrogation by the CIA when he was released from the hospital on April 15, 2002.[94]

(U) Another category of information that the Study's flawed analytical methodology excludes is corroborative information. If a detainee subjected to enhanced interrogation provided information that was already available to the CIA or other elements of the Intelligence Community from another source, then the methodology dictates that such information cannot be considered to support a CIA effectiveness representation. This result occurs even in situations in which the detainee's information clarified or explained the significance of the prior information. Another exclusion category applies if the Study determined that there was no causal relationship between the information obtained from a detainee after the use of enhanced interrogation and the operational success claimed by the CIA. In these case studies, we often found documentary evidence that supported direct causal links between such detainee information and the operational success represented by the CIA. The final category excludes detainee information about terrorist plots when there was a subsequent assessment by intelligence and law enforcement personnel that such plots were infeasible or never operationalized.

(U) This flawed analytical methodology often forced the Study to use absolute language such as, "no connection," "no indicadon," "played no role," or "these representations were inaccurate." Our review of the documentary record often found valid counter-examples that disproved such absolute claims. We also found that when we invalidated the claims in the initial case studies, there was often a cascading effect that further undermined claims in the subsequent case studies. Here we summarize the claims for the case studies we examined and our alternate analysis of those claims.

(U) Our Analytical Methodology

(U) Our analytical methodology simply focuses on the significant inherent weaknesses contained in the analytical categories of the Study's methodology. For example, in case studies where the Study claims there was no relationship between the use of enhanced interrogation techniques and the operational success, it often uses absolute language such as, "no connection," "no indication," "played no role," or "these representations were inaccurate." This greatly simplified our analytical task, because the main problem with absolute claims is that it usually only takes one valid counter-example to disprove the claim. We did not have too much difficulty using the documentary record to: establish connections; find indications; identify the roles; and demonstrate the accuracy of certain representations. We suspect that this task would have been even easier if there had been an opportunity to speak to the relevant witnesses.

(U) The same can be said with respect to the Study's treatment of the "otherwise available categories." In these case study claims, the Study would point to documents that "provided similar information" or contained "corroborative" information. The usual problem with these claims is that they failed to analyze the weight and significance of the information provided by the particular detainee. We found documentary evidence indicating that the CIA often had not understood or properly exploited previously acquired intelligence information until after its significance was clarified by a particular detainee or detainees.

(U)   Also,   we   were   less   inclined   to   dismiss   the significance of certain plots and threats just because there was   documentary   evidence   indicating   that   some intelligence professionals found them infeasible or had not yet become operational. Often, the most difficult part of a terrorist plot is getting the terrorists into a position where they can attack. If the terrorists are not neutralized, they have additional time to refine their plans, adjust to new targets, or gain access to better weapons and equipment. The   evolving   nature   of   the   Karachi   terrorist   plots demonstrates this point quite well.[95]

(U) Re-organization of the "Effectiveness" Case Studies

(U) In general, we have tried to organize our analysis of these   case   studies   sequentially   into   six   logical   and chronological groupings. For example, since Abu Zubaydah was   the   first   CIA   detainee   subjected   to   enhanced interrogation techniques, we begin with the case studies which examine the significant intelligence information that he disclosed to his interrogators. Despite claims made by the Study, we found that, over time, information obtained from Abu Zubaydah was very useful in the subsequent interrogation of other detainees and sometimes even helped lead to the capture of other terrorists, which in turn, often disrupted developing terrorist plots.

(U) The next logical grouping of case studies centers geographically in Pakistan during the March 2002 through April   2003   time-frame   and   concerns   the   Intelligence

135

Community's efforts to locate and capture the al-Qa'ida terrorists in that country. For example, we trace how Abu Zubaydah's information helped ████████████ ████████████ Pakistani authorities conduct important raids on several key safe houses in Karachi on September 10-11, 2002, which resulted in a treasure trove of collected physical evidence and intelligence information, as well as the capture of Ramzi bin al-Shibh, Abu Badr, Abdul Rahim Gulam Rabbani, Hassan Muhammad, Ali bin Attash, and other al-Qa'ida members. We turn next to the capture of KSM in Rawalpindi in March 2003 and then examine the various Karachi terrorist plots, which were largely neutralized by the September 2002 safe house raids, but were not finally disrupted until the capture of Ali Abdul Aziz Ali and Khallad bin Attash on April 29, 2003, in Karachi. This grouping ends with our discussion of the Heathrow and Canary Wharf Plots, which were fully disrupted with the captures of Ramzi bin al-Shibh, KSM, Ali Abdul Aziz Ali, and Khallad bin Attash.

(U) The third grouping takes us briefly to Southeast Asia and our analysis of how detainee information helped lead to the capture of Riduan Isamuddin, also known as "Hambali," in Thailand during August 2003, the disruption of the Second Wave plots, and the capture of his Al-Ghuraba Group in Karachi, Pakistan.

(U) Our fourth grouping consists of the case studies that primarily involved information provided by KSM. We begin with an analysis of four case studies where KSM provided helpful information during 2003: the critical intelligence on Jaffar al-Tayyar (also known as Adnan el-

Shuknjumah); the arrest of Saleh al-Marri; the capture of Iyman Faris; and the identification and arrests of Uzhair and Saifullah Paracha.

(U) The fifth grouping examines three case studies that are factually unrelated but depend upon detainee information that was provided in 2004. The first involves the tactical intelligence provided on Shkai, Pakistan, by Hassan Ghul. The second involves the thwarting of the Camp Lemonier plotting in Djibouti and the third examines how CIA detainees subjected to enhanced interrogation provided information useful in the validation of CIA sources.

(U) Our final chronological group covers the identification of Usama Bin Ladin's courier. Here, we demonstrate that detainee information played a significant role in leading CIA analysts to the courier Abu Ahmad al-Kuwaiti, who in turn, led the Intelligence Community to Usama Bin Ladin.

(U) The Domino Effect

(U) Our reorganization of these case studies away from the Study's confusing primary and secondary "effectiveness representations" frame of reference into a more traditional chronological analytical framework clearly exposes the fatal flaw in the structure of the Study's current analysis. In essence, the Study's analysis resembles a very large and carefully lined-up set of dominoes. The claims made in those first few dominoes are absolutely crucial in maintaining the structure and validity of many of the claims made and repeated in the dominoes that follow. Our analysis demonstrates that the claims in these initial case studies are simply not supported by the factual documentary record. This led to an analytical chain reaction in which many of the Study's subsequent claims became invalid, in part, because of their dependence on the first few factually inaccurate claims.

(TS// ████████████ //NF) A good example of this "Domino Effect" is the factually incorrect claim made by the Study that the use of enhanced interrogation techniques played "no role in the identification of Jose Padilla, because Abu Zubaydah provided the information about Padilla during an interrogation by FBI agents who were "exclusively" using "rapport-building" techniques against him more than three months prior to the CIA's "use of DOJ-approved enhanced interrogation techniques."[96] The facts demonstrate, however, that Abu Zubaydah had been subjected to "around the clock" interrogation that included more than four days of dietary manipulation, nudity, as well as a total of 126.5 hours (5.27 days) of sleep deprivation during the 136-hour (5.67 day) period by the time the FBI finished up the 8.5-hour interrogation shift which yielded the identification of Jose Padilla.[97] Since these three enhanced interrogation techniques were used in combination with the FBI's "rapport building" technique during this particular interrogation, it is simply absurd to claim that they played "no role" in obtaining the information about Padilla from Abu Zubaydah. Consistent with the "Domino Effect" analogy, when this factually incorrect claim falls, it can no longer be cited as support for other claims. This specific factually incorrect claim, sometimes used in slightly different variations, is repeated at least 19 times throughout the Study.[98]

(U) Ultimately, our analysis of these case studies leads us to conclude that there are simply not enough "dominoes" left standing to support the Study's explosive conclusion – that the "CIA's justification for the use of its enhanced interrogation techniques rested on inaccurate claims of their effectiveness." It is very disappointing that the Study has leveled such serious accusations against the personnel involved in the CIA's Detention and Interrogation Program, when so many of the Study's own claims are demonstrably false.

Δ

Endnotes

[92] SSCI Study, Findings and Conclusions, December 3, 2014, p. 2.

[93] We have combined the KSM as the "mastermind" of the September 11, 2001, terrorist attacks case study with the KSM "Mukhtar" alias case study. We did not have time to adequately address the Majid Khan, Sajid Badat, and Dhiren Barot case studies.

[94] *See infra*, pp. 150-155.

[95] *See infra*, pp. 181-183.

[96] SSCI Study, Executive Summary, December 3, 2014, pp. 230-231 and 230 n.1315; *see infra*, pp.150-155.

[97] *See infra*, pp. 150-155.

[98] *See* SSCI Study, Executive Summary, December 3, 2014, pp. 209-210, 230, 230 n.1314, 234; SSCI Study, Volume I, March 31. 2014, pp. 624 and 636; and SSCI Study, Volume II, April 1, 2014, pp. 57, 75. 75 n.274. 79, 343, 349. 358, 409. 445 n.2245, 530, 532. 535, and 1089.

(U) The Identification of Khalid Shaykh Mohammad as the Mastermind of the 9/11 Attacks and His "Mukhtar" Alias

Study Claim:

~~(TS//~~ ████████████████ ~~//NF)~~ "On at least two prominent occasions, the CIA represented, inaccurately, that Abu Zubaydah provided [information identifying KSM as the mastermind of 9/11] after the use of the CIA's enhanced interrogation techniques."[99]

~~(TS//~~ ████████████████ ~~//NF)~~ "In at least one instance in November 2007... the CIA asserted that Abu Zubaydah identified KSM as 'Mukhtar' after the use of the CIA's enhanced interrogation techniques."[100]

~~(TS//~~ ████████████████ ~~//NF)~~ "There is no evidence to support the statement that Abu Zubaydah's information – obtained by FBI interrogators prior to the use of the CIA's enhanced interrogation techniques and while Abu Zubaydah was hospitalized – was uniquely important in the identification of KSM as the 'mastermind' of the 9/11 attacks."[101]

Fact:

(U) Neither of the occasions cited with respect to the "Mastermind of 9/11" information were "prominent." The first occasion was not even a CIA representation, but rather a mistake made by the Department of Justice in one of its legal opinions.[102] The second occasion was a set of November 2007 documents and talking points for the CIA Director to use in a briefing with the President. Although these briefing materials did contain some erroneous information about KSM's interrogation, the Study fails to demonstrate whether this erroneous information was "represented" to the President during that timeframe.[103]

(U) The one instance where the CIA asserted that Abu Zubaydah identified KSM as "Mukhtar" after the use of enhanced interrogation techniques was contained in the same November 2007 briefing materials used by the CIA Director to brief the President.[104] Again, the Study fails to demonstrate whether this erroneous information was "represented" to the President during this timeframe.

(U) There is considerable evidence that the information Abu Zubaydah provided identifying KSM as "Mukhtar" and the mastermind of 9/11 was significant to CIA analysts, operators, and FBI interrogators. Both the Congressional Joint Inquiry into the 9/11 Attacks and the 9/11 Commission discussed the importance of this information to the Intelligence Community in understanding KSM's role in the attacks and in the al-Qa'ida organization.

(U) We have combined our analysis of these two case

studies because they share common facts and analytical issues. The Study's claims with respect to the CIA's alleged misrepresentations about KSM's "Mukhtar" alias and being the mastermind of 9/11 are themselves inaccurate. Also, the Study's absolute claim that "there is no evidence" that Abu Zubaydah's information was uniquely important in the identification of KSM as the mastermind of 9/11 is contradicted by the documentary record and publicly available information.

(U) Our analysis of the Study's erroneous claims about the supposed CIA "representations" is dispositive. For the first "prominent" occasion, the Study mistakenly alleges that the CIA made an inaccurate representation about Abu Zubaydah providing information identifying KSM as the mastermind of 9/11 after the use of the CIA's enhanced interrogation techniques.[105] It turns out that this particular inaccurate representation *was not made by the CIA,* but rather was expressed in a written legal opinion by the Office of Legal Counsel at the Department Justice (DOJ). [106] The Study confirms its own mistake by pointing out that the CIA briefing notes provided to DOJ in support of their request for the OLC opinion *correctly stated,* "Within months of his arrest, Abu Zubaydah provided details about al-Qa'ida's organization structure, key operatives, and modus operandi. It was also Abu Zubaydah, *early in his detention, who identified KSM as the mastermind of 9/11.*"[107] DOJ is accountable for this negligible mistake, not the CIA.

(S//OC//NF) With respect to the second "prominent" occasion, the CIA does admit that "in one instance – a supporting document for a set of DCIA talking points for a

142

meeting with the President – we mischaracterized the information as having been obtained after the application of enhanced interrogation techniques."[108] However, while this information in Director Hayden's briefing materials about KSM was inaccurate, the Study fails to explain how the CIA supposedly "represented" these inaccuracies to the President or other executive branch officials during this November 2007 timeframe. Without talking to witnesses, we have no proof that any such inaccurate representation ever occurred. What we do know is that President Bush got this issue right in a speech that he delivered nearly a year before this particular error was inserted into Director Hayden's briefing materials. Specifically, President Bush said,

> After he recovered, Zubaydah was defiant and evasive. He declared his hatred of America. During questioning, he at first disclosed what he thought was nominal information – and then stopped all cooperation. Well, in fact the 'nominal' information he gave us turned out to be quite important. For example, Zubaydah disclosed Khalid Sheikh Mohammed – or KSM – was the mastermind behind the 9/11 attacks, and used the alias 'Muktar.'"[109]

The President's speech is the "representation" that mattered most, regardless of whether the erroneous information in Director Hayden's briefing materials was discussed during a classified Presidential briefing one year later. We conclude that if there was any error here, it was harmless.

(S//OC//NF) The Study's claim in the second case study is essentially identical to the first, except that Director

143

Hayden's briefing materials for the November 2007 meeting with the President contained an erroneous assertion that Abu Zubaydah identified KSM as "Mukhtar" after the use of the CIA's enhanced interrogation techniques.[110] Analytically, this is a distinction without a difference and we reach the same conclusion – if there was any error here, it was harmless.

(S// ███████ //NF) Turning now to the Study's "no evidence" claim, numerous Intelligence Community documents show that Intelligence Community analysts believed that Zubaydah's information identifying KSM as the mastermind of 9/11 was important. Soon after the interrogation that revealed KSM as the masterrmind of 9/11 and identification as "Mukhtar," the CIA disseminated an intelligence report, ███████ within the Intelligence Community ████████████████ ████████ detailing the information.[111] Responses ████████████████████ indicated they followed up and requested more information ████████ on him.[112]

(S//NF) Zubaydah's FBI interrogator Ali Soufan also described the information from Zubaydah on KSM as significant. In 2008, Soufan told Committee staff that when Zubaydah provided that information, "we had no idea at the time that Mukhtar was the KSM from 9/11.... Because we had been working so diligently on trying to figure out the puzzles of 9/11 and who is Mukhtar, and when Abu Zubaydah said that, I think the picture was complete."[113] On May 13, 2009, Soufan also told the Senate Judiciary Committee that prior to Zubaydah providing information on KSM's role as the mastermind of the 9/11 attacks, "we had no idea of KSM's role in 9/11 or of his importance in the al Qaeda leadership structure."[114]

(U) Moreover, a summary of the Program released publicly by the Director of National Intelligence in 2006 explained both the significance of this information and how other previously collected intelligence had not stood out to analysts until the information from Zubaydah. According to the summary, "during initial interrogation, Abu Zubaydah gave some information that he probably viewed as nominal. Some was important, however, including that KSM was the 9/11 mastermind and used the moniker "Mukhtar." This identification allowed us to comb previously collected intelligence for both names, opening up new leads to this terrorist plotter – leads that eventually resulted in his capture."[114]

(TS// ███████████████ //NF) The Senate and House Intelligence Joint Inquiry Into the Intelligence Community Activities Before and After the Terrorist Attacks of September 11, 2001, adopted with the support of four members who also voted in favor of the Study, said that "although the Intelligence Community knew of KSM's support for terrorism since 1995 and later learned of his links to al-Qa'ida, he was not recognized as a senior al-Qa'ida lieutenant. In April 2002, the Intelligence Community learned that KSM and his group conceived the September 11 plot."[116] If there is any doubt that the report was referring to the information from Zubaydah, CIA operational cable traffic from April 2002 confirms: "[Abu Zubaydah] stated the idea of September 11 was conceived by [KSM] and his group."[117]

(U) The 9/11 Commission Report also made clear diat the Intelligence Community did not recognize KSM's importance prior to 9/11. "KSM, who had been indicted in January 1996 for his role in the Manila air plot, was seen primarily as another freelance terrorist, associated with Ramzi Yousef."[118] The Commission noted that because KSM was being targeted for arrest, responsibility for tracking him was in CIA's Renditions Branch, which did not focus on analytic connections. "When subsequent information came, more critical for analysis than for tracking, no unit had the job of following up on what the information might mean."[119] As one of ten "Operational Opportunities" that were missed prior to 9/11, the Commission wrote, "August 2001, the CIA does not focus on information that Khalid Sheikh Mohammed is a key al Qaeda lieutenant or connect information identifying KSM as the 'Mukhtar' mentioned in other reports to the analysis that could have linked 'Mukhtar' with Ramzi Binalshibh and Moussaoui."[120] The 9/11 Commission adds:

> The final piece of the puzzle arrived at the CIA's Bin Ladin unit on August 28 [2001] in a cable reporting that KSM's nickname was Mukhtar. No one made the connection to the reports about Mukhtar that had been circulated in the spring. This connection might have also underscored concern about the June reporting that KSM was recruiting terrorists to travel, including to the United States. Only after 9/11 would it be discovered that Mukhtar/KSM had communicated with a phone that was used by Binalshibh, and that Binalshibh used the same phone to communicate with Moussaoui.'[121]

(U) Finally, the 9/11 Commission notes that the information connecting KSM to the Binalshibh phone came from detainee interviews with Binalshibh in late 2002 and 2003 and with KSM in 2003, well after Abu Zubaydah identified KSM as Mukhtar and the 9/11 mastennind.[122] It is also worth noting that, like this information, all of the information for chapters 5 and 7 of the 9/11 Commission report, which explain what the Commission knew about al-Qa'ida's planning for the 9/11 attacks, "rel[ies] heavily on information obtained from captured al Qaeda members," mostly in CIA's interrogation program.[123]

Δ

Endnotes

[99] SSCI Study, Executive Summary, December 3, 2014, p. 312.

[100] SSCI Study, Executive Summary, December 3, 2014, p. 315.

[101] SSCI Study, Executive Summary, December 3, 2014, p. 313.

[102] *See* SSCI Study, Executive Summary, December 3. 2014, p. 313, n.1748.

[103] *See* DCIA Talking Points: Waterboard, 06 November 2007, pp. 1-3. This document was sent to DCIA on November 6 in preparation for a meeting with POTUS.

[104] *See* DCIA Talking Points: Waterboard, November 6. 2007, pp. 1-3.

[105] *See* SSCI Study, Executive Summary, December

3, 2014, p. 312-313.

[106] *See* Memorandum for John A. Rizzo from Steven Bradbury, Re: Application of United States Obligations Under Article 16 of the Convention Against Torture to Certain Techniques that May Be Used in the Interrogation of High Value al Qaeda Detainees, May 30, 2005, p. 10.
[http://www.justice.gov/sites/default/files/olc/legacy/201 3/10/21/memo-bradbury2005.pdf]

[107] Briefing Notes on the Value of Detainee Reporting, April 8. 2005, p. 5. (emphasis added)

[108] CIA Study Response, Case Studies (TAB C), June 27, 2013, p. 20.

[109] President George W. Bush, *Trying Detainees; Address on the Creation of Military Commissions,* Washington, D.C., September 6, 2006.
[http://georgewbush-whitehouse.archives.gov/news/releases/2006/09/20060906 -3.html]

[110] *See* SSCI Study, Executive Summary, December 3, 2014, p. 315.

[111] *See* CIA,

[112] *See* CIA,

[113] SSCI Transcript, Staff Interview of FBI Special Agent All Soufan, April 28, 2008 (DTS 2008-2411).

[114] Ali Soufan, Statement for the Record, before the United States Senate Committee on the Judiciary. May 13, 2009.

[115] Summary of the High Value Terrorist Detainee Program, Office of the Director of National

Intelligence, p. 1.

[116] The Joint Inquiry Into the Intelligence Community Activities Before and After the Terrorist Attacks of September 11, 2001, December 2002, p. 310.

[117] CIA, ███████ 10065, April 18, 2002, p. 3.

[118] 9/11 Commission Report, p. 276.

[119] 9/11 Commission Report, p. 276.

[120] 9/11 Commission Report, p. 356.

[121] 9/11 Commission Report, p. 277. The CIA acknowledged that this intelligence report identified KSM as "Mukhtar" prior to Abu Zubaydah's information. After reviewing its records, the CIA concluded that "our officers simply missed the earlier cable." CIA Study Response, Studies (TAB C), June 27, 2013. p. 22.

[122] 9/11 Commission Report, Chapter 7, n.163.

[123] 9/11 Commission Report, p. 146.

(U) The Thwarting of the Dirty Bomb / Tall Buildings Plot and the Capture of Jose Padilla

Study Claim:

(TS// ███████████████████ //NF) "A review of CIA operational cables and other CIA records found that the use of the CIA's enhanced interrogation techniques played no role in the identification of 'Jose Padilla' or the thwarting of the Dirty Bomb or Tall Buildings plotting. CIA records indicate that:... (3) Abu Zubaydah provided this information to FBI officers who were using rapport-building techniques, in April 2002, more than three months prior to the CIA's 'use of DOJ-approved enhanced interrogation techniques,'...."[124]

Fact:

(TS// ███████████████████ //NF) CIA records clearly indicate that sleep deprivation played a significant role in Abu Zubaydah's identification of Jose Padilla as an al-Qa'ida operative tasked to carry out an attack against the United States. Abu Zubaydah provided this information to FBI agents during an interrogation session that began late at night on April 20, 2002, and ended on April 21, 2002. Between April 15, 2002 and April 21, 2002, Abu Zubaydah was deprived of sleep for a total of 126.5 hours (5.27 days) over a 136 hour (5.6 day) period – while only being permitted several brief sleep breaks between April 19, 2002 and April 21,2002, which totaled 9.5 hours.

(TS// ███████████████████ //NF) This particular Study claim gives the false impression that enhanced interrogation techniques played no role in obtaining important threat information about Jose Padilla during the interrogation of Abu Zubaydah on April 20-21, 2002, and implies that such information was really just the result of the "rapport-building" techniques used by the FBI agents that evening.

~~(TS//~~ ███████████████ ~~//NF)~~ The CIA documentary record is clear that Abu Zubaydah was subjected to an extended period of sleep deprivation and other enhanced interrogation techniques during his interrogation between April 15, 2002 and April 21, 2002. [125] Specifically, during this time period when FBI agents and CIA officers were working together in rotating, round-the-clock shifts, some of the interrogation techniques used on Abu Zubaydah included nudity, liquid diet,[126] sensory deprivation,[128] and extended sleep deprivation.[129]

~~(TS//~~ ███████████████ ~~//NF)~~ The sleep deprivation of Abu Zubaydah began on April 15, 2002.[130] By April 19, 2002, Abu Zubaydah had been subjected to 76 straight hours of sleep deprivation in the form of intensive interrogation sessions and his ability to focus on questions and provide coherent answers appeared to be compromised to a point where sleep was required.[131] Abu Zubaydah was allowed three hours of sleep at that time.[132] On April 20, 2002, the FBI began its late-night interrogation shift atapproximately 10:30 p.m. with Abu Zubaydah and continued until about 7:00 a.m. the next morning. During that shift, Abu Zubaydah was given a two-hour sleep break; time for prayer, food, and water; and a medical check-up. [133] By April 21, 2002, the day he identified Jose Padilla as a terrorist inside the United States, CIA records indicate that Abu Zubaydah had only been permitted several brief sleep breaks between April 19, 2002 and April 21, 2002, which only totaled 9.5 hours of sleep over a 136-hour period.[134] *That means Abu Zubaydah had been sleep deprived for a total of 126.5 hours (5.27 days) over a 136-hour (5.6 day) period by the time his FBI interrogators were finished with him at the end of that shift.*

~~(TS//~~ █████████████████████████ ~~//NF)~~ A CIA chart, not included in the Study, which describes both the standard and enhanced techniques used on Abu Zubaydah, notes for April 21, 2002, "two sessions; sleep deprivation (136 hours)" under the heading "enhanced techniques."[135] Moreover, the FBI interrogator, identified in the press as █████████████████████████ who was questioning Zubaydah at the time he provided the Padilla information, told the OIG that "during the CIA interrogations Zubaydah 'gave up' Jose Padilla and identified several targets for future al-Qaeda attacks.[136] In other words, while Special Agent █████████████ obtained the information on Padilla, it was during a period that the FBI and CIA officers were using the CIA's techniques.

~~(TS//~~ █████████████████████████ ~~//NF)~~ When the CIA and FBI interrogators entered the room late on the night of April 20, 2002, Abu Zubaydah was totally naked. He had been subjected to at least four days of dietary manipulation and had been deprived of 126.5 hours of sleep during the past 136 hours.[138] According to FBI Special Agent Ali Soufan, they gave him a towel. They took some Coke and tea into the room and "started talking about different things." Sometime during the next morning, Abu Zubaydah "came back to his senses and he started cooperating again. And this is when he gave us Padilla."[139] Rather than concede that Abu Zubaydah was being subjected to a combination of at least three enhanced interrogation techniques while the FBI agents were using an additional rapport-building technique, the Study includes this perplexing footnote text: "While Abu Zubaydah was subjected to nudity and *limited* sleep deprivation prior to this date by the CIA, *he had been allowed to sleep* prior to being questioned by the FBI officers, who were exclusively using rapport-building interrogation techniques when the information was acquired."[140] Like the claim in this case study, this footnote is simply at odds with what really happened.

~~(TS//~~ ███████████████████ ~~//NF)~~ There is no reasonable way to reconcile these facts with the claim that enhanced interrogation techniques played "no role" in Abu Zubaydah's identification of Jose Padilla. Sleep deprivation for 126.5 hours over a 136-hour period – which was hardly "limited" – was an enhanced interrogation technique regardless of whether the Department of Justice formally labeled it as such a couple of months later. The Study cannot dismiss the use of these enhanced interrogation techniques simply because they were used before the Department of Justice eventually approved them. The Study's assertion that the FBI was "exclusively" using rapport-building techniques fails to recognize the reality that this interrogation technique was used in combination with at least three other enhanced interrogation techniques. In judging what caused Abu Zubaydah to give up valuable intelligence, including information on Jose Padilla, it is impossible to separate or disaggregate enhanced interrogation techniques from rapport-building techniques after enhanced techniques are applied. Enhanced interrogation techniques are designed to compel detainees to cooperate with questioning and are used in conjunction with traditional questioning methods or interrogation techniques. The simple fact is that Abu Zubaydah gave up Padilla during that interrogation, after being subjected to enhanced interrogation techniques. It is simply not factually accurate for the Study to claim that Abu Zubaydah gave up the information on Padilla *before* he was subjected to enhanced interrogation techniques. Nor is it factually accurate to claim that enhanced interrogation techniques played no role in identifying Padilla as a terrorist threat.

(TS// ███████████████ //NF) The direct refutation of this Study claim illustrates the Study's flawed analytical methodology. As we detail in many of the case studies below, Zubaydah provided much of the key initial information that caused the Intelligence Community to recognize the significance of certain events, future threats, terrorist networks, and even potential assets. The Study repeatedly and incorrectly alleges that the FBI obtained this information prior to the application of CIA's enhanced interrogation techniques.[141] As a result, this mistaken allegation is taken as a settled premise in the Study's analysis of other case studies and related issues, which has the practical effect of undermining the Study's analyses of those matters.

(TS// ███████████████ //NF) Under its flawed

154

methodology, the Study was able to disregard the significance of the large amount of information provided by Abu Zubaydah between April 15, 2002 and August 4, 2002, by incorrectly categorizing it as not being obtained from the use enhanced interrogation techniques. We now know that all of the information obtained from Abu Zubaydah on and after April 15, 2002, was provided after he had been subjected to enhanced interrogation. The practical result of this fact is that information obtained from Abu Zubaydah after April 15, 2002, can no longer be disregarded by the Study and must be factored into the assessment of the executive branch's effectiveness claims concerning the enhanced interrogation techniques along with the significant amount of important information obtained from Zubaydah following his second period of enhanced interrogation, which began on August 4, 2002. Given the breadth of the information provided by Abu Zubaydah after April 15, 2002, and its attendant impact on subsequent intelligence efforts by the United States government and its allies, we conclude that this information supports the CIA's specific representations about the effectiveness of its Detention and Interrogation Program, including the use of enhanced interrogation techniques, in relation to the thwarting of the Dirty Bomb / Tall Buildings plot and the capture of Jose Padilla.

Δ

Endnotes

[124] SSCI Study, Executive Summary, December 3, 2014, pp. 229-231.

[125] *See* CIA, ▮▮▮▮ 10043, April 15. 2002, p. 2;
CIA, ▮▮▮▮ 10047, April 16, 2002, p. 2.

[126] SSCI Transcript, Staff Interview of FBI Special
Agent Ali Soufan, April 28. 2008, p. 22. (DTS 2008-
2411)

[127] *See* CIA, ▮▮▮▮ 10090, April 21, 2002, p. 5.

[128] *See* CIA, ▮▮▮▮ 10116, April 25, 2002, pp. 3-4;
CIA, ▮▮▮▮ 10016, April 12, 2002, pp. 4-5.

[129] *See* CIA, ▮▮▮▮ 10094, April 21, 2002, p. 3;
CIA, ▮▮▮▮ 10071, April 19. 2002, p. 2; CIA,
▮▮▮▮ 10091, April 21, 2002, p. 2. Dietary
manipulation, nudity, and sleep deprivation (more than
48 hours) were also subsequently authorized as
enhanced interrogation techniques by the Department
of Justice. See Memorandum for John A. Rizzo, Senior
Deputy General Counsel, Central Intelligence Agency,
from Steven G. Bradbury, Principal Deputy Assistant
Attorney General, Office of Legal Counsel,
Department of Justice, May 30, 2005, Re: Application
of United States Obligations under Article 16 of the
Convention Against Torture to Certain Techniques
that May be Used in the Interrogation of High value Al
Qaeda Detainees (DTS 2009-1810, Tab-11).
[http://www.justice.gov/sites/default/files/olc/legacy/201
3/10/21/memo-bradbury2005.pdf]

[130] *See* FBI Letter to Pasquale J. (Pat) D'Amuro,
Assistant Director, Counterterrorism Division, April
16, 2002, p. 2 ("The interview with ABU ZUBAYDA
is continuing around the clock and we will advise you
of any further information ASAP").

[131] *See* CIA, ▮▮▮▮ 10071, April 19, 2002, p. 2.

[132] *See* CIA, ▮▮▮▮ 10071, April 19, 2002, p. 2.

[133] *See* FBI Draft Report on Abu Zubaida interview

session from approximately 10:30 p.m., April 20, 2002, to about 7:00 a.m., on April 21, 2002, p. 1.

[134] *See* CIA, ████████ 10094, April 21. 2002, p. 2; CIA Assessment of the accuracy of facts stated in the SSCI Minority's response to the Study of the Central Intelligence Agency's Detention and Interrogation Program, June 27, 2013, p. 1.

[135] CIA, Interrogations Using Standard and Enhanced Techniques, Ahu Zubaydah, undated, p. 1.

[136] Department of Justice Inspector General, *A Review of the FBI's Involvement in and Observations of Detainee Interrogations in Guantanamo Bay, Afghanistan, and Iraq*, May 2008, p. 69 (DTS 2008-2188). [http://www.justice.gov/oig/special/s0805/final.pdf#page =112]

[137] *See* SSCI Transcript. Staff Interview of FBI Special Agent Ali Soufan, April 28, 2008. p. 22. (DTS 2008-2411).

[138] *See* CIA, ████████ 10094, April 21, 2002, p. 2; CIA, ████████ 10090, April 21, 2002, p. 5.

[139] SSCI Transcript, Staff Interview of FBI Special Agent Ali Soufan, April 28, 2008, p. 19. (DTS 2008-2411).

[140] SSCI Study, Executive Summary, April 3, 2014, p. 226 n.1292 (emphasis added). *But see* FBI Draft Report on Abu Zubaida interview session from approximately 10:30 p.m., April 20, 2002, to about 7:00 a.m., on April 21, 2002, p. 1. It appears from this draft report that Abu Zubaydah was permitted a two-hour sleep break sometime during the FBI shift, which seems to clearly demonstrate that the FBI interrogators were aware that Abu Zubaydah was being subjected to sleep deprivation.

[[The December 3, 2014, revision of footnote 1292 in the April 3, 2014 version of the Executive Summary continues to misrepresent the events surrounding Abu Zubaydah's interrogation by editing the footnote to read, "While Abu Zubaydah was subjected to sleep deprivation and nudity prior to this date by the CIA, he had been allowed to sleep *shortly* prior to being questioned *on this matter* by the FBI *special agents*, who were exclusively using rapport-building interrogation techniques when this information was acquired from Abu Zubaydah (who was covered with a towel)." (emphasis added). *Compare* SSCI Study, Executive Summary, April 3, 2014, p. 226 n.1292 *with* SSCI Study, Executive Summary, December 3, 2014, p. 230. n.1315.]]

[141] *See* SSCI Study, Executive Summary, December 3, 2014, pp. 209-210, 230, 230 n.1314, 234; SSCI Study, Volume I, March 31, 2014, pp. 624 and 636; and SSCI Study, Volume II, April 1, 2014, pp. 57, 75, 75 n.274, 79, 343, 349, 358, 409, 445 n.2245, 530, 532, 535, and 1089.

(U) The Capture of Ramzi bin al-Shibh

Study Claim:

(TS// ██████████████████ //NF) "A review of CIA records found no connection between Abu Zubaydah's reporting on Ramzi bin al-Shibh and Ramzi bin al-Shibh's capture.... While CIA records indicate that Abu Zubaydah provided information on Ramzi bin al-Shibh, there is no indication that Abu Zubaydah provided information on bin al-Shibh's whereabouts. Further, while Abu Zubaydah provided information on bin al-Shibh while being subjected to the CIA's enhanced interrogation techniques, he provided similar information to FBI interrogators prior to the initiation of the CIA's enhanced interrogation techniques."[142]

Fact:

(TS// ██████████████████ //NF) CIA records demonstrate that Abu Zubaydah was subjected to enhanced interrogation techniques during two separate periods in April 2002 and August 2002. During these timeframes, Abu Zubaydah made several photographic identifications of Ramzi bin al-Shibh and provided information that bin al-Shibh had been in Kandahar at the end of 2001, but was then working with KSM in Karachi, Pakistan. More important, Abu Zubaydah provided information about how he would go about locating Hassan Ghul and other al-Qa'ida associates in Karachi. This information caused ██████████████████ Pakistani authorities to intensify their efforts and helped lead them to capture Ramzi bin al-Shibh and other al-Qa'ida associates during the Karachi safe house raids conducted on

September 10-11, 2002.

~~(TS//~~ █████████████████ ~~//NF)~~ The claim made in this case study relies, in part, upon the factually incorrect premise that Abu Zubaydah was not subjected to enhanced interrogation techniques until August 4, 2002.[143] As previously demonstrated, Abu Zubaydah was first subjected to the enhanced interrogation techniques of sleep deprivation, nudity, and dietary manipulation on April 15, 2002. Abu Zubaydah's second period of enhanced interrogation, which included the use of the waterboard, began on August 4, 2002.[145]

~~(TS//~~ █████████████████ ~~//NF)~~ The Study also incorrectly claims that "there is no indication in CIA records that Abu Zubaydah provided information on bin al-Shibh's whereabouts."[146] While the CIA Study Response appears to concede this point unnecessarily,[147] CIA and FBI records establish that Abu Zubaydah did provide locational information about Ramzi bin al-Shibh. Specifically, he noted that he had seen bin al-Shibh in Kandahar, Afghanistan, at the end of 2001, and that he was aware that bin al-Shibh was presently working with KSM in Karachi, Pakistan.

~~(TS//~~ █████████████████ ~~//NF)~~ On April 18, 2002, during Abu Zubaydah's first period of enhanced interrogation, an FBI interrogator showed him a photograph of Ramzi bin al-Shibh. According to the FBI, Abu Zubaydah said that he knew the man in the photograph as "Ramzi bin al-Shiba" and that he had seen him with a group of Arabs shortly after a missile strike in Kandahar, Afghanistan, on the house of Taib Agha, Mullah

Omar's secretary.[148] This information appears to place bin al-Shibh in Kandahar in the November 2001 timeframe, roughly five months prior to this interview with Abu Zubaydah. On June 2, 2002, the FBI again showed Abu Zubaydah a photograph of bin al-Shibh. This time Abu Zubaydah provided some additional information, stating that he knew this man as "Al-Sheeba," whom he saw with KSM in Kandahar around December 2001, near the end of Ramadan. He also noted that al-Shibh speaks Arabic like a Yemeni and that he had seen al-Shibh in the media after the September 11, 2001, terrorist attacks.[149] On August 21, 2002, during his second period of enhanced interrogation, Abu Zubaydah "immediately recognized the photograph of Ramzi bin al Shibh."[150] Abu Zubaydah mentioned that he had heard "that al-Shibh had stayed at the secret guest house in Qandahar that Mukhtar had established for the pilots and others destined to be involved in the 9/11 attacks."[151]

(TS// ████████████████████ //NF) On May 19, 2002, and May 20, 2002, Abu Zubaydah identified a picture of bin al-Shibh as "al-Shiba" and "*noted that he is always with (KSM).*" If that assertion was true, then Abu Zubaydah was essentially suggestingthat bin al-Shibh was with KSM in or around Karachi, Pakistan, because he had also informed his interrogators that KSM was located in or around Karachi. [153] Abu Zubaydah confirmed this association while being subjected to enhanced interrogation on August 21, 2002, when he stated that bin al-Shibh was "one of the operatives working for Mukhtar aka Khalid Shaykh Mohammad,"[154] again suggesting that bin al-Shibh was likely in Karachi.

(TS// ████████████████████ //NF) The Study's claim that it found "no connection" between Abu Zubaydah's reporting and Ramzi bin al-Shibh's capture is the result of poor analysis. On August 20, 2002, during his second period of enhanced interrogation, when asked how he would find his former al-Qa'ida associates if he were set free, Abu Zubaydah told CIA interrogators that he would contact the well-known associate of Hassan Ghul, who could put him in touch with Hassan Ghul and other senior al-Qa'ida members.[155] The Study frames this interchange much more narrowly. It asserts that "Abu Zubaydah was asked specifically how he would find Hassan Ghul. In response, Abu Zubaydah provided corroborative reporting: that Hassan Ghul could possibly be located through a well-known associate."[156] This narrow framing of the question and response enables the Study to conclude incorrectly that the capture of bin al-Shibh was an "unexpected" result of the raids that failed to capture Hassan Ghul.[157] The Study's approach fails to understand the causal link between Abu Zubaydah's information and the successful Karachi safe house raids of September 11, 2002, which resulted in the collection of important intelligence information and the capture of 11 al-Qa'ida associates, including Ramzi bin al-Shibh.

(TS// ████████████████████ //NF) About six weeks before Abu Zubaydah identified the significance of the well-known associate of Hassan Ghul, Pakistani authorities ████████████████████████████ ██████████████ raided the well-known associate of Hassan Ghul's home ████████████ in early July

2002. The well-known associate of Hassan Ghul was interviewed on the spot and cooperated with Pakistani authorities ███████████████████████████████████████ ███████████████████████████████████████. The known associate of Hassan Ghul even sent ████████████ with the Pakistani officers to identify a home where Hassan Ghul formerly resided.[158] The CIA officers observed that the location was "extremely close to (if not an exact match)" to a location where KSM once resided, according to a June 18, 2002, report from the FBI.[159]

~~(TS//~~███████████████████████~~//NF)~~ The Study dismisses Abu Zubaydah's identification of the well-known associate of Hassan Ghul as mere "corroborative reporting," and does not attach the appropriate significance to this information because of its rigid adherence to its flawed analytical methodology, which presumes that anything corroborative cannot be considered as "otherwise unavailable actionable intelligence."[160] The facts tell a different story, Abu Zubaydah was a recognized senior member of al-Qa'ida who had direct ties to multiple high-ranking terrorists, including Usama Bin Ladin. The CIA was focused on Hassan Ghul, another well-connected senior member of al-Qa'ida, and "other" al-Qa'ida associates of Abu Zubaydah. Therefore, Abu Zubaydah's disclosures were deemed by the CIA as significant and actionable intelligence. When Abu Zubaydah identified the well-known associate of Hassan Ghul as the first person he would contact to reconnect with Hassan Ghul and other al-Qa'ida associates, it is very likely that collecting additional intelligence from the well-known associate of Hassan Ghul became a top operational priority for U.S. and Pakistani officials.

(TS// ████████████████████ //NF) It is not surprising that CIA Headquarters ████████████ ████████████████████████ on August 29, 2002, to request that Pakistani officials "reinterview the well-known associate of Hassan Ghul for additional intelligence on Hassan Ghul."[161] On September 3, 2002, ████████████████████████ reported that Pakistani officials had re-interviewed the well-known associate of Hassan Ghul an unknown number of times and that these officials noted that at times the well-known associate of Hassan Ghul contradicted himself.[162] On September 9, 2002, Pakistani officials returned to the well-known associate of Hassan Ghul's home and interviewed another well-known associate of Hassan Ghul who had recently returned to ████████████████████████████. The other well-known associate of Hassan Ghul cooperated and disclosed the location of ████████████████████████ Hassan Ghul's apartment, which was promptly raided but found to be empty.[163] Pakistani authorities interviewed ████████ ████████████████████████████████ ████████████ and learned that while Hassan Ghul had vacated the apartment, he was scheduled to return to the complex ████████████████████████████████ ████████████████████████████████████. The Pakistani authorities subsequently placed the complex under surveillance in an effort to capture Hassan Ghul.[164]

(TS// ████████████████████ //NF) On September 10, 2002, Pakistani authorities arrested two individuals believed to be Hassan Ghul and his driver outside of the apartment complex.[165] These individuals turned out to be Muhammad Ahmad Ghulam Rabbani, a.k.a. Abu Badr and Muhammad Madni, Abu Badr's driver.[166] Information obtained from Madni led to a series of raids on September 11, 2002, by Pakistani authorities of the identified safe houses, resulting in the arrest of 11 individuals, including Ramzi bin al-Shibh, Abdul Rahim Gulam Rabbani, Hassan Muhammad Ali bin Attash, and other al-Qa'ida members. [167] These raids also resulted in the collection of important al-Qa'ida operational documents, including financial records and the coded "perfume letter."[168]

(TS// ▮▮▮▮▮▮▮▮▮▮▮▮▮▮▮▮▮ //NF) The Study's claims with respect to the capture of Ramzi bin al-Shibh do not hold up under a close examination of the CIA documentary record. There was a direct causal connection between the information provided by Abu Zubaydah during his second period of enhanced interrogation and bin al-Shibh's capture. Abu Zubaydah had informed his interrogators that bin al-Shibh was one of KSM's operatives in Karachi. Zubaydah confirmed the importance the well-known associate of Hassan Ghul to locate Hassan Ghul and other al-Qa'ida associates operating in Karachi, including bin al-Shibh.

(U) Since the Study's claims on this topic do not hold up to factual scrutiny, its criticisms of the CIA representations with respect to Ramzi bin al-Shibh and President Bush's references to bin al-Shibh in his September 6, 2006, speech on the CIA's Detention and Interrogation Program are not valid. The CIA said Abu Zubaydah's "knowledge of al-

Qa'ida lower-level facilitators, modus operandi and safehouses... played a key role in the ultimate capture of Ramzi bin al-Shibh."[169] Far from a "misrepresentation," that statement was completely accurate and consistent with the circumstances that led to bin al-Shibh's ultimate capture. Similarly, the text in President Bush's September 6, 2006, speech on the CIA's Detention and Interrogation Program noting that "the information Zubaydah provided helped lead to the capture of Binalshibh" was also accurate.[170]

(U) The capture of Ramzi bin al-Shibh and the other al-Qa'ida terrorists during ▮▮▮▮▮▮▮▮▮▮▮▮▮▮▮▮▮▮▮▮ ▮▮▮▮▮▮▮ raids of September 10-11, 2002, were stunning operational successes, made possible, in part, by the CIA's Detention and Interrogation Program.

Δ

Endnotes

[142] SSCI Study, Executive Summary, December 3, 2014, p. 318.

[143] *Compare* SSCI Study, Executive Summary, December 3, 2014, p. 323 *with supra*, pp. 150-155.

[144] *See supra*, pp. 150-155. The CIA began subjecting Abu Zubaydah to monitored sleep deprivation on April 15, 2002, the day he was discharged from the hospital. He was continued on a liquid diet and subjected to nudity. All three of these interrogation techniques were subsequently and formally categorized by the Department of Justice as "enhanced interrogation techniques." *See* CIA, ▮▮▮▮▮▮▮ 10043, April 15, 2002, p. 2; CIA, ▮▮▮▮▮▮▮ 10047, April 16,

2002, p. 2; Memorandum for John A. Rizzo, Senior Deputy General Counsel, Central Intelligence Agency, from Steven G. Bradbury, Principal Deputy Assistant Attorney General, Office of Legal Counsel, Department of Justice, May 30, 2005, Re: Application of United States Obligations under Article 16 of the Convention Against Torture to Certain Techniques that May be Used in the Interrogation of High value Al Qaeda Detainees (DTS 2009-1810, Tab-11). [http://www.justice.gov/sites/default/files/olc/legacy/201 3/10/21/memo-bradbury2005.pdf]

[145] *See* CIA, 10586, August 04, 2002, p. 4.

[146] SSCI Study, Executive Summary, December 3, 2014, p. 318.

[147] *See* CIA Study Response, Case Studies (TAB C), June 27, 2013. p. 23 ("It is true that Abu [Zubaydah] provided no information *specifically* on Bin al-Shibh's whereabouts....") (emphasis added).

[148] *See* FBI draft report of the interrogation of Abu Zubaydah. April 18, 2002, 6:10 a.m. to 10:40 a.m., p. 1.

[149] *See* FBI draft report of the interrogation of Abu Zubaydah, June 3, 2002, 4:00p.m. to 8:30p.m., p. 3; CIA, ▮▮▮▮▮▮▮ 10428, June 7, 2002, p. 5.

[150] *See* CIA, ▮▮▮▮▮▮▮ 10656, August 21, 2002, p. 2. See also CIA, ▮▮▮▮▮▮▮ 10654, August 21, 2002, p. 1-2.

[151] CIA, ▮▮▮▮▮▮▮ 10656, August 21, 2002, p. 3.

[152] CIA, DIRECTOR ▮▮▮▮▮▮▮▮▮▮ - ▮▮▮▮▮▮▮▮▮▮ May 27, 2002, p. 4.

[153] The draft report of this interview states: (1) "Abu Jafar told [Abu Zubaydah] that he and his friend had to get to Karachi because they had business with

Muhktar"; (2) "This [group of 11 Filipinos or Malaysians] was on their way to Karachi to meet up with Muhktar"; (3) "the American and Kenyan [Zubaydah] sent to Muhktar in mid-March 2002... [Zubaydah] actually sent them to Hassan Ghul and Amanullah (in Karachi) who would have then arranged for them to be taken to Muhktar"; and (4) "Subject advised that, prior to his arrest he was trying to coordinate a trip to Karachi to meet with Muhktar." FBI draft report of the interrogation of Abu Zubaydah, May 20, 5:25 p.m. to 8:40 p.m., pp. 3 and 5.

[154] CIA, DIRECTOR ███████████ August 26, 2002, p. 4.

[155] *See* Captures Resulting From Detainee Information: Four Case Studies, November 26, 2003, p. 2; CIA, ████████ 10644, August 20; 2002, pp: 2-3; and CIA. ALEC ███████████ August 29, 2002, p. 2.

[156] SSCI Study, Executive Summary, December 3, 2014, p. 323.

[157] *See* SSCI Study, Executive Summary, December 3, 2014, pp. 75, 318, and 320.

[158] *See* CIA, CIA CABLE 11755 ████████████-████████

[159] *See* CIA, CIA CABLE 11755 ████████████-████████

[160] *See* SSCI Study, Executive Summary, December 3, 2014, p. 323.

[161] CIA, ALEC ██████████ August 29, 2002, p. 3.

[162] *See* CIA, CIA CABLE 12207, September 5, 2002, p. 2.

[163] *See* CIA, CIA CABLE 12249, September 9, 2002,

p. 2.

[164] *See* CIA, CIA CABLE 12249, September 9, 2002, pp. 2-3.

[165] *See* CIA, CIA CABLE 12251, September ███, 2002, p. 2; CIA, CIA ████████████████ ███████ September ███, 2002, p. 2.

[166] *See* CIA, CIA CABLE 33363, September 11, 2002, p. 2. Abu Badr is the brother of Abdul Rahim Gulam Rabbani, aka Abu Rahama, who ran the KSM safe house used by the 9/11 al-Qa'ida terrorists. Abu Zubaydah made photographic indentification of Abu Badr and called him KSM's man in Karachi. *See* CIA, ALEC ████████████ ████████████████████ █████ CIA, CIA CABLE 12267, September 11, 2002, p. 2.

[167] *See* CIA, ALEC ███████████ September 11, 2002, pp. 2-3. Madni informed the arresting officers that Abu Badr was a major al-Qa'ida [facilitator]." *See also* CIA, CIA CABLE 12267, September 11, 2002, pp. 2-4. He also gave ████ ███████████████████ information about the locations of al-Qa'da-affiliated residences and safe houses in Karachi. CIA, CIA CABLE 12251, September ███, 2002, p. 2; CIA, █████ █████ ████████████████████████ September ███, 2002, pp. 3-4.

[168] *See* CIA, ALEC ██████████ October 3, 2002, p. 2.

[169] CIA, Memorandum to the Inspector General from James Pavitt, CIA Deputy Director for Operations, Comments to Draft IG Special Review, Counterterrorism Detention and Interrogation Activities, February 27, 2004.

[170] President George W. Bush, *Trying Detainees; Address on the Creation of Military Commissions*,

Washington, D.C., September 6, 2006.
[http://georgewbush-whitehouse.archives.gov/news/-releases/2006/09/20060906-3.html]

[171] SSCI Study, Executive Summary, December 3, 2014, p. 327.

(U) The Capture of Khalid Shaykh Mohammad

Study Claim:

~~(TS//~~ █████████████████████ ~~//NF)~~ "[T]here
are no CIA records to support the assertion that Abu
Zubaydah, Ramzi bin al-Shibh, or any other CIA
detainee played any role in the 'the planning and
execution of the operation that captured Khalid Sheikh
Mohammed.'"[171]

Fact:

~~(TS//~~ █████████████████████ ~~//NF)~~
Information obtained from CIA detainee Abu
Zubaydah was essential to furthering the CIA's
understanding of KSM's role in the September 11,
2001, terrorist attacks and helped lead to the capture of
Ramzi bin al-Shibh. The █████████████████████
█████████████████████ interrogation of bin al-
Shibh and DETAINEE R provided key insights about
KSM █████████████████████. Information
produced through detainee interrogation was pivotal to
the retention of a key CIA asset whose cooperation led
directly to the capture of KSM.

~~(TS//~~ █████████████████ ~~//NF)~~ The Study almost
exclusively attributes the capture of KSM to a "unilateral
CIA asset."[172] We agree with the Study that this asset
provided information that was crucial to KSM's capture in
Rawalpindi, Pakistan, on March 1, 2003.[173] We also
acknowledge that the CIA had met with the asset as early as
fall 2001 and that the asset had provided good intelligence
information related to KSM. However, the Study fails to
acknowledge the cascading sequence of revelations that

began with Abu Zubaydah's identification of the importance of the well-known associate of Hassan Ghul and culminated in the information provided by the asset which led directly to the capture of KSM. Moreover, the Study does not recognize that, but for the fortuitous intervention of a CIA officer – who was aware of recently obtained detainee information which corroborated the asset's claims concerning KSM – the asset would have been terminated as a CIA source prior to providing the crucial pre-capture information about KSM.[174]

~~(TS//~~   ~~//NF)~~ As stated previously, information obtained from Abu Zubaydah about KSM prior to the use of enhanced interrogation techniques was key to the CIA's realization of KSM's operational significance. The CIA disseminated an intelligence report, ▮▮▮▮▮▮▮▮ within the Intelligence Community ▮▮▮▮▮▮▮▮▮▮▮▮▮▮▮▮▮▮▮▮detailing KSM's identification as "Mukhtar" and his role as the mastermind of 9/11.[175] Responses ▮▮▮▮▮▮▮▮▮▮▮▮ ▮▮▮▮▮▮▮▮▮▮▮▮▮▮▮▮▮▮▮▮▮▮▮▮ indicated they followed up and requested more information ▮▮▮▮▮▮▮▮▮▮▮▮▮▮▮▮ on him.[176] Zubaydah's FBI interrogator Ali Soufan also described the information from Zubaydah on KSM as significant. In 2008, Soufan told Committee staff that when Zubaydah provided that information, "we had no idea at the time that Mukhtar was the KSM from 9/11........ Because we had been working so diligently on trying to figure out the puzzles of 9/11 and who is Mukhtar, and when Abu Zubaydah said that, I think the picture was complete."[177] Also, on May 13, 2009,

Soufan told the Senate Judiciary Committee that prior to Zubaydah providing information on KSM's role as the mastermind of the 9/11 attacks, "we had no idea of KSM's role in 9/11 or of his importance in the al Qaeda leadership structure."[178]

(TS// ███████████████ //NF) The chain of events leading to KSM's capture begins in earnest with Zubaydah's interrogation on August 20, 2002, when, during his second period of being subjected to enhanced interrogation techniques, he was asked how he would go about locating Hassan Ghul and other al-Qa'ida associates if he were to be released.[179] Zubaydah responded to this question by stating that he would reach out to [the well-known associate of Hassan Ghul] ███████████████
███████████████ reconnect with Ghul and others.[180] As explained in greater detail in our discussion about the capture of Ramzi bin al-Shibh, this information from Zubaydah caused ███████████████ Pakistani authorities to intensify their investigative efforts [the well-known associate of Hassan Ghul] ███████████████
███████ who had previously located, interviewed, and surveilled.[181] These investigative efforts resulted in ███████████████ Pakistani raids of safe houses in Karachi on September 10-11, 2002.[182] Ramzi bin al-Shibl was among those captured during these raids.

(TS// ███████████████ //NF) Ramzi bin al-Shibh becomes one of the next links in the effort to track down and capture KSM. Shortly after his capture in Karachi, bin al-Shibh was transferred ███████████████

173

████████████████████████████ In late 2002, ██████████
██
██
██

Ramzi indicated ████████ that the best way to find KSM is to find ██████████████████████████████████ 'Ammar' who is also in Karachi."[183] A few days later, in a photographic identification, bin al-Shibh confirmed that 9/11 financier, Ali Abdul Aziz Ali, was Ammar al-Baluchi, ████████████
██
██
██

████████████ [184] The Study asserts that "Ammar al-Baluchi played no role in the operation that captured KSM, which centered around ██████████████████████████████
██████████████████████████████ [185] While Ammar might not have played a direct role in the "operation" that captured KSM, bin al-Shibh's key insights about Ammar clarified his importance such that Alec Station highlighted bin al-Shibh's photo-identification of Ammar al-Baluchi as a break-through.[186]

(TS//██████████████████████████//NF) Moreover, according to the CIA, bin al-Shibh's information about Ammar al Baluchi was used to interrogate DETAINEE R. [187] This claim is supported by a CIA requirements cable which contained numerous questions concerning KSM ██████████████████████████ [188] In late 2002, DETAINEE R provided background and physical details on KSM ██████████████████████████████████████
██

174

███ [189] ██████████████████████ the next day, DETAINEE R ████████████████████████

████████████████████████████████████
████████████████████████████████████
████████████████████████████████████

██████████████████████████████ [190] The next day ██████████████████████ the CIA inter-rogators continuing their questioning of DETAINEE R on the topic of KSM ███████████████████████

██████ DETAINEE R provided ████████████

████████████████████ [191] In late 2002 ██████
██████████████████ DETAINEE R was rendered into CIA custody and subjected to enhanced interrogation techniques. ██████████████████████████████
██████████████████████████████ CIA ████
████████████████████ reported that ████
██████████████ "said in no uncertain terms that none of the information provided by DETAINEE R has been of any use and ██████████████████████████████
██████████ wasted time here chasing people and places that are probably bogus." CIA ██████████████ urged interrogators to readdress the issues with DETAINEE R and acquire more – and more accurate – information.[192] ████
██████████████████████████████████

DETAINEE R was asked to provide as much locational information as possible on ████████████████
████████████████████████████████
████████████████████████████████
████████████████████████████████

175

(TS// ~~████████████████~~ //NF) This brings us to ASSET X, who was initially undervalued by the CIA, despite his repeated claims that he could help locate KSM in Paldstan. In ████████████████ 2001 the asset declined to work the CIA because his proposed financial compensation package had been rejected. In ████████2002, the Counterterrorism Center directed recruiters to reconnect with ASSET X.[194] By ████████████ of that same year, he was assigned to a new case officer. The case officer was unfamiliar with ASSET X's potential to provide information that might lead to the location of KSM, and the cables he sent to CIA Headquarters in pursuit of guidance in handling the asset went unread and unanswered when they were re-routed to a compartmented team which had been disbanded.[195]

(TS// ~~████████████████~~ //NF) Having heard nothing back from CIA Headquarters, the case officer was on the verge of terminating the CIA's relationship with the asset in ████████████2002. When the case officer met with his Chief of Base to discuss the termination, by chance, another CIA officer with prior operational contact with the asset[196] overheard their conversation as he was waiting to meet with the Chief of Base. This other CIA officer ██████████████████████████████ having come from ████████████████████████████ that reported inforaiation from DETAINEE R ████████████████████████████ ████████████████████████████████ ██████████████████████████████████. The officer's current mission included trying to track down KSM. He recognized ASSET X's information ████████████████- ████████████████████████████████████- ████████████████████████████████████- ██████████████████████████████████████.

He advised ASSET X's current case officer and the Chief of Base against proceeding with the termination, and joined in a meeting between the current case officer and ASSET X]. ASSET X was subsequently able to provide information that resulted in KSM's capture on March 1, 2003.

(TS// ████████████████████ //NF) Although ASSET X's contributions were clearly important to KSM's capture, the true linchpin in the operation was the visiting officer's familiarity with the crucial information that the detainees had provided about KSM. Information from DETAINEE R background and ████████████████████████████- ████ information on KSM ████████████████████ lies at the end of a causal chain that traces back through Ramzi bin al-Shibh and Abu Zubaydah. Absent this collective body of information, the requisite understanding of KSM's activities, organizational stature, ████████████████- ████████████████████ would have eluded analysts, to make nothing of the fact ASSET X's relationship with the CIA would have been terminated in ███████████████ 2002; months in advance of KSM's March 2003 capture.

Δ

Endnotes

[172] SSCI Study, Executive Summary, December 3, 2014, p. 327.

[174] *See* CIA Oral History Program, Interview of [REDACTED] by [REDACTED], October 14, 2004, pp. 5-7.

[175] *See* CIA, █████████████████████

[176] *See* CIA, █████████████████████

[177] SSCI Transcript, Staff Interview of FBI Special Agent, Ali Soufan, April 28, 2008 (DTS 2008-2411).

[178] Ali Soufan, Statement for the Record, before the United States Senate Committee on the Judiciary, May 13, 2009.

[179] *See* CIA, ALEC ████████, August 29, 2002, pp. 2-3.

[180] *See* CIA, ALEC ████████, August 29, 2002, pp. 2-4.

[181] *See supra*, pp. 159-166.

[182] *See* CIA, CIA CABLE 12251, September ██, 2002, p. 2; CIA, CIA 468392 / ███████████████████, September ██, 2002, pp. 3-4.

[183]

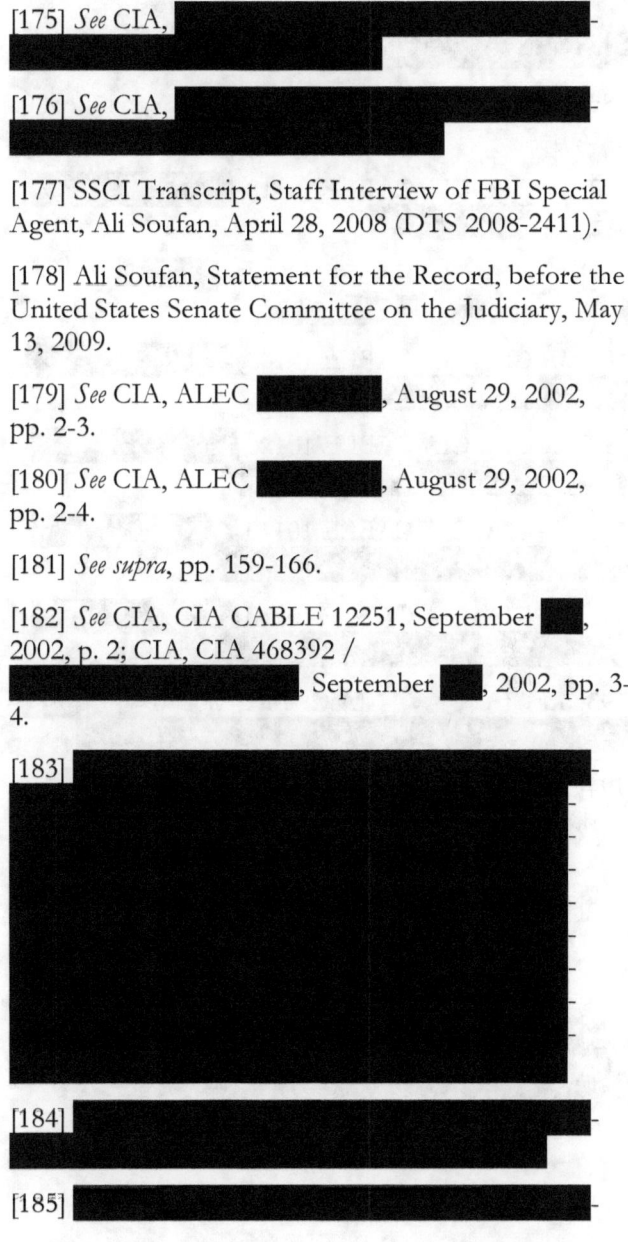

[184] ███████████████████████

[185] ███████████████████████

[186] *See* CIA, CIA CABLE ████████, September 30, 2002, p. 2.

[187] *See* CIA, CIA CABLE 10118, ████████-████████

[188] *See* CIA, CIA CABLE 530341, ████ -████

[189] *See* CIA, CIA CABLE 10103, ████ -████

[190] *See* CIA, CIA CABLE 10120 ████ -

[191] *See* CIA, CIA CABLE 10140 ████ -

[192] *See* CIA, CIA CABLE 10250 ████ -

[193] *See* CIA ████ CIA CABLE] 30266 ████ -

[194] *See* CIA Oral History Program, Interview of [REDACTED] by [REDACTED], October 14, 2004, p. 3.

[195] *See* CIA Oral History Program, Interview of [REDACTED] by [REDACTED], October 14 2004 p. 4.

[196] ████████

(U) The Disruption of the Karachi Hotels Bombing Plot

Study Claim:

~~(TS//~~ ██████████████████████ ~~//NF)~~ "[T]he CIA's enhanced interrogation techniques – to include the waterboard – played no role in the disruption of the Karachi Plot(s)."[198]

Fact:

(U) CIA documents show that key intelligence collected through the CIA's Detention and Interrogation Program, including information obtained after the use of enhanced interrogation techniques, played a major role in disrupting the Karachi hotels bombing plot.

~~(TS//~~ ██████████████████ ~~//NF)~~ As the Study notes, the reference to the "Karachi Plot(s)" refers to:

terrorist plotting that targeted a variety of U.S. and western interests in the Karachi area, to include the U.S. Consulate, named hotels nearthe airport and beach, U.S. vehicles traveling between the Consulate and the airport, U.S. diplomatic housing, potential sniperattacks against U.S. personnel, as well as Pakistan's Faisal Army Base.[199]

~~(S//NF)~~ The CIA has acknowledged that on several occasions, including in prominent representations such as President's Bush's 2006 speech, it mischaracterized the impact of the reporting acquired from detainees on the Karachi plots. Instead of claiming that the information "helped stop a planned attack on the U.S. Consulate in Karachi," the CIA should have stated that it "revealed ongoing attack plotting against the U.S. official presence in Karachi that prompted the Consulate to take further steps to protect its officers."[200]

(TS// ███████████████ //NF) Our analysis will demonstrate that the intelligence collected through the CIA's Detention and Interrogation Program, including information obtained after the use of enhanced interrogation techniques, played a key role in the disruption of the Karachi hotels bombing plot. The Study notes that the CIA had information regarding the Karachi terrorist plotting as early as September 11, 2002, in the form of the "perfume letter," which was obtained during a ███████ raid

███

███ of a safe house in Karachi, Pakistan.[201] What the Study fails to point out, however, is that Abu Zubaydah provided crucial information which played a big role in leading to the ███████ raids of the al-Qa'ida safe houses on September 11, 2002 – the same raids that yielded the "perfume letter" and disrupted the Karachi hotels plot. Specifically, ███████████████ Pakistani raids were the direct result of information provided by Abu Zubaydah on August 20, 2002, during his second period of enhanced interrogation.[202]

(TS// ███████████████ //NF) When asked how he would go about finding his former al-Qa'ida associates if he were set free, Abu Zubaydah told CIA interrogators that he would contact a well-known associate of Hassan Ghul who could put him in touch with Ghul and other senior al-

Qa'ida members.[203] CIA officers then asked Pakistani officials to question the well-known associate of Hassan Ghul, who on September 7, 2002, provided vague information the Pakistanis assessed was untruthful.[204] The Pakistanis continued to watch the residence and, when another well-known associate of Hassan Ghul returned to the residence, questioned the other well-known associate of Hassan Ghul as well. The other well-known associate of Hassan Ghul cooperated and provided the location of Ghul's last apartment.[205] This information led to the arrest, on September 9, 2002, of an individual thought to be Ghul[206], but who turned out to be another al-Qa'ida terrorist.[207] Abu Zubaydah then positively identified this terrorist as Abu Badr, "KSM's driver and KSM's man in Karachi," facilitating the movement of al-Qa'ida operatives. [208] Badr's driver, who was also arrested, identified information about several al-Qa'ida safehouses and residences in Karachi.[209]

(TS// ██████████████████ //NF) Based on this information, on September 11, 2002, ████████████████ ████████████████████████████ conducted ████████ raids, which resulted in the arrests of several terrorists and key documents, including one dubbed the "perfume letter" because the word "perfumes" was used as a codeword.[210] In this May 2002 letter, KSM told Hamza Zubayr, a terrorist killed in the same raids, he would provide him with $30,000, with another $20,000 available upon request, and that "we have acquired the green light that is strong for the [hotels]" clearly indicating a plot of some kind.[211] More troubling, the letter suggested "[increasing] the number to make it three instead of one."[212] Were it not for Abu Zubaydah's original information about the significance of the well-known associate of Hassan Ghul, which led to the Karachi safe house raids, it is unclear if the "perfume letter" would ever have been found.

~~(TS//~~ ████████████████████ ~~//NF)~~ Abu Zuhaydah's value, however, did not end with providing the true significance of the well-known associate of Hassan Ghul. Zubaydah subsequently translated the "perfume letter" for the CIA, identified the key word in the letter – "hotels" – that had not been previously translated, and told the CIA that the reference to "Khallad" in the letter may be the "one legged Yemeni." A CIA analyst noted that the one-legged Yemeni was terrorist Khallad bin Attash, who was later arrested and admitted to his involvement in the plot.[213]

~~(TS//~~ ████████████████████ ~~//NF)~~ By early October 2002, the CIA had completed a search of the individuals identified in the "perfume letter" and concluded that most of those who had been assigned roles in support of the hotels operation had been arrested or killed by the Pakistani authorities during the September 11, 2002 raids.[214] Although the Karachi hotels plot had been thwarted by these raids, at least one of the individuals identified by Abu Zubaydah in the letter, Khallad bin Attash, a known al-Qa'ida operative, remained at large.[215] Eventually, on April 28, 2003, ████████████████████████████ ██████████████████████████ was able to capture several al-Qa'ida operatives, including Ammar al-Baluchi and bin Attash. ████████████ also successfully confiscated explosives, detonators, and ammunition as part of the capture operation.[216]

(TS// ████████████████████ //NF) On May 17, 2003, Khallad bin Attash confirmed that Ammar al-Baluchi had intended to use the explosives stashed for that operation to target the U.S. Consulate.[217] The next day, ████████ ████████████████ indicated its clear understanding of how these interrelated Karachi plot events had improved the U.S. security posture in the area when it noted that although its options to enhance security:

> may appear limited... ██████████████████-
> ████████████████ and what
> we have seen over past months as an increased
> aggressiveness of local authorities have provided some
> protection from these threats. We point specifically to
> the 11 September 2002 raids in Karachi, the 1 March
> 2003 take-down of KSM, and to the recent arrests of
> al-Baluchi and ba Attash as examples of how ████-
> ████████████ have thwarted attacks.[218]

Δ

Endnotes

[197] ████████████████████████-

[198] SSCI Study, Executive Summary, December 3, 2014, p. 242.

[199] SSCI Study, Executive Summary, December 3, 2014, p. 239; *see also* CIA, ████████ 11454, April 30,

2003, pp. 1-4.

[200] CIA Study Response, Case Studies (TAB C), June 27, 2013, p. 6.

[201] *See* SSCI Study, Executive Summary, December 3, 2014, p. 242; CIA, ALEC ▮▮▮▮ October 3, 2002, pp. 2-4. *and* CIA, ALEC ▮▮▮▮ October 3, 2002, pp. 2-4.

[202] *See* CIA, Captures Resulting From Detainee Information: Four Case Studies, November 26, 2003, p. 2.

[203] *See* CIA, Captures Resulting From Detainee Information: Four Case Studies, November 26, 2003, p. 2.; CIA, ▮▮▮▮ 10644, August 29, 2002, pp. 1-2; CIA, ALEC ▮▮▮▮ August 29, 2002, pp. 2-3.

[204] *See* CIA, ALEC ▮▮▮▮ ▮▮▮▮ CIA, CIA CABLE 12207, September 05. 2002, pp. 2-3.

[205] *See* CIA, CIA CABLE 12249, September 09, 2002, p. 2.

[206] *See* CIA, CIA CABLE 12251, September ▮▮, 2002, p. 2.

[207] *See* CIA, CIA CABLE 12254, September 10, 2002, p. 4; CIA, ALEC ▮▮▮▮ ▮▮▮▮.

[208] CIA, ALEC ▮▮▮▮ ▮▮▮▮

[209] *See* CIA, CIA CABLE 12251, September ▮▮, 2002, p. 2.

[210] *See* CIA, CIA CABLE 12267, September 11, 2002, p. 2; CIA, CIA CABLE ▮▮▮▮ October 03. 2002, p. 2.

[211] CIA, CIA CABLE 33804, September 19, 2002, p. 4; After his capture on April 1, 2003, KSM would confirm that the Karachi plot referenced in the "perfume letter" was the plot directed at three named hotels, chosen because they were frequented by American and German guests. *See* SSCI Study, Volume II, April 1, 2014, pp. 592-593.

[212] CIA, CIA CABLE 33804, September 19, 2002, p. 4.

[213] *See* E-mail from: CIA analyst; to: ██████████████████; subject: Re: AZ on the perfume letter; date: October 10, 2002, at 9:50 A.M., p. 6.

[214] *See* CIA, ALEC ████████ October 3, 2002, pp. 2-12.

[215] *See* CIA, ALEC ████████ October 3, 2002, pp. 2-12.

[216] *See* CIA, CIA CABLE 45028, ██████████████ ████████████

[217] *See* CIA, [CIA CABLE] 38405, May 17, 2003, p. 4.

[218] *See* CIA, CIA CABLE 14510 ██████████████ ████████

[219] SSCI Study, Executive Summary, December 3, 2014, pp. 297-298.

(U) The Heathrow and Canary Wharf Plots

Study Claim:

"[C]ontrary to CIA representations, information acquired during or after the use of the CIA's enhanced interrogation techniques played no role in 'alert[ing]' the CIA to the threat to – or the 'disrupt[ing]' the plotting against – Heathrow Airport and Canary Wharf."[219]

Fact:

~~(TS//~~ ████████████████████ ~~//NF)~~ The CIA interrogation program played a key role in disrupting the Heathrow and Canary Wharf plotting.

~~(TS//~~ ████████████████ ~~//NF)~~ Despite its claim that information acquired during or after the use of enhanced interrogation techniques played "no role" in the disruption of the Heathrow Airport and Canary Wharf plots, the Study twice concedes these plots were "fully disrupted" with the detentions of Ramzi bin al-Shibh, KSM, Ammar al-Baluchi, and Khallad bin Attash.[220] The Study then incorrectly asserts that "[t]here are no CIA records to indicate that any of the detainees was captured as a result of CIA detainee reporting.[221] As we have previously demonstrated, information obtained from the CIA interrogation program played a key role in the capture of al-Shibh and KSM.[222] Also, Ramzi bin al-Shibh provided information about Ammar al-Baluchi and Abu Zubaydah provided information about Khallad bin Attash prior to their arrests.[223] The same detainee information that helped lead to the capture of these terrorists also played a key role in fully disrupting the Heathrow Airport and Canary Wharf plots.

~~(TS//~~ ███████████████ ~~//NF)~~ Thus far, the following analytical dominoes have fallen in relation to the Heathrow and Canary Whaif plots: (1) "There is considerable evidence that the information Abu Zubaydah provided identifying KSM as "Mukhtar" and the mastermind of 9/11 was significant to CIA analysts, operators, and FBI interrogators";[224] (2) "Abu Zubaydah provided information about how he would go about locating Hassan Ghul and other al-Qa'ida associates in Karachi. This information caused ████████████ Pakistani authorities to intensify their efforts and helped lead them to capture Ramzi bin al-Shibh and other al-Qa'ida associates during the Karachi safe house raids conducted on September 10-11, 2002";[225] (3) "Information produced through detainee interrogation was pivotal to the retention of a key CIA asset whose cooperation led directly to the capture of KSM";[226] (4) Zubaydah told the CIA that the reference to "Khallad" in the letter may be the "one legged Yemeni";[227] and (5) Pakistan's arrest of al-Qa'ida terrorists Ammar al-Baluchi and Khallad Bin Attash disrupted the al-Qa'ida plot to attack the U.S. Consulate in Karachi.[228] Taken together, these significant operational accomplishments, most of them resulting from information obtained from CIA detainees, also had the added bonus of disrupting the Heathrow and Canary Wharf plots.

~~(TS//~~ ███████████████ ~~//NF)~~ The Study undercuts its own argument that the CIA interrogation program played no role in the disruption of the Heathrow and Canary Wharf plotting almost immediately after its narrative on the plots begins. The Study says "records indicate the Heathrow Airport plotting had not progressed beyond the initial planning stages when the operation was fully disrupted with the detention of Ramzi bin al-Shibh (detained on September 11, 2002), KSM (detained on March 1, 2003), Ammarai-Baluchi (detained on April 29, 2003), and Khallad bin Attash (detained on April 29, 2003)."[229] As we explained previously, Ramzi bin al-Shibh was detained as a result of information provided by Abu Zubaydah during a period of enhanced interrogation.[230] By asserting that the detention of Ramzi bin al-Shibh played a role in the disruption of the plot, certainly the detainee information that led to his detention also played a role in the plot's disruption.

(TS// █████████████████████ //NF) Additionally, while the Study claims that the CIA already had information in its possession prior to the detention and interrogation of those detainees the CIA credits with providing information on the plot (KSM, Ammar al-Baluchi, and Khallad bin Attash), much of that reporting, including identification of Heathrow airport as the target, came from interrogations of Ramzi bin al-Shibh occurring prior to CIA custody. Again, ████████████████ ████████████ were only able to detain and question Ramzi bin al-Shibh because information provided by Abu Zubaydah in CIA detention led to bin al-Shibh's arrest.

(TS// █████████████████████ //NF) While the Study cites a CIA document to support its claim that the plot "was

190

fully disrupted" with the arrests of the four previously mentioned terrorists, the CIA document says that the plot was "disrupted," not "fully disrupted."[231] Perhaps for that reason, the CIA continued to interrogate detainees about the plot, long after the arrests of both Ramzi bin al-Shibh and KSM, to uncover more details about the plot and any operatives. For example, the CIA confronted Ramzi bin al-Shibh and KSM about e-mail addresses found in KSM's computer that belonged to the two Saudi-based operatives who could have been used in the plot, Ayyub and Azmari. [232] Although the Study notes that these two operatives were "unwitting" of the Heathrow plot, they appear to have been willing terrorist operatives, as the CIA learned that Ayyub participated in a suicide attack in Riyadh, Saudi Arabia on May 12, 2003, that killed 36 individuals and injured more than 160 others. Azmari was arrested on July 1, 2003 for his connections to the attack.[233]

(TS// █████████████ //NF) Additionally, as noted in several papers and briefings by the CIA, in mid-March 2003, the CIA questioned KSM about a hand-drawn illustration in his notebook of what appeared to be an I-beam with the term "Wharf" written in Enghsh, and "Cannery Wharf" in Arabic.[234] KSM told interrogators it was part of the "Heathrow program" to target Canary Wharf in London as well, a target that had not been previously discussed by other detainees.[235]

(TS// ██████████████ //NF) After the detention in April 29, 2003, of Khailad bin Attash and Ammar al-Baluchi, debriefers used the reporting from KSM and bin al-Shibh to confront them. In a document explaining the value of detainee reporting provided to the Department of Justice, CIA explained:

> Khallad admitted to having been involved in the plot and revealed that he directed group leader Hazim al-Sha'ir to begin locating pilots who could hijack planes and crash them into the airport. Khallad said he and operative Abu Talha al-Pakistani considered ███████████ countries as possible launch sites for the hijacking attempts and that they narrowed the options to the ███████████████████ - ███████████████████ Khailad's statements provided leverage in debriefings of KSM. KSM fleshed out the status of the operation, including identifying an additional target in the United Kingdom, Canary Wharf.[236]

(U) In the years that followed the initial arrest of Ramzi bin al-Shibh, CIA officers continued to unravel the details of this plotting and provided information that helped lead to the detention and questioning of several other individuals involved in the plot.[237] In light of the information cited above, the Study's assertion that the CIA interrogation program played "no role" in the disruption of this plotting makes little sense, especially when the Study's own 62-page chart identifying the intelligence on the Heathrow plot devotes most of the pages to information from detainees in CIA's program or to Ramzi bin al-Shibh, who was captured because of CIA detainee information.[238]

Δ

Endnotes

[220] *See* SSCI Study, Executive Summary, December

3, 2014, pp. 295 and 299.

[221] SSCI Study, Executive Summary, December 3, 2014, p. 299.

[222] *See supra*, pp. 159-178.

[223] *See supra*, pp. 173 and 184.

[224] *See supra*, pp. 140-147.

[225] *See supra*, pp. 159-166.

[226] *See supra*, pp. 171-178.

[227] E-mail from: CIA analyst; to: ███████████ ; subject: Re: AZ on the perfume letter; date: October 10, 2002, at 9:50 AM, p. 6.

[228] *See* CIA Study Response, Case Studies (Tab C), p. 6.

[229] SSCI Study, Volume II, April 1, 2014, pp. 1000-1062.

[230] *See supra*, pp.159-166.

[231] SSCI Study, Volume II, April 1, 2014, pp. 976-78.

[232] *See* SSCI Study, Volume II, April 1, 2014, p. 983.

[233] SSCI Study, Volume II, p. 983 n.4387.

[234] CIA, WASHINGTON DC ███████████ CIA, ██████ 10787, March 13, 2003, p. 3.

[235] *See* CIA, 10787, March 13, 2003, p. 3.

[236] CIA, Briefing Notes on the Value of Detainee Reponing, April 8, 2005, 10:47am, p. 4.

[237] *See* SSCI Study, Volume II, April 1, 2014, pp. 1000-1062.

[238] *See* SSCI Study, Volume II, April 1, 2014, pp. 1000-1062.

(U) The Capture of Hambali

Study Claim:

~~(TS//~~ ███████████████ ~~//NF)~~ "A review of CIA operational cables and other records found that information obtained from KSM during or after the use of the CIA's enhanced interrogation techniques played no role in the capture of Hambali."[239]

Fact:

~~(TS//~~ ███████████████ ~~//NF)~~ CIA documents show that the interrogation of KSM and al-Qa'ida operative Zubair, during and after the use of enhanced interrogation techniques on both individuals, played a key role in the capture of Hambali.

~~(TS//~~ ███████████████ ~~//NF)~~ The Study's claim that the enhanced interrogation of KSM played "no role" in the capture of Hambali is not accurate, because two detainees subjected to enhanced interrogation techniques, KSM and Mohd Farik bin Amin, a senior member of Jemaah Islamiya (JI) and more commonly known as "Zubair,[240] provided significant information that helped lead to the capture of Hambali.

(TS// ███████████████ //NF) The claim that the enhanced interrogation of KSM played "no role in the capture of Hambali ignores the fact that KSM provided the crucial piece of information permitting the CIA to recognize the significance of, and act upon, previously known connections that would ultimately lead to Hambali's capture. The Study correctly points out that on March 6, 2003, Majid Khan told foreign government ███████████ ████████ interrogators about his travel to Bangkok in December 2002 and provision of $50,000 to an individual named "Zubair" at the behest of al-Qa'ida.[241] While the Study would like the reader to infer that Majid Khan provided a sufficient connection to Hambali, the Study ignores the fact that Khan never mentioned that the money was destined for Hambali. Moreover, the Study excludes the CIA's answer to the following question for the record: "Was there enough other information linking Zubair and Hambali?" The CIA's answer states:

> No. We assess, and believe the documentary record indicates that otherwise available intelligence was not sufficient to enable officers at the time to conclude Zubair was a targeting inroad to Hambali. A targeting study on Hambali in the late December timeframe, for example, lists a number of potential inroads but not Zubair. A look at the contemporaneous records as well as a plot summary from years later provide no evidence that Zubair played a role in the Bali Bombings.[242]

While Majid Khan's information was still an important piece of the puzzle, it is clear that something more was needed to help locate Hambali. That "something more" would come from KSM several days later.

(TS// ███████████████████ //NF) KSM had been rendered into CIA custody on March ███, 2003, and immediately subjected to enhanced interrogation.[243] On March 11, 2003, KSM admitted to providing Hambali with $50,000 to conduct a terrorist attack in "approximately November 2002." KSM reported, however, that the money was "necessary materials" for a Hambali operation that was approaching "zero hour," information that created a sense of urgency for the CIA to uncover more about Hambali's location.During this interrogation, KSM made no reference to Majid Khan or Zubair.[245] On March 13, 2003, CIA ████ ███████████████████ sent a cable saying that in light of KSM's information that he arranged to send $50,000 to Hambali in November 2002 to procure materials for an operation that was approaching "zero hour," "we view [the information] from Majid Khan on his trip to Bangkok for an alleged money transfer between 26-29 December with ever greater concern."[246] Moreover, the same cable makes clear that at the time of KSM's reporting, the CIA did not know whether the information from KSM and Majid Khan were about the same transaction. The cable says, "KSM's information and Majid's 'story' maybe unrelated, but it appears too premature to judge at this juncture, and we must assume they possibly are until additional facts are learned."[247]

(TS// ███████████████████ //NF) On March 17, 2003, KSM was questioned about the Majid Khan network. KSM positively identified a picture of Majid Khan as "Majid aka Yusif, the al-Qa'ida courier" KSM used to deliver the $50,000 for the next big Hambali operation, through

"Hambali representatives in Thailand."[248] Significantly, KSM said that Khan had not been informed that the money was ultimately for Hambali and that KSM did not know who Hambali's intermediary was.[249] Days later, CIA officers still seemed to be trying to understand the connection between the KSM and the Majid Khan reporting. According to a March 20, 2003, cable, KSM's reporting that he used Majid Khan as a courier to transport al-Qa'ida funds to Hambali, "appears to confirm station [sic] earlier concerns that the $50,000 transfer involving KSM and Hambali may be one in the same with the $50,000 al-Qa'ida transfer facilitated by Khan.[250] Questioned again on March 22, 2003, Khan acknowledged that his trip to Thailand to deliver the $50,000 was at KSM's request.[251]

(U) While it would be difficult to know conclusively without talking to the analysts involved, CIA documents indicate it was the combination of reporting from KSM and Majid Khan that led to the efforts to find Hambali through Zubair. A CIA summary of Hambali's capture timeline states, while "numerous sources had placed Hambali in various Southeast Asian countries, it was captured al-Qa'ida leader KSM who put ████████████████ ████████████████████████████████ on Hambali's trail" – contradicting the Study's claim that the KSM interrogation played "no role."[252]

(TS// ████████████████████ //NF) On June 8, 2003, Zubair was detained by the Government of Thailand. ████████████████████████████████, Zubair reported on ████████████████████████████████████ ██

and corroborated reporting on Business Q.[253] On June ███, 2003, Zubair was transferred into CIA custody and was immediately subjected to enhanced interrogation techniques.[254] Zubair told his interrogators about

█████████████████████████████████████

█████████████████████████████████████

█████████████████████████████████████

█████████████████████████████████████

████████████████████ [255] Zubair also explained

how he █████████████████████████████████

█████████████████████████████████████

█████████████████████████████████████

█████████████████████████████████████

█████████████████████████████████████

█████████████████████████████████████

█████████████████████████████████████

█████████████████████████████████████

█████████████████████████████████████.

[256] This information was consistent with the information he had provided ████████████████████████

█████████

(TS// ███████████████████ //NF) ████████

█████████████████████████████████████

█████████████████████████████████████

█████████████████████████████████████

█████████████████████████████████████

█████████████████████████████████████

█████████████████████████████████████

██████████████████████████ the CIA planned an operation to find Hambali by watching ████████ ██████████████████████████ and waiting for Hambali's

198

facilitators ███████████████████████████████. It appears that Zubair provided key information about these Hambali facilitators after being subjected to the CIA's enhanced interrogation techniques. Specifically, CIA documents show that analysts assessed that it would be "Zubair cohort and former roommate Lilie" ██████████ ████████████████████████████████████ because "per the Zubair debriefings, Lilie is now ██████████ ██████████████████████████████████████ ██████████████████████ and "finding Lilie, therefore, may be tantamount to finding Hambali."[258] ████████████ ██████████████████████████████████

███ Hambali associate Amer, who actually ██████████ ████████████████████████████████ was tracked and Zubair identified a picture of him and speculated that "Lilie likely tasked [Amer] to handle ██████████████████ ████ thus following Amer would likely lead to finding Lilie."[259] Amer was arrested on August 11, 2003, and cooperated in locating Lilie hours later.[262] Lilie was found to have a key fob in his possession imprinted with an address, which Lilie said was the address of two apartments he used for Hambali's activities, one of which was Hambali's residence.[261] Hambali was captured at the address found on the key fob several hours later.[262] It appears that Zubair's cooperation after being subjected to enhanced interrogation techniques played a significant role in the capture of Hambali through Amer and Lilie.

Δ

Endnotes

[239] SSCI Study, Executive Summary, December 3, 2014, p. 305.

[240] The Study acknowledges that Zubair was immediately subjected to CIA enhanced interrogation techniques upon being transferred into CIA custody on June ███, 2003. *See* SSCI Study, Executive Summary, December 3, 2014, p. 309. It attempts to downplay this fact by noting that: (1) "CIA records indicate that Thai authorities were unilaterally following investigative leads related to Hambali and Zubair" and that "[i]t is unknown what specific investigative steps were taken by Thai authorities (or the CIA) between early June 2003 and July 16, 2003, to investigate [BUSINESS Q] ███████ ████████████████████ and (2) the CIA has never represented "to policymakers that the information obtained from Zubair after the use of the CIA's enhanced interrogation techniques led to Hambali's capture." *See* SSCI Study, Executive Summary, December 3, 2014, pp. 309, n.1737. Although we might not know what specific "unilateral" steps were taken by the Thai authorities related to ████████████████████, if any, CIA records provide a good description of the information provided Zubair after the use of enhanced interrogation techniques and the subsequent steps taken by the CIA, including ████████████-████████████████████, to track down and capture Hambali. The absence of a CIA representation about Zubair does not invalidate the assertion that the information he provided after being subjected to enhanced interrogation techniques may have helped lead to the capture of Hambali, especially since this assertion is supported by the CIA documentary record.

[241] SSCI Study, Executive Summary, December 3, 2014, pp. 307-308.

[242] CIA Response to SSCI Request for Information, October 25, 2013, p. 4 (DTS 2013-3152). This answer contradicts the assertion by the Study that "[b]y this time, the CIA had significant information – prior to KSM's capture – indicating that a 'Zubair' played a central supporting role in the JI, was affiliated with al-Qa'ida figures like KSM, had expertise in ████████-████████████████████ in Southeast Asia, and was suspected of playing a role in Hambali's October 12, 2002, Bali bombings." SSCI Study, Executive Summary. December 3, 2014, p. 306-307.

[243] *See* CIA, [CIA CABLE] 34491, March 5, 2003, pp. 1-3.

[244] CIA, ██████ 10755, March 11, 2003.

[245] *See* CIA, ██████ 10755, March 11, 2003, pp. 1-3.

[246] CIA, CIA CABLE, 81697, ████████████████████████

[247] *See* CIA, CIA CABLE, 81697, ████████████████████████

[248] CIA, ██████ 10865, March 17, 2003, p. 3.

[249] *See* CIA, ██████ 10865, March 17, 2003. p. 3.

[250] CIA, CIA CABLE 81990, March 20, 2003, p. 2.

[251] *See* CIA, CIA CABLE 13890, ████████████ ██████

[252] CIA., Hambali Capture/Detention Timeline, no date. p. 6.

[253] *See* CIA Study Response, Case Studies (TAB C),

June 27, 2013, p. 19.

[254] *See* CIA [CIA CABLE] 40568, ██████████
██████████

[255] *See* CIA, Hambali Capture/Detention Timeline, no date, p. 7; CIA, [CIA CABLE] 40915 ██████████ CIA, [CIA CABLE] 41017, ██████████

[256] *See* CIA, Hambali Capture/Detention Timeline, no date, p. 7: CIA, [CIA CABLE] 40915 ██████████

[257] *See* CIA, Hambali Capture/Detention Timeline, no date, p. 7-8; CIA, ALEC ██████████

[258] CIA, Hambali Capture/Detention Timeline, no date, p. 2.

[259] CIA, Hambali,Capture/Detention Timeline, no date, p. 5.

[260] CIA, Hambali Capture/Detention Timeline, no date, p. 5.

[261] CIA, Hambali Capture/Detention Timeline, no date, p. 6.

[262] CIA, Hambali Capture/Detention Timeline, no date, p. 5.

[263] SSCI Study, Executive Summary, December 3, 2014, p. 251. This claim has been modified from the version that appeared in the report that was approved by the Committee at the end of the 112th Congress. For example, it no longer claims that the CIA's interrogation program, excluding the use of enhanced interrogation techniques, did not play a role in the thwarting of the al-Ghuraba Group. It also substitutes

the words "discovery or thwarting" in place of the original "identification *and* disruption." (emphasis added).

(U) The Thwarting of the Second Wave Plots and Discovery of the Al-Ghuraba Group

Study Claim:

~~(TS//~~ ███████████████████ ~~//NF)~~ "A review of CIA operational cables and other documents found that the CIA's enhanced interrogation techniques played no role in the 'discovery' or thwarting of either 'Second Wave' plot. Likewise, records indicate that the CIA's enhanced interrogation techniques played no role in the 'discovery' of a 17-member 'cell tasked with executing the 'Second Wave.'"[263]

Fact:

~~(TS//~~ ███████████████ ~~//NF)~~ The CIA interrogation program played a key role in disrupting the "Second Wave" plot and led to the capture of the 17-member al-Ghuraba group.

~~(TS//~~ ███████████████ ~~//NF)~~ The Study asserts that because Hambali's brother, Gun Gun Ruswan Gunawan, first identified a group of 17 Malaysian and Indonesian Jemaah Islamiya (JI) affiliated students in

203

Karachi, "the use of the CIA's enhanced interrogation techniques against Hambali did not result in the 'discovery' of 'the Ghuraba Cell' that was 'tasked with executing the 'Second Wave' plotting.'"[264] While Gunawan did identify the group of JI students in Karachi, the Study ignores that KSM, who had also been subjected to the CIA's enhanced interrogation techniques, provided information months earlier on this same roup of JI students and their location in Karachi – information that had helped lead to the capture of Gunawan himself. The Study also ignores information provided by other detainees in CIA's interrogation program.

(TS// ████████████ //NF) In April 2003, KSM provided information about Gunawan's role in Karachi as a communications conduit between Hambali and al-Qa'ida and reported that he was living in the dormitory where he was enrolled at Abu Baki'-Sadeeq University.[265] KSM also drew a map with the location of a house he called "Colony Gate" where he met Gunawan, where he said a group of JI students would meet.[266] According to CIA information, while the CIA was already aware of Gunawan, "KSM's identification of his role as Hambali's potential successor prioritized his capture. Information from multiple detainees, including KSM, narrowed down [Gunawan's] location and enabled his capture in September 2003."[267] This information was excluded from the Study. Hambali provided very similar information after his capture in August 2003 ████████████████████████. [268]

(TS// ████████████ //NF) On August 20,

2003, CIA headquarters provided information on Gunawan ██████████ █████████ "which solidly ties Rusman Gunawan to al-Qa'ida and al-Qa'ida's terrorist attacks" ██████████ ████████████████████ ████████████████████████████ [269] The information provided was largely from interrogations of KSM, including information about Gunawan working as a communications conduit for Hambali and al-Qa'ida, his location in Karachi, a description of Gunawan, but also provided information from another detainee in CIA custody, Ammar al-Baluchi.[270] Gunawan was arrested on ████████████████████████████, at the Abu Bakr Madrassa, locational information first provided by KSM, along with most of JI student group.[271]

~~(TS//~~ ████████████████████████ ~~//NF)~~ After Gunawan's arrest he was caught trying to send a coded message which he admitted was intended to warn the group of JI-affiliated students about his arrest.[272] ████████████████████ ████ participating in the interrogation recognized Gunawan's information about this group of mostly Malaysian students as similar to intelligence reporting provided previously by KSM that he was planning to recruit Malaysians in a "next wave of attacks."[273] The officers asked that Hambali be questioned about the reporting.[274]

~~(TS//~~ ████████████████████████ ~~//NF)~~ During a CIA interrogation of Hambali days later, Hambali, now in CIA custody and undergoing enhanced interrogation, provided more information about the group, identifying them as the "al-Ghiiraba" group and describing how they were set up by Hambali and sent to Karachi because of its "proximity to Afghanistan and the availability of military-style training facilities there."[275] He said the Program was designed to "give a select few the opportunity for military-style training to prepare them for jihad" and identified two who were ready for operations.[276] Hambali provided information about the identities and backgrounds of several of the al-Ghuraba group members and described conversations he had with KSM about possible future attacks on the United States.[277] In a subsequent interrogation, Hambali said the group was not yet ready for operations, but may be in 2003-2004 (it was already late 2003 when he provided this information) and he named individuals who were being groomed as suicide and other operatives.[278]

(TS// ████████████████ //NF) ████████████ ████████████████████ arrested the members of the al-Ghuraba group during raids on ███████████████ ████████████████ A cable describing the arrests said, "[W]e captured this cell based on the debriefings of captured senior al-Qa'ida operatives, who stated that some members of this cell were to be part of senior al-Qa[']ida leader Khalid Shaykh Muhammad (KSM)['s] [']second wave['] operation to attack the United States using the same modus operandi as was used in the September 11, 2001 attacks."[279]

(TS// ████████████████████ //NF) In a seeming effort to suggest CIA's assessment of the threat posedby the al-Ghuraba group had diminished over time, the Study identified an October 27, 2006, CIA cable that stated, "[A]ll of the members of the former al-Ghuraba cell have now been released."[280] It also cited an April 18, 2008, CIA intelligence report focusing on the Jemaah Islamiya and referencing the al-Ghuraba group that makes no reference to the group serving as potential operatives for KSM's 'Second Wave' plotting."[281]

(TS// ███████████████████ //NF) These statements are misleading in several ways. The April 18, 2008 intelligence report was about Jemaah Islamiya in Pakistan, not the al-Ghuraba group, and provided only a minor description of the "al-Ghuraba cell in Karachi," but did mention that its leader was in direct contact with Hambali and "al-Qa'ida external operations chief Khalid

Shaykh Muhammad."[282] The Study omitted a report focused on Jemaah Islamiya's al-Ghuraba group published five months later that said "members of the cell had also been identified by Khalid Shaykh Muhammad, the mastermind of the attacks of 11 September 2001, and senior al-Qa'ida and JI operative Hambali as candidates for post-11 September attacks against the U.S. Homeland," including for "second wave suicide hijacking operations in the Unites States and Europe."[283] Far from suggesting the CIA was unconcerned about the al-Ghuraba group, this report devoted 20 pages to describing the threat from its members including their "jihad activities" and the caution that "as this group of radicalized militants reconnects and mingles with other young Southeast Asian Muslims, it poses a revived threat to US and Western interests."[284] ███████

████████████████████████████████████
████████████████████████████████████
████████████████████████

Δ

Endnotes

[264] SSCI Study, Executive Summary, December 3, 2014, pp. 255-256.

[265] *See* CIA, ████████ 11192, April 8, 2003, p. 3.

[266] *See* CIA, ████████ 11212, April 11, 2003, p. 2.

[267] CIA, *Detainee Reporting Pivotal for the War Against Al-Qa'ida,* June 1, 2005, p. 2 (DTS 2009-1387). [http://documents.nytimes.com/c-i-a-reports-on-interrogation-methods#p=245]

[268] *See* CIA, CIA CABLE 87551, August 15, 2003, pp. 4-5.

[269] CIA, ALEC ██████████████████
████████████████████

[270] CIA, ALEC ██████████████████
████████████████████

[271] *See* CIA, CIA CABLE 15252, ████████████
████████████

[272] *See* CIA, CIA CABLE 15359, ████████████
████████████

[273] CIA, CIA CABLE 15359, ██████████████
████████████

[274] *See* CIA, CIA CABLE 15359, ████████████
████████████

[275] CIA, [CIA CABLE] 45915, September 14, 2003, p. 2.

[276] CIA, [CIA CABLE] 45915, September 14. 2003, p. 2.

[277] *See* CIA, [CIA CABLE] 45915, September 14, 2003, p. 2.

[278] CIA, [CIA CABLE] 45953, September 15. 2003. p. 3.

[279] CIA, CIA CABLE 52981, ███████████

[280] CIA, CIA CABLE 131396, October 27, 2006, p. 2.

[281] *See* CIA, Jemaah Islamiya: Counterterrorism Scrutiny Limiting Extremist Agenda in Pakistan, April 18, 2008.

[282] CIA, Jemaah Islamiya: Counterterrorism Scrutiny Limiting Extremist Agenda in Pakistan, April 18, 2008, p. 1.

[283] CIA, Southeast Asia: Jemaah Islamiya's Al-Ghuraba Cell Coalescing, September 17, 2008, pp. 1 and 2.

[284] CIA, Southeast Asia: Jemaah Islamiya's Al-Ghuraba Cell Coalescing, September 17, 2008, pp. 1-2.

(U) Critical Intelligence Alerting the CIA to Jaffar al-Tayyar

Study Claim:

> (TS// ~~██████████~~ //NF) "CIA representations [about detainee reporting on Jaffar al-Tayyar] also omitted key contextual facts, including that... (2) CIA detainee Abu Zubaydah provided a description and information on a KSM associate named Jaffar al-Tayyar to FBI Special Agents in May 2002, prior to being subjected to the CIA's enhanced interrogation techniques... and (5)CIA records indicate that KSM did not know al-Tayyar's true name and that it was Jose Padilla – in military custody and being questioned by the FBI – who provided al-Tayyar's true name as Adnan el-Shukrijumah."[286]

Fact:

> (TS// ~~██████████~~ //NF) Abu Zubaydah provided a description of and information about Jaffar al-Tayyar to FBI special agents in May 2002 *after* being subjected to enhanced interrogation between April 15, 2002 and April 21, 2002. Although KSM did not know al-Tayyar's true name, he did report that Padilla might know al-Tayyar's true name. Padilla subsequently confirmed Jaffar's true name as Adnan El Shukrijumah.

(TS// ~~██████████~~ //NF) On May 20, 2002, while in CIA custody, Abu Zubaydah provided information on an associate of KSM by the name of Abu Jaffar al-Thayer. Abu Zubaydah provided a detailed description of Abu Jaffar al-Thayer, including that he spoke English well and may have studied in the United States.[287] The Study incorrectly claims that this May 20, 2002, interrogation took place prior to the initiation of the CIA's enhanced interrogation techniques.[288] Abu Zubaydah had already been subjected to an extended period of sleep deprivation and other enhanced interrogation techniques during his interrogation between April 15, 2002 and April 21, 2002, about one month *prior* to his May 20 interrogation.[289]

(TS// ███████████████████ //NF) The Study also cites as a key contextual fact omitted from CIA representations that KSM did not know al-Tayyar's true name, and it was Jose Padilla, in military custody and being questioned by the FBI, who provided al-Tayyar's true name as Adnan el-Shukrijumah.[290] However, this omission was rendered moot because, as the Study itself notes a few pages later,[291] the "FBI began participating in the military debriefings [of Padilla] in March 2003, *after KSM reported Padilla might know the true name of a US-bound al-Qa'ida operative known at the time only as Jaffar al-Tayyar.* Padilla subsequently confirmed Jaffar's true name as Adnan El Shukrijumah."[292]

Δ

Endnotes

[285] CIA, Southeast Asia: Jemaah Islamiya's Al-Ghuraba Cell Coalescing, September 17, 2008, p. 2.

[286] SSCI Study, Executive Summary, December 3, 2014, pp. 358-359.

[287] *See* FBI draft report of the interrogation of Abu

Zubaydah, May 20, 2002, 5:25 p.m. to 8:40 p.m., p. 3.

[288] *See* SSCI Study, Executive Summary, December 3, 2014, p. 362.

[289] *See supra*, pp. 33-36.

[290] *See* SSCI Study, Executive Summary, December 3, 2014, pp. 359.

[291] *See* SSCI Study, Executive Summary, December 3, 2014, p. 365.

[292] *See* CIA, Briefing Notes on the Value of Detainee Reporting, April 15, 2005, p. 3 (emphasis added); *See also* CIA, ALEC ▮▮▮▮▮ March 21, 2003, p. 6 ("Our service has developed new information, based on leads from detained al-Qa'ida operations chief Khalid Shaykh Muhammad (KSM), that al-Qa'ida operative Jafar al-Tayyar's true niame is Adnan Shukri Jumah and he could be involved in an imminent suicide attack in the United States").

(U) The Identification and Arrest of Saleh al-Marri

Study Claim:

~~(TS//~~ ███████████████ ~~//NF)~~ The Study correctly asserts, "[t]he CIA represented to the CIA Office of Inspector General that 'as a result of the lawful use of EITs,' KSM 'provided information that helped lead t[o] the arrests of terrorists including... Saleh Almari, a sleeper operative in New York.'"[293]

Fact:

~~(TS//~~ ███████████████ ~~//NF)~~ KSM provided valuable intelligence that helped to clarify Saleh al-Marri's role in al-Qa'ida operations and played a significant role in al-Marri's prosecution.

~~(TS//~~ ███████████████ ~~//NF)~~ The Study cites an interview between the OIG and the Deputy Chief of the Counterterrorist Center, in which the deputy chief claims that information from KSM helped lead to the arrest of al-Marri.[294] As the Study makes clear, al-Marri was not arrested based on information from KSM, and could not have been, because al-Marri was arrested in December 2001, before the detention of KSM in March 2003. Two days after the interview with the IG, the deputy chief wrote in an email that al-Marri "had been detained on a material witness warrant based on information linking him to the 9/11 financier Hasawi."[295] The Study correctly notes that this inaccuracy appears in the final version of the OIG's May 2004 Special Review[296], as referenced in an Office of Legal Counsel memorandum analyzing the legality of the

CIA's enhanced interrogation techniques.[297] In its response to the Study, the CIA concedes that the agency erred in describing detainee reporting as contributing to al-Marri's arrest. However, the agency stresses that KSM did provide valuable intelligence on ul-Marri – intelligence that played a significant role in al-Marri's prosecution.[298]

(TS// ███████████████████ //NF) The Study's focus on this factual error is out of proportion with its significance. The IG's Special Review section on effectiveness contains approximately six pages of discussion, including numerous success stories attributed to intelligence collected from detainees.[299] Incorrectly characterizing the manner in which detainee intelligence was valuable – arrest versus prosecution – for one item in a list of terrorists identified, captured, and prosecuted does not diminish the overall value that detainee intelligence provided in helping to identify, capture, and prosecute terrorists.

(TS// ███████████████████ //NF) The Study also notes that the CIA and the FBI had information about al-Marri prior to KSM's interrogation, in an apparent attempt to downplay the importance of the information obtained from KSM.[300] It was KSM who identified a photograph of al-Marri and described him as an al-Qa'ida sleeper operative sent to the United States shortly before 9/11. KSM said his plan was for al-Marri, who "had the perfect built-in cover for travel to the United States as a student pursuing his advanced degree in computer studies at a university near New York," was to serve as al-Qa'ida's point of contact to settle other operatives in the United States for follow-on attacks after 9/11.[301] KSM also said that al-Marri trained at the al-Faruq camp and had poisons training and said al-Marri offered himself as a martyr to Bin Ladin.[302] Prior to the information from KSM, al-Marri was charged with credit card fraud and false statements. After the information from KSM, al-Marri was designated as an enemy combatant. In 2009, after being transferred to federal court, al-Marri pled guilty to one count of conspiracy to provide material support to al-Qa'ida. In his plea, he admitted that he attended terrorist training camps and met with KSM to offer his services to al-Qa'ida, who told him to travel to the United States before 9/11 and await instructs – *all information initially provided by KSM.*

Δ

Endnotes

[293] SSCI Study, Executive Summary, December 3, 2014, p. 366.

[294] SSCI Study, Executive Summary, December 3, 2014, p. 366 n.2064.

[295] Email from: ███████████████████████ to: ████████████████████; et al.; subject: value of detainees; date: July 18, 2003, at 2:30 PM.

[296] *See* CIA Office of Inspector General, Special Review: Counterterrorism Detention and Interrogation Activities (September 2001 – October 2003), May 7, 2004, p. 87 (DTS 2004-2710). [http://media.washingtonpost.com/wp-srv/nation/documents/cia_oig_report.pdf]

[297] *See* Memorandum for John A. Rizzo, Senior

Deputy General Counsel, Central Intelligence Agency, from Steven G. Bradbury, Principal Deputy Assistant Attorney General, Office of Legal Counsel, May 30, 2005, Re: Application of United States Obligations Under Article 16 of the Convention Against Torture to Certain Techniques that May be Used in the Interrogation of high Value A1 Qaeda Detainees, p. 9 (DTS 2009-1810, Tab 11).
[http://www.justice.gov/sites/default/files/olc/legacy/201 3/10/21/memo-bradbury2005.pdf]

[298] *See* CIA Study Response, Case Studies (TAB C), June 27, 2013, p. 35.

[299] *See* CIA Office of Inspector General, Special Review: Counterterrorism Detention and Interrogation Activities (September 2001 – October 2003), May 7, 2004, pp. 85-91 (DTS 2004-2710).
[http://media.washingtonpost.com/wp-srv/nation/documents/cia_oig_report.pdf]

[300] *See* SSCI Study, Executive Summary, December 3, 2014, pp. 367-368.

[301] CIA, WASHINGTON DC ▮

[302] *See* CIA, CIA WASHINGTON DC ▮

(U) The Arrest and Prosecution of Iyman Faris

Study Claim:

(U) "Over a period of years, the CIA provided the 'identification,' 'arrest,' 'capture,' 'investigation,' and 'prosecution' of Iyman Faris as evidence for the effectiveness of the CIA's enhanced interrogation techniques. These representations were inaccurate."[303]

Fact:

(U) CIA, FBI, and Department of Justice documents show that information obtained from KSM after he was waterboarded led directly to Faris's arrest and was key in his prosecution.

(U) The Study correctly points out that CIA statements implying that detainee information had led to the "identification" or "investigation" of Iyman Faris were inaccurate. However, contrary to the Study's claims, the CIA representations that information obtained from KSM after he was subjected to enhanced interrogation techniques directly led to the arrest and prosecution of Iyman Faris were accurate.

(S//OC/NF) The CIA has admitted that, in a few cases, it incorrectly stated or implied that KSM's information led to the investigation of Iyman Faris when it should have stated that KSM's reporting informed and focused the investigation.[304] The CIA's mistake is somewhat understandable, given that the CIA only began to focus on Iyman Faris in March 2003 and was not aware that the FBI had opened and closed a preliminary investigation on Faris back in 2001. In essence, Faris was a new investigative target to the CIA in March 2003.[305] Regardless, the CIA's representation concerning the identification and initial investigation of Faris is much less important than the details that led to his arrest and prosecution.

(TS// ███████████████████ FISA/NF) On March 5, 2003, Majid Khan, an al-Qa'ida operative directly subordinate to KSM, was taken into custody by Pakistani authorities.[306] That same day, the FBI's authorized electronic surveillance of Majid Khan's residence in Maryland indicated ███████████████████, Majid Khan's ████████████ made a suspicious call to an individual, later confirmed to be Iyman Faris. They spoke about the possible arrest of Majid Khan and ███████████████████ s suspicions that he was under FBI surveillance. ███████████████████ asked Faris whether he had been approached or questioned and warned Faris not to contact anyone using his phone.[307] The FBI reopened its international terrorism investigation on Iyman Faris soon thereafter.[308]

(TS// ███████████████████ //NF) On March 10, 2003, in response to a requirements cable from CIA Headquarters reporting that al-Qa'ida was targeting U.S. suspension bridges,[309] KSM stated that any such plans were "theoretical" and only "on paper." He also stated that no one was currently pursuing such a plot.[310]

(TS// ███████████████████ //NF) On March 11, 2003, Majid Khan identified a photograph of Iyman Faris before he was in CIA custody. Among other details, Khan said that Faris was a 35-year old truck driver of Pakistani origin who was a "business partner of his ███████████" ████████████████████████[311] The next day, Majid Khan described Faris as "an Islamic extremist,"[312] On March 14, 2003, Majid Khan provided the following additional details on Faris: (1) Faris was a mujahedeen "during the Afghan/Soviet period"; (2) Faris was a close associate of Maqsood Khan, a known al-Qa'ida associate in contact with senior al-Qa'ida members and Majid's uncle; and (3) Faris had contacted Majid Khan's family after the capture of KSM became public and requested that the family pass a message to Maqsood Khan regarding the status of KSM.[313]

(TS// ████████████████ //NF) On March 16, 2003, when asked again about the targeting of U.S. suspension bridges, KSM repeated his earlier assertions, noting that, while Usama Bin Ladin officially endorsed attacks against suspension bridges in the United States, he "had no planned targets in the [United States] which were pending attack and that after 9/11 the [United States] had become too hard a target."[314] KSM never referenced Iyman Faris during his March 10 and March 16 interrogations. Thus far, none of the information collected by the U.S. Intelligence Community would have been sufficient to prosecute Iyman Faris on charges of material support to terrorism.

(TS// ████████████████ //NF) On March 17 and 18, 2003, the CIA questioned KSM about Majid Khan's family and KSM stated that another Khan relative, whom he identified from a picture of Faris, was a "truck driver in Ohio."[315] On March 18, 2003, KSM told interrogators he tasked the truck driver to procure specialized machine tools that would be useful to al-Qaida in loosening the nuts and bolts of suspension bridges in the United States. KSM said he was informed by an intermediary that Faris could not find the tools.[316] This revelation would turn out to be a key piece of incriminating evidence against Iyman Faris.

(TS// ▓▓▓▓▓▓▓▓▓▓▓▓▓▓▓▓▓ //NF) The Study excluded information found in CIA documents which shows that, immediately after obtaining information from KSM and Majid Khan regarding Faris, the CIA queried the FBI for "additional details" on Faris, "including a readout on his current activities and plans for FBI continued investigation."[317] The cable specifically noted that "KSM seems to have accurately identified" Faris from a photograph as the "truck driver in Ohio." On March 20, 2003, the FBI picked Faris up for questioning and conducted a consent search of his apartment, seizing his laptop. When our staff asked the FBI why Faris was picked up, they cited the cables from CIA.[318] The FBI investigators went into this interview armed with the information revealed by KSM and Majid Khan, which enabled them to explore Faris's ties with KSM and al-Qa'ida plotting in the United States.[319] The Study notes that when approached by law enforcement, Iyman Faris voluntarily provided information and self-incriminating statements.[320] This gives a false impression that the information provided by KSM was unnecessary to securing the arrest and prosecution of Faris by omitting the important context that the FBI questioned

Faris armed with incriminating information obtained from KSM on March 17 and 18, 2003.[321]

(U) There is further proof that the incriminating revelations obtained from KSM after he was subjected to enhanced interrogation techniques led directly to the successful arrest and prosecution of Iyman Faris – On May 1, 2003, Faris pled guilty to "casing a New York City bridge for al Qaeda, and researching and providing information to al Qaeda regarding the tools necessary for possible attacks on U.S. targets," *the exact terrorist activities described by KSM.*

Δ

Endnotes

[303] SSCI Study, Executive Summary, December 3, 2014, p. 276.

[304] CIA Study Response, Case Studies (TAB C), June 27, 2013, p. 13.

[305] *See* CIA Study Response, Case Studies (TAB C); June 27, 2013, p. 14.

[306] *See* CIA, CIA CABLE 13658, March 5, 2003, pp. 1-2.

[307] CIA, CIA CABLE ███████, March 6, 2003, p. 4.

[308] SSCI Study, Executive Summary, December 3, 2014, p. 280; FBI information confirmed by the FBI on November 30, 2010, SSCI Study, Executive Summary, December 3, 2014, p. 280, n.1581.

[309] CIA, ALEC ███████ March 7, 2003, p. 1.

[310] CIA, ALEC ███████ 10752, March 10, 2003, p. 2; CIA, DIRECTOR ███████ March 12, 2003, p. 5. *See also* ███████.

[311] CIA, CIA CABLE 13758, ███████-███████

[312] CIA, CIA CABLE 13765, ███████-███████

[313] CIA, CIA CABLE 13785, ███████-███████

[314] CIA, ███████ 10858, March 9, 2003, p. 2.

[315] CIA, ███████ 10886, March 18, 2003, pp. 5-6.

[316] CIA, ███████ 10886, March 18, 2003, pp. 5-6.

[317] CIA, ███████-███████ Information from KSM on Majid Khan.

[318] Phone call from the FBI responding to Staff questions from a document review, January 25, 2013.

[319] *See* CIA Study Response, Case Studies (TAB C), June 27, 2013, p. 13; FBI WASH 040537Z, April 4, 2003, p. 2.

[320] SSCI Study, Executive Summary, December 3, 2014, pp. 283-284.

[321] SSCI Study, Executive Summary, December 3, 2014, pp. 281-282.

(U) The Arrest and Prosecution of Uzhair Paracha and the Arrest of Saifullah Paracha

Study Claim:

(TS// ███████████ //NF) "The CIA represented that information obtained through the use of the CIA's enhanced interrogation techniques produced otherwise unavailable intelligence that led to the identification and/or arrest of Uzhair Paracha and his father Saifullah Paracha (aka, Sayf al-Rahman Paracha). These CIA representations included inaccurate information and omitted significant material information, specifically a body [of] intelligence reporting – acquired prior to CIA detainee reporting – that linked the Parachas to al-Qa'ida-related terrorist activities."[322]

Fact:

(TS// ███████████ //NF) Information obtained from KSM during his enhanced interrogation on March 25, 2003, about alleged explosives smuggling into the United States, attacks on U.S. gas stations, and related material support to al-Qa'ida, motivated the FBI to track down and arrest Uzhair Paracha in New York a few days later on March 31,2003. The Intelligence Community continued its pursuit of Saifullah, who was later arrested ███████ on July 6, 2003. Among other charges, Uzhair was successfully convicted on November 23, 2005, of providing material support to al-Qa'ida and sentenced to 30 years in prison. KSM's description of Uzhair's involvement in the gas station plots and his claim that

223

Uzhair may have provided other logistical support for
Majid's entry into the United States was consistent with
the press release's description of some of the evidence
used during Uzhair's trial.

~~(TS//~~ █████████████████████ ~~//NF)~~ On March 25,
2003, while being subjected to enhanced interrogation
techniques, KSM provided U.S. domestic threat information
concerning Saifullah Paracha and his son, Uzhair Paracha.
KSM stated that Saifullah Paracha was a Pakistani
businessman in Karachi, who owned a textile business with
a branch in New York City. KSM alleged that his nephew,
Ammar al-Baluchi, and Majid Khan had discussed a plan
with Saifullah to use his textile business to smuggle
explosives into the United States. According to this plan,
the explosives would be shipped in containers that Saifullah
used to ship the clothes that he sold in the United States.
KSM stated that Saifullah agreed to the plan, but he was
unclear how much Uzhair Paracha knew about it.[323] KSM
added that Majid Khan planned to rent a storage space in
whatever area of United States he chose, not necessarily
close to New York City, and that the explosives would be
used in al-Qa'ida's campaign against economic targets in
the United States.

~~(TS//~~ █████████████████████ ~~//NF)~~ KSM was also
aware that Ammar al-Baluchi and Majid Khan had
approached Saifullah and Uzhair to help resettle Majid
Khan in the United States, where Majid had plans *to blow up
several gas stations.* KSM stated that Ammar was hoping that
Paracha could sponsor Majid's entry into the United States,
if necessary. KSM also told his interrogators that "*Uzhair
may have provided other logistical supportfor Majid's entry into*

224

the United States." Finally, KSM noted that Saifullah owned a media company in Pakistan and had traveled to Kandahar, Afghanistan, in 1999 to meet with Usama Bin Ladin for the purpose of offering al-Qa'ida the services of his media company.[326]

~~(TS//~~ █████████████████ ~~//NF)~~ Threat information related to the allegation of explosives smuggling motivated the FBI to begin searching in earnest for Saifullah and Uzhair Paracha. The next day, on March 26, 2003, the FBI's field division in Washington, DC requested the CIA to approve the following tearline based upon KSM's reporting:

> Subject: Sayf Al-Rahman Paracha's Possible
> Involvement in Plot to Smuggle Explosives to the
> United States. It has come to our attention that one
> Sayf al-Rahman Paracha, a Pakistani businessman and
> owner of an import-export textile business in Karachi,
> Pakistan, may be involved in a plan to smuggle
> explosives to the United States for al-Qa'ida terrorist
> related activities. There is a possibility that Mr.
> Paracha's son Uzhair may be involved as well. Our
> information indicates that Uzhair traveled from
> Pakistan to the U.S. circa 17 February 2003. We seek
> your assistance in providing any information you may
> have regarding these individuals, their activities, and
> personalities. Your cooperation and assistance in this
> matter is greatly appreciated.[327]

In the same cable request, the FBI noted that it had conducted routine records checks and that both Parachas

████████████████████████████████

████████████████████████████ [328]

~~(TS//~~ █████████████████ ~~//NF)~~ The FBI arrested

Uzhair in New York on March 31, 2003. The CIA was able to develop an operation that lured Saifullah Paracha out of Pakistan, which resulted in his arrest ████████████ ████████████████████████████████████ on July 6, 2003. [329] On November 23, 2005 – after a two-week jury trial – Uzhair was convicted on all charges in the five-count indictment of providing material support to al-Qa'ida and sentenced to 30 years in prison.[330] The press release announcing the trial results stated,

> The evidence at trial proved that PARACHA, 26, agreed with his father, Saifullah Paracha, and two al Qaeda members, Majid Khan and Ammar Al-Baluchi, to provide support to al Qaeda by, among other things, *trying to help Khan obtain a travel document that would have allowed Khan to re-enter the United States to commit a terrorist act.* Statements from Khan admitted at trial revealed that, once inside the United States, *Khan intended to carry out an attack on gasoline stations.*[331]

The decision to conduct the "late night" interrogation session with KSM on March 25, 2003, was made after reviewing recent intelligence obtained from Majid Khan and Iyman Faris.[332] The March 22, 2003, interview of Majid Khan was conducted ██████████████████ ████████████████████████████████████ [333] The resulting cable from that interview explained the relationship between the Parachas and al-Qa'ida, specifically Majid Khan and Ammar al-Baluchi.[334] It also provided details explaining how Uzhair impersonated Majid Khan by using Majid's debit card and a phone conversation between Uzhair and Majid Khan related to Majid's bank account and "calls to the INS."[335]

information from the March 22, 2003, interrogation of Majid Khan was consistent with the charges described in Uzhair Paracha's indictment, although it did not include any reference to the gas station attacks mentioned by KSM.[336]

(TS// ███████████████████ //NF) Based on these facts, we conclude that KSM's allegations of Saifullah Paracha's involvement in a plan to smuggle explosives into the United States motivated the FBI to track down and arrest Uzhair Paracha in New York just a few days later, on March 31, 2003. The CIA was able to develop an operation that lured Saifullah Paracha out of Pakistan, which resulted in his arrest in ████████████████████ on July 6, 2003. There appears to be a direct causal link between the information provided by KSM and the subsequent actions by the Intelligence Community that led to the arrests of Saifullah and Uzhair Paracha. Moreover, KSM's description of Uzhair's involvement in the gas station plots and his claim that Uzhair may have provided other logistical support for Majid's entry into the United States was consistent with the description of evidence used during Uzhair's trial that was included in the press release announcing the trial results.[337]

(TS// ███████████████████ //NF) The Study asserts that KSM's allegations of explosives smuggling were inaccurate because Saifullah Paracha and others denied being involved in such a plot and at least one senior CIA counterterrorism official questioned the validity of the smuggling plot.[338] The fact that Saifullah Paracha and his alleged co-conspirators denied their involvement in an explosives smuggling plot is not persuasive. Also, we have no intention of countering the CIA official's speculative judgment about the alleged plot with further speculation of our own. Regardless of whether the allegations of explosives smuggling were true, the allegations alone were sufficient to trigger the immediate responsive actions by the FBI and CIA that helped lead to the capture of these two terrorists.

(TS// ███████████████ //NF) The Study also attempts to lessen the significance of the information provided by KSM by suggesting that the Intelligence Community had sufficient information prior to KSM's reporting to identify and arrest Saifullah and Uzhair Paracha. In support of this assertion, the Study identifies what it considers to be "significant material information" acquired by the Intelligence Community prior to any reporting from CIA detainees.[339] Quibbling about the omission of "significant material information," – including previously obtained information about an individual named Paracha other than Uzhair and Saifullah or contained in un-disseminated FBI case files[340] – seems largely tangential to the fact that detainee information, including some information obtained after using enhanced interrogation techniques, helped lead to the successful arrests of both men and was consistent with evidence used in the successful prosecution of Uzhair Paracha.

Δ

Endnotes

[322] SSCI Study, Executive Summary, December 3,

2014, p. 352.

[323] CIA, DIRECTOR ███████████████████
████████████

[324] CIA, DIRECTOR ███████████████████
████████████████████████

[325] CIA, DIRECTOR ███████████████████
██████████

[326] CIA, DIRECTOR ███████████████████
████████████████████. During a subsequent
interrogation, KSM provided additional incriminating
information about Saifullah Paracha. The cable reports
that "[i]n light of Paracha's past history of handling
money for al-Qa'ida, [KSM] approached Paracha with
approximately U.S. $260,000-275,000 in cash and asked
him to hold it for al-Qa'ida. [KSM] told Paracha not to
invest the money in any business ventures and
instructed him to keep the money in a safe at his
office." KSM had received these funds from Usama
Bin Ladin. CIA, ████████ 11123, April 3, 2003, p. 3.

[327] FBI, WASH 261909Z, March 26, 2003, pp. 2-3.

[328] FBI, WASH 261909Z, March 26, 2003, p. 2.

[329] CIA Study Response, Case Studies (TAB C), June
27, 2013, p. 31.

[330] DOJ, United States Attorney, Southern District
of New York, *Pakistani Man Convicted of Providing
Material Support to Al Qaeda Sentenced to 30 Years in
Federal Prison*, July 20, 2006, p. 1.
[http://www.justice.gov/usao/nys/pressreleases/July06/par
achasentencingpr.pdf]

[331] DOJ, United States Attorney, *Southern District of
New York, Pakistani Man Convicted of Providing Material
Support to Al Qaeda Sentenced to 30 Years in Federal Prison*,

July 20, 2006, p. 2.
[http://www.justice.gov/usao/nys/pressreleases/July06/par
achasentencingpr.pdf#page=2]

[332] CIA, ███████ 10984, March 24, 2003, p. 2
("Base decided to hold a late night session with KSM
upon reviewing latest Karachi readout on [Majid Khan]
debriefs [CIA CABLE 13890] and FBI intel report...
from debriefings of... [Iyman Faris]").

[333] CIA, CIA CABLE 13890, ████████████
███████████

[334] CIA, CIA CABLE 13890, ████████████
███████████

[335] CIA, CIA CABLE 13890, ████████████
███████████

[336] *Compare* CIA, CIA CABLE 13890
████████████████, *with* Indictment, United
States v. Uzair Paracha, United States District Court,
Southern District of New York. Our review of the
initial cables related to the plan to attack gas stations in
the United States revealed that on March 18, 2003,
Majid Khan was the first to disclose KSM's interest in
"operational procedures of U.S. gas stations and the
tanker trucks that service them," but provided no real
details about specific plans other than being later
tasked by KSM to investigate the procedures for
purchasing gas stations in Pakistan. CIA CIA CABLE
13816, March 18, 2003, p. 3. On March 18, 2003, KSM
provided incriminating details about his conspiracy
with Majid Khan to attack gas stations in the United
States. *See* CIA, ████████ 10886, March 18, 2003,
pp. 2-4.

[337] *Compare* DOJ, United States Attorney, Southern
District of New York, *Pakistani Man Convicted of
Providing Material Support to Al Qaeda Sentenced to 30 Years*

in Federal Prison, July 20, 2006, p. 1
[http://www.justice.gov/usao/nys/pressreleases/July06/par
achasentencingpr.pdf] *with* CIA, DIRECTOR ████████
████████████████████████████████.

[338] SSCI Study, Executive Summary, December 3,
2014, p. 352.

[339] SSCI Study, Executive Summary, December 3,
2014, pp. 352-355.

[340] *See* SSCI Study. Executive Summary, December
3. 2014, pp. 354-355; see also, CIA Study Response,
Case Studies, June 27, 2013, pp. 31-32.

(U) Tactical Intelligence on Shkai, Pakistan

~~(TS//~~ ████████████████████ ~~//NF)~~ The Study asserts that the "CIA representation that the use of the CIA's enhanced interrogation techniques produced *otherwise unavailable* tactical intelligence related to Shkai, Pakistan, was provided to senior policymakers and the Department of Justice between 2004 and 2009."[341] Here is the actual text of the CIA representation at issue:

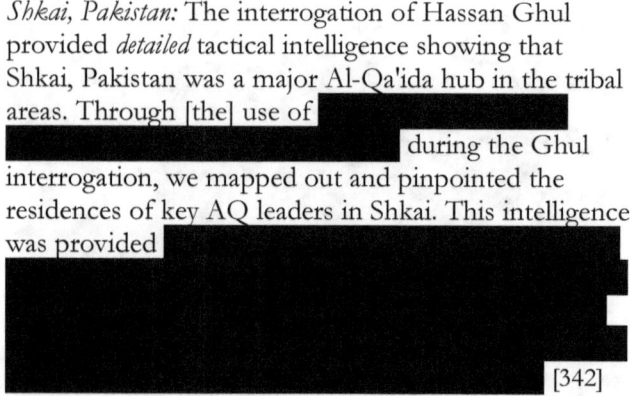

> *Shkai, Pakistan:* The interrogation of Hassan Ghul provided *detailed* tactical intelligence showing that Shkai, Pakistan was a major Al-Qa'ida hub in the tribal areas. Through [the] use of ████████████ ████████████████████████ during the Ghul interrogation, we mapped out and pinpointed the residences of key AQ leaders in Shkai. This intelligence was provided ████████████████
>
> [342]

This representation does not assert that the intelligence was "otherwise unavailable" tactical intelligence, but rather, "detailed" tactical intelligence. More important, while the Study's paraphrase of the representation is not accurate, the CIA's representation itself was factually accurate.

(TS ████████████████████ OC/NF) The CIA Response to the Study makes it clear that Ghul provided detailed tactical intelligence on Shkai, Pakistan, after he was subjected to enhanced interrogation techniques. Specifically, he sat down with ███████████████ experts and pointed to specific locations where he had met some of the senior al-Qa'ida members who the CIA was trying to find.[343] Ghul also revealed his understanding about how Hamza Rabia, a then little-known al-Qa'ida operative, had taken over the group's lead attack coordinator after the capture of KSM in 2003. [344] He used ███████████████ to give more details about the "Bachelor House," the "Ida Khan Complex" and a separate compound used by a group of al-Qa'ida-aligned Uzbeks. He even described the group's evacuation plans in the event of an attack on Shkai.[345] During an interrogation on January 28, 2004, Hassan Ghul drew a detailed map of the locations of a training camp/safehouse near Shkai, provided route information to the site, provided a detailed sketch of the compound and specified the rooms where explosives were stored. Ghul was shown the area and located the route ███████████████████████████████[346] He also identified nine al-Qa'ida members – including Hamza Rabia, Abu Faraj al-Libia, and Spin Ghul – who were located at the safehouse as of June 2003.[347]

(TS// ███████████████████████ //NF) Senior U.S. officials presented the CIA's analysis of Ghul's debriefings and other intelligence about Shkai ████████████████

███████████████████████████████████████
███████████████████████████████████████
███████████████████████████████████████
███████████████████████████████████████
███████████████████████████████████████
███████████████████████████████████████

██████████████████████████████████

██████████████████████████████████

████████████ [348] As the Study notes, a July 2004 CIA report says that t████████████████████████████████

██████████████████████████████████

██████████████████████████████████

██████████████████████████████████

██████████████████████████████████

████████████████████████████████ "[a]l-Qaida's senior operatives who were in Shkai ██████████████ ██████████████████████████████ remained in South Waziristan as of mid-June [2004]."[349] However, the CIA report also notes that ████████████████████████

██████████████████████████████████

██████████████████████████████████

██████████████████████████████████

██████████████████████████████████

██████████████████████████████████

██████████████████████████████████

██████████████████████████████████

██████████████████████████████████

██████████████████████████████████

██████████████████████████████████

██████████████████████████████████

██████████████████████████████████

██████████████████████████████████

██████████████████████████████████

██████████████████████████████████

██████████████████████████████████

██████████████████████████████████

██████████████████████████████████

██████████████████████████████████

██████████████████████████████████

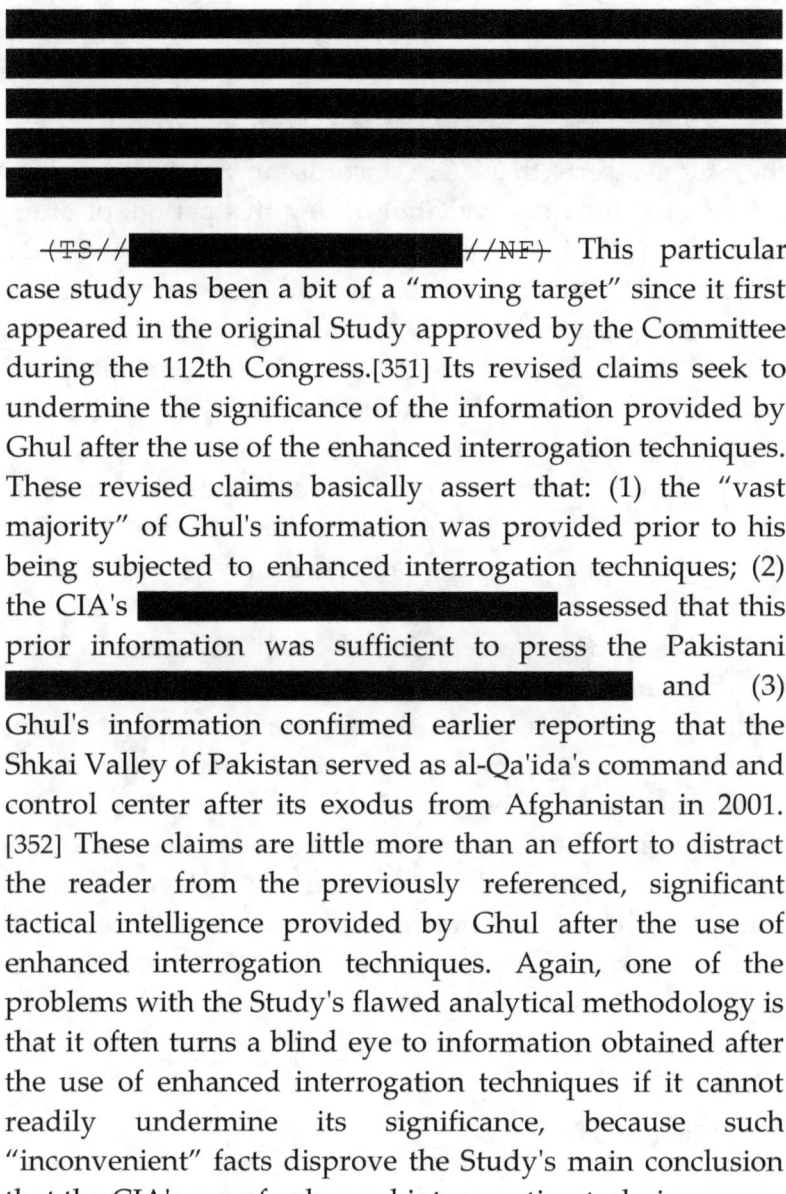

(TS// ███████████████████ //NF) This particular case study has been a bit of a "moving target" since it first appeared in the original Study approved by the Committee during the 112th Congress.[351] Its revised claims seek to undermine the significance of the information provided by Ghul after the use of the enhanced interrogation techniques. These revised claims basically assert that: (1) the "vast majority" of Ghul's information was provided prior to his being subjected to enhanced interrogation techniques; (2) the CIA's ███████████████████ assessed that this prior information was sufficient to press the Pakistani ███████████████████████████████ and (3) Ghul's information confirmed earlier reporting that the Shkai Valley of Pakistan served as al-Qa'ida's command and control center after its exodus from Afghanistan in 2001. [352] These claims are little more than an effort to distract the reader from the previously referenced, significant tactical intelligence provided by Ghul after the use of enhanced interrogation techniques. Again, one of the problems with the Study's flawed analytical methodology is that it often turns a blind eye to information obtained after the use of enhanced interrogation techniques if it cannot readily undermine its significance, because such "inconvenient" facts disprove the Study's main conclusion that the CIA's use of enhanced interrogation techniques was not an effective means of acquiring intelligence or gaining cooperation from detainees.

(TS// ████████████████ //NF) In a similar vein, the Study asserts that "CIA records do not indicate that information provided by Ghul during this period, or after, resulted in the identification or capture of any al-Qa'ida leaders."[353] In fact, prior to the use of enhanced interrogation techniques, Hassan Ghul speculated that Abu Ahmad al-Kuwaiti: (1) could be one of three people with Usama Bin Ladin; and (2) may have handled Bin Ladin's needs, including sending messages to his gatekeeper, Abu Faraj al-Libi. After the use of enhanced interrogation techniques, Hassan Ghul cooperated by telling his interrogators that Abu Ahmad specifically passed a letter from Bin Ladin to Abu Faraj in late 2003 and that Abu Ahmad had "disappeared" from Karachi, Pakistan, in 2002. This information was not only more concrete than Ghul's earlier speculations, but it corroborated information from another detainee, Ammar al Baluchi, that Abu Ahmad served as a courier for Bin Ladin.[354] While this information technically didn't result in the "identification" or "capture" of Bin Ladin, it most certainly played a crucial role in the U.S. Government's successful efforts to locate and neutralize Bin Ladin in his Abbottabad compound in Pakistan on May 2, 2011.

Δ

Endnotes

[341] SSCI Study, Executive Summary. December

3,2014, p. 370 (emphasis added).

[342] CIA Memorandum for Steve Bradbury at Office of Legal Counsel, Department of Justice, dated March 2, 2005, from CIA attorney, ▮▮▮▮ Legal Group, DCI Counterterrorist Center, subject "Effectiveness of the CIA Counterterrorist Interrogation Techniques" (emphasis added).

[343] CIA Study Response, Case Studies (TAB C), June 27, 2013, p. 36; ALEC ▮▮▮▮ February ▮, 2004, pp. 5 and 11.

[344] CIA, CIA CABLE 20397, February ▮, 2004, p. 5.

[345] CIA, CIA CABLE ▮▮▮▮, February ▮, 2004, pp. 10 and 12; CIA, CIA CABLE 1299, January ▮, 2004, pp. 2-3.

[346] CIA, CIA CABLE ▮▮▮▮, February ▮, 2004, pp. 10 and 12; CIA, CIA CABLE 1299, January ▮, 2004, pp. 2-3.

[347] CIA, CIA CABLE ▮▮▮▮, February ▮, 2004, pp. 10 and 12; CIA, CIA CABLE 1299, January ▮, 2004, pp. 2-3.

[348] CIA, ALEC ▮▮▮▮ February ▮, 2004, pp. 1-2; CIA, CIA CABLE 67575, May 6, 2004, p. 1-2; CIA, CIA CABLE 66803, April 26, 2004, pp. 1-11.

[349] SSCI Study Response, Executive Summary, December 3, 2004, p. 378; CIA, DIRECTOR ▮▮▮▮ CIA, Al-Qaida's Waziristan Sanctuary Disrupted but Still Viable, July 21, 2004, p. 1, (DTS 2004-3240).

[350] CIA, Al-Qaida's Waziristan Sanctuary Disrupted but Still Viable, July 21, 2004, p. 1, (DTS 2004-3240).

[351] *Compare* CIA Study Response, Case Studies (TAB C), June 27, 2013, p. 36 (citing the original Study claims concerning the CIA's representation about Ghul's tactical intelligence on Shkai in the appendix to the Study's original findings and conclusions) *with* SSCI Study, Executive Summary, December 3, 2014, p. 368.

[352] SSCI Study, Executive Summary, December 3, 2014, p. 369.

[353] SSCI Study, Executive Summary, December 3, 2014, p. 376.

[354] CIA, DIRECTOR ████████████████ ██████████.

(U) The Thwarting of the Camp Lemonier Plotting

~~(TS//~~ ████████████████████ ~~//NF)~~ In a September 6, 2006 speech, President Bush highlighted the thwarting of a planned strike against Camp Lemonier in Djibouti as an example of the value of information obtained as a part of CIA's Detention and Interrogation Program. The core claim in this section of the Study is not only inaccurate; it was never made.

Study Claim:

> ~~(TS//~~ ████████████████████ ~~//NF)~~ "The CIA represented that intelligence derived from the use of CIA's enhanced interrogation techniques thwarted plotting against the U.S. military base, Camp Lemonier, in Djibouti. These representations are inaccurate."[355]

Fact:

> ~~(TS//~~ ████████████████████ ~~//NF)~~ Representations about the thwarting of an attack against Camp Lemonier in Djibouti, specifically President Bush's 2006 comments that "Terrorists held in CIA custody have also provided information that helped stop a planned strike on U.S. Marines at Camp Lemonier in Djibouti," were accurate and have been mischaracterized by the Study.[356]

~~(TS//~~ ████████████████████ ~~//NF)~~ In this section of the Executive Summary, the Study fundamentally mischaracterizes two representations attributed to President Bush and the CIA. The first representation, which comes from the President's September 6, 2006, speech, is attributed to the CIA by the Study because of the CIA's vetting of the speech. In his speech, the President stated, "[t]errorists held in CIA custody have also provided information that *helped stop a planned strike* on U.S. Marines at Camp Lemonier in Djibouti..."[357] Contrary to the Study's assertions, the President did not attribute the thwarting of this plot exclusively to the use of enhanced interrogation techniques, but information from "[t]errorists held in CIA custody." In addition, the President never stated that the plot was disrupted exclusively because of information from detainees in CIA custody. The President was clear that information from detainees "helped" to stop the planned strike. This idea that detainee reporting builds on and contextualizes previous and subsequent reporting is repeated a few lines later in the speech, when the President makes clear, "[t]he information we get from these detainees is corroborated by intelligence... that we've received from other sources, and together this intelligence has helped us connect the dots and stop attacks before they occur."[358] This is another example of where the President and the CIA are pilloried by the Study for representations they actually never made.

(TS// ████████████████ //NF) The second example cited in the Study is pulled from a set of talking points drafted for use in an October 30, 2007, briefing to then-Chairman of the House Defense Appropriations Subcommittee, former Congressman John Murtha. In the written talking points, theCIA states, "[A CIA detainee] informed us of an operation underway to attack the U.S. military at Camp Lemonier in Djibouti. We believe our understanding of this plot helped us prevent the attack."[359] Setting aside the question of whether these talking points were ever actually employed (which is virtually unanswerable, given the passing of Congressman Murtha in 2010 and the Study's failure to interview the relevant intelligence officers), this representation, like the President's 2006 speech, does not include a reference to enhanced interrogation techniques. Moreover, as was previously the case, the CIA does not claim that the attacks were thwarted solely because of detainee information. They clearly point to their "understanding of this plot," which was a mosaic based on many different sources of intelligence.

(TS// ███████████ //NF) The President's claim that "[t]errorists held in CIA custody have also provided information that helped stop a planned strike on U.S. Marines at Camp Lemonier in Djibouti" was accurate. [360] The detention of two terrorists by the CLA, KSM and Guleed Hassan Ahmed, affected al-Qa'ida's ongoing plotting against Camp Lemonier. The March 3, 2003, arrest of KSM came days after a late-February meeting with Abu Yasir, al-Qa'ida's link to affiliated terrorist cells in Somalia and Kenya, and prevented KSM from attending a follow-on meeting, at which he was to discuss the provision of operational funds with al-Qa'ida leaders in East Africa, some of whom were plotting an attack against Camp Lemonier.[361] Guleed Hassan Ahmed, who conducted reconnaissance of Camp Lemonier for al-Qa'ida, provided information about the Camp Lemonier plot and al-Qa'ida's Somali support network.[362] The information Guleed

241

provided, both prior to and after being transferred into CIA custody, combined with intelligence derived from other sources and methods, was central in driving CIA's targeting of al-Qa'ida proxies based in East Africa.[363] Although these events are not independently responsible for thwarting the plot against Camp Lemonier, they undoubtedly "helped" or contributed to the disruption of the plot.

(TS// ███████████████████ //NF) Finally, the Study claims that plotting against Camp Lemonier "did not 'stop' because of information acquired from CIA detainee Guleed in 2004, but rather, continued well into 2007," implying that continued terrorist targeting of Camp Lemonier excludes the possibility a planned strike was thwarted.[364] This assertion undervalues Camp Lemonier's appeal as a terrorist target, and is willfully blind to the victory even a single obstructed terrorist plot represents. Camp Lemonier is the only major U.S. military base in sub-Saharan Africa, hosting approximately 1,600 military personnel.[365] It is also located within striking distance of, and an active threat to, al-Qa'ida operatives throughout the Horn of Africa. It stands to reason that Camp Lemonier exists as a target of sustained terrorist focus.

Δ

Endnotes

[355] SSCI Study, Executive Summary, December 3, 2014, p. 336.

[356] President George W. Bush. *Trying Detainees;*

Address on the Creation of Military Commissions, Washington, D.C., September 6, 2006. [http://georgewbush-whitehouse.archives.gov/news/-releases/2006/09/20060906-3.html]

[357] President George W. Bush, *Trying Detainees; Address on the Creation of Military Commissions*, Washington, D.C., September 6, 2006. (emphasis added). [http://georgewbush-whitehouse.archives.gov/-news/releases/2006/09/20060906-3.html]

[358] President George W. Bush, *Trying Detainees; Address on the Creation of Military Commissions*, Washington, D.C., September 6, 2006. [http://georgewbush-whitehouse.archives.gov/news/-releases/2006/09/20060906-3.html]

[359] SSCI Study, Executive Summary, Dec. 3, 2014, p. 338; DCIA Meeting with Chairman Murtha re: Rendition and Detention Programs, Oct 30, 2007, p. 1.

[360] President George W. Bush, *Trying Detainees; Address on the Creation of Military Commissions*, Washington, D.C., September 6, 2006. [http://georgewbush-whitehouse.archives.gov/news/-releases/2006/09/20060906-3.html]

[361] CIA, DIRECTOR ██████████ CIA, HEADQUARTERS ████████ ██████████

[362] CIA, CIA ████████ █ ████████ ██████████

[363] CIA, HEADQUARTERS ████████ ██████████

[364] SSCI Study, Executive Summary, December 3, 2014, p. 338.

[365] CIA, CIA CABLE 207044, May 22, 2003, p. 9.

(U) CIA Detainees Subjected to EITs Validated CIA Sources

Study Claim:

~~(TS//~~ ██████████████████████ ~~//NF)~~ "[T]he CIA also represented that its enhanced interrogation techniques were necessary to validate CIA sources. The claim was based on one CIA detainee – Janat Gul – contradicting the reporting of one CIA asset."[366]

Fact:

~~(TS//~~ ██████████████████████ ~~//NF)~~ Contrary to the Study's claim, the CIA representations cited by the Study do not assert that enhanced interrogation techniques helped to validate sources. Rather, the representations only make reference to "detainee information" or detainee "reporting." Also contrary to the Study's claim, we found evidence in the documentary record where the CIA representations about Janat Gul also contained additional examples of source validation. Moreover, the three items of information that the Study asserts should have been included in the Janat Gul asset validation representations were not "critical" and their inclusion does not alter the fact that Gul's persistent contradiction of the asset's claims did help the CIA "validate" that particular asset.

~~(TS//~~ ██████████████████████ ~~//NF)~~ The Study complains that the CIA justified the use of enhanced interrogation techniques by repeatedly using the same Janat Gul example of detainee reporting to determine that one of its assets had fabricated information. The Study first provides the following representation made by CIA Director Hayden during one of our Committee hearings:

> Detainee information is a key tool for validating clandestine sources. In fact, in one case, the detainee's information proved to be the accurate story, and the clandestine source was confronted and subsequently admitted to embellishing or fabricating some or all of the details in his report.

The Study also provides one other example of an asset validation justification:

> Pakistan-based facilitator *Janat Gul's most significant reporting* helped us validate a CIA asset who was providing information about the 2004 pre-election threat. The asset claimed that Gul had arranged a meeting between himself and al-Qa'ida's chief of finance, ShaykhSa'id, a claim that Gul vehemently denied. Gul's reporting was later matched with information obtained from Sharif al-Masri and Abu Talha al-Pakistani, captured after Gul. With this reporting in hand, CIA ███████████████ the asset, who subsequently admitted to fabricating his reporting about the meeting.[368]

Contrary to the Study's claim here, the first observation that should be made about these representations is that they do not contain any reference to the use of "enhanced interrogation techniques." In the first representation, Director Hayden uses the words "detainee information." In the second, the briefing notes simply use the terra "reporting."

(TS// ██████████████████ //NF) Another part of the Study's claim is also factually inaccurate. The Study asserts that the CIA's representation "was based on *one* CIA detainee – Janat Gul...."[369] During our review of the documentary record we found numerous copies of the "Briefing Notes on the Value of Detainee Reporting," that contained the exact representation cited by the Study above, although the version we selected did not place special emphasis on "Janat Gul's most significant reporting."[370] More important, the representations in the August 2005 version contain the following additional examples under the same heading of "Helping to Validate Other Sources":

> In other instances, detainee information has been useful in identifying clandestine assets who are providing good reporting. *For example*, Hassan Ghul's reporting on Shkai *helped us validate several assets* in the field who also told us that al-Qa'ida members had found safehaven at this location....

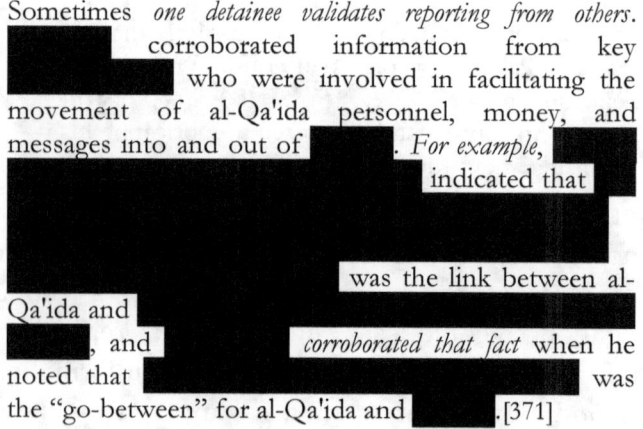

Sometimes *one detainee validates reporting from others.* ████████ corroborated information from key ████████ who were involved in facilitating the movement of al-Qa'ida personnel, money, and messages into and out of ████. *For example,* ████ indicated that ████████ was the link between al-Qa'ida and ████ , and ████████ *corroborated that fact* when he noted that ████████ was the "go-between" for al-Qa'ida and ████ .[371]

Ironically, the Study's omission of these additional examples of source validation from its own analysis deprives the reader of "significant context."

(TS// ████████████████████ //NF) The Study seems to imply that the omission of certain "critical" contextual information from the CIA's representations about source validation somehow nullifies the Janat Gul example.[372] Our examination of the three items of contextual information cited by the Study leads us to conclude that the Janat Gul case remains illustrative of detainee information helping to determine that a CIA source had fabricated certain aspects of his reporting.

(TS// ████████████████████ //NF) First, the Study faults the CIA for failing to include in its representations that the asset's reporting about the 2004 pre-election threat was doubted by CIA officers prior to the use of enhanced interrogation techniques against Janat Gul.[373] This concern is easily dismissed because a review of the e-mail reveals that the concerns raised by the CIA officers were not about the credibility of the sources, but more about the possibility that al-Qa'ida might be using this threat information to test the sources who had provided the pre-election threat information. The email raising the concern specifically states, "this is not to say that either ASSET Y or [source name REDACTED] are wrong or that the AQ statement below[374] is anything more than dis-information."[375] The reply email stated that it was possible the sources were just hearing the same rumors, but recollected that when al-Qa'ida put out similar rumors in the summer of 2001, those turned out to be true.[376] These emails do not support any inference about early suspicions of the source's credibility nor do they dismiss the legitimacy of the threat information provided by the sources.

(TS// ███████████████ //NF) The Study criticizes the asset validation representations by the CIA because they did not acknowledge that the source's fabricated reporting was the reason that Janat Gul was subjected to the enhanced interrogation techniques.[377] There are two problems with this criticism. First, the CIA believed that the source's allegations about Janat Gul meeting with Shayk Sa'id, al-Qa'ida's chief of finance, were truue when they began to use enhanced interrogation techniques against Gul between August 3, 2004, and August 10,2004, and then again from August 21, 2004, to August 25, 2004.[378] The CIA source did not recant some of the underlying threat information pertaining to Gul until October ██ and ██, 2004, *more than two months after Gul's enhanced interrogation began and 15 days after his enhanced interrogation ended.* It is also important to understand that the source's information was not the only information that caused the CIA to believe that Gul was an al-Qa'ida facilitator with connections to multiple high value targets. The source's information was also not solely responsible for the request and authorization to subject Gul to enhanced interrogation techniques.[379] The CIA cable requesting interrogation authorities makes clear those authorities were being pursued to "collect critical threat, locational, and other high priority information."[380] This same communication cited a previous cable detailing CIA approval to detain Gul, in which Gul's apprehension was justified on grounds that he was "one of the highest level extremist facilitators remaining in Pakistan, and multiple source reporting indicates that he has connections to various HVTS."[381]

(TS// ███████████████████ //NF) Second, the Study does not fully support its claim that the CIA source's representations about the pre-election threat were inaccurate.[382] Specifically, the cable reporting the fabrication by one of these sources in October 2004 clearly indicates that some of the source's pre-election threat information was considered to be "generally truthful." The Study states that the source "was deceptive in response to questions regarding... the pre-election threat."[383] This assertion is not entirely accurate. In fact, the cited cable indicated that the source ██████████████████ ██████████ on the issue of the pre-election threat ████████ ██ ███████████████████████████████.[384] Moreover, the assessment paragraph in the cited cable states: "Based on [the source's] seemingly genuine concern and constant return to the issue, COB believes that [the source] is being generally truthful about his discussions... on the pre-election threat."[385]

(TS// ███████████████████ //NF) The Study's final piece of "critical" contextual information that was missing from the CIA representations on this issue was the failure of the CIA to disclose that it eventually concluded that Janat Gul was not a high-level al-Qa'ida figure and never had threat information.[386] This seems to miscast Janat Gul as a hapless victim of circumstance, when in fact he was a known terrorist facilitator. Beyond that, the question of whether every accusation made against Gul was proven or not, is fundamentally immaterial to the matter of his detainee reporting being used to validate – or, in this instance, invalidate – an intelligence source.

(TS// ▮▮▮▮▮▮▮▮▮▮▮▮▮▮▮▮▮ //NF) Our analysis has demonstrated that this claim suffers from multiple fatal defects: (1) the representations do not reference enhanced interrogation techniques; (2) representations in the documentary record were found to have additional examples of asset validation beyond the Janat Gul example; and (3) including any of the three problematic contextual items raised by the Study would not alter the fact that Janat Gul's persistent contradiction of the asset's claims did help the CIA "validate" that particular asset.

Δ

Endnotes

[366] *See* SSCI Study, Executive Summary, December 3, 2014, p. 342.

[367] SSCI Study, Executive Summary, December 3, 2014, p. 342 (citing General Michael Hayden, Director, Central Intelligence Agency, Classified Statement for the Record, Senate Select Committee on Intelligence, April 12, 2007, p. 8 (DTS 2007-1563)).

[368] SSCI Study, Executive Summary, December 3, 2014, p. 343 (citing CIA. Briefing for Obama National Security Team – "Renditions, Detentions, and Interrogations (RDI)" including "Tab 7," named "RDG Copy – Briefing on RDI Program 09 Jan. 2009." (emphasis in original).

[369] SSCI Study, Executive Summary, December 4, 2014, p. 342 (emphasis added).

[370] CIA, Briefing Notes on the Value of Detainee Reporting, August 2005, p. 8. This document is attached as Appendix II, *see infra*, p. II-1.

[371] CIA, Briefing Notes on the Value of Detainee Reporting, August 2005, pp. 8-9 (emphasis added).

[372] SSCI Study, Executive Summary, December 4, 2014, p. 343.

[373] *See* SSCI Study, Executive Summary, December 4, 2014, pp. 343.

[374] The referenced statement was issued by al-Qa'ida on March 17, 2004, and asserted that al-Qa'ida would not operate any large-scale operation prior to the election.

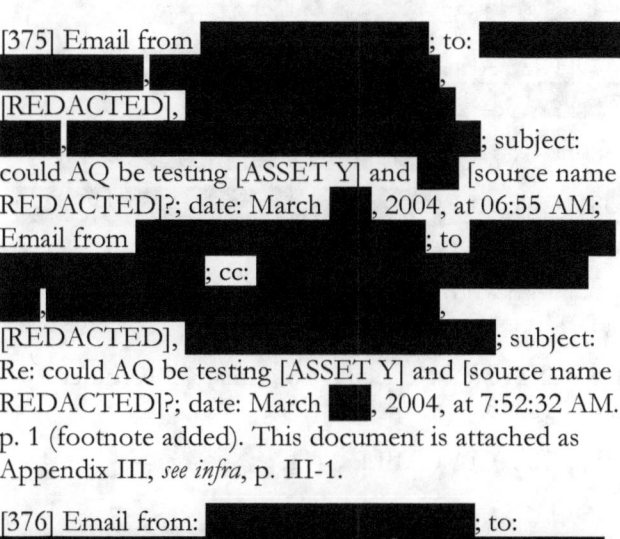

[375] Email from ███████████; to: ███████ [REDACTED], ███████; subject: could AQ be testing [ASSET Y] and ██ [source name REDACTED]?; date: March ██, 2004, at 06:55 AM; Email from ███████; to ███████; cc: ███████ [REDACTED], ███████; subject: Re: could AQ be testing [ASSET Y] and [source name REDACTED]?; date: March ██, 2004, at 7:52:32 AM. p. 1 (footnote added). This document is attached as Appendix III, *see infra*, p. III-1.

[376] Email from: ███████; to: ███████, [REDACTED], ███████; subject: could AQ be testing [ASSET Y] and [source name REDACTED]?; date: March ██, 2004, at 06:55 AM; Email from: ███████; to ███████;

cc: ████████████████████████ ████████ █████████, [REDACTED], ██████████ ███████; subject: Re: could AQ be testing [ASSET Y] and [source name REDACTED]?; date: March ██, 2004, at 7:52:32 AM, p. 1 (footnote added). This email confirms that the sensitive source who subsequently admitted to fabricating information was not the only source providing information related to a possible pre-election threat.

[377] SSCI Study, Executive Summary, December 4, 2014, p. 343.

[378] CIA, ██████████ 1512, ████████████ 2004, p.2; CIA, ████████ 1545, ████████, 2004, p. 1; CIA, ████████ 1603. ███████████ 2004, p. 3; and CIA, ████████ 1632, ████████ 2004, p. 2.

[379] CIA, ALEC ████████████ ████████████ ████████████████

[380] CIA, ██████████ 1484, ████████, 2004, p. 2.

[381] CIA, ALEC ████████ ██████████████

[382] See SSCI Study, Executive Summary, December 3, 2014, p. 417.

[383] SSCI Study, Executive Summary, December 3, 2014, p. 348.

[384] CIA, CIA CABLE 1411, ████████████, 2004, p. 4.

[385] CIA, CIA CABLE 1411, ████████████, 2004, p. 5.

[386] SSCI Study, Executive Summary, December 3, p. 343.

(U) The Identification of Bin Ladin's Courier

~~(TS//~~ ████████████████████ ~~//NF)~~ Shortly after the May 2011 raid on the Usama Bin Ladin compound, current and former CIA employees highlighted the role of reporting from the CIA Detention and Interrogation Program in the operation. These officials represented that CIA detainees provided the "tip-off information on Abu Ahmad al-Kuwaiti (variant Abu Ahmed al-Kuwaiti), the Bin Ladin courier who ultimately led to finding Bin Ladin.[387] As we show below, these representations were accurate.

Study Claim:

> ~~(TS//~~ ████████████████████ ~~//NF)~~ "[T]he 'tipoff' on Abu Ahmad al-Kuwaiti in 2002 did not come from the interrogation of CIA detainees and was obtained prior to any CIA detainee reporting."[388]

Fact:

> ~~(TS//~~ ████████████████████ ~~//NF)~~ CIA documents show that detainee information served as the "tip-off" and played a significant role in leading CIA analysts to the courier Abu Ahmad al-Kuwaiti. While there was other information in CIA databases about al-Kuwaiti, this information was not recognized as important by analysts until after detainees provided information on him.

~~(TS//~~ ████████████████████ ~~//NF)~~ In the days immediately after the Bin Ladin raid, CIA analysts and operators testified before the Committee about how they tracked down Bin Ladin. The CIA described the lead information as being provided by detainees in U.S. custody at CIA secret sites and the detention facility at Guantanamo Bay, Cuba, and from detainees in the custody of foreign governments that helped the CIA recognize the importance of Bin Ladin's courier, Abu Ahmad al-Kuwaiti.[389] CIA officers were clear that the information was from detainees, but never portrayed the information as originating solely from detainees held by the CIA.

(TS// ███████████████ //NF) CIA documents show that even before the raid took place, CIA analysts prepared briefings and papers on their analysis of what led them to the courier. These briefings and papers clearly described the key role that detainee reporting played in this analytical and operational process. A CIA paper in November 2007 noted that "over twenty mid to high-value detainees have discussed Abu Ahmad's ties to senior al-Qa'ida leaders, including his role in delivering messages from Bin Ladin and his close association with former al-Qa'ida third-in-command Abu Faraj al-Libi."[390] The report highlighted specific reporting from two detainees, Hassan Ghul and Ammar al-Baluchi, who both identified Abu Faraj al-Libi's role in communicating to Bin Ladin through Abu Ahmad. It was this and similar reporting from other detainees that helped analysts realize Abu Faraj's categorical denials that he even knew anyone named Abu Ahniad al-Kuwaiti, "almost certainly were an attempt to protect Abu Ahmed," thus showing his importance.[391]

(TS// ███████████████ //NF) Additionally, a retrospective prepared by the CIA's Study for the Center of Intelligence after the raid also made clear in its report that detainee information was significant in the identification of the courier. The report noted that High-Value Terrorist analysts, targeters, and their managers told the Center that:

> debriefing al-Qa'ida detainees provided them with unparalleled expertise and knowledge of the organization. The ability to cross-check detainee statements against one another – specifically Abu Faraj's with that of numerous other detainees – ultimately led to the assessment that Abu Ahmad was directly serving as Bin Ladin's facilitator and possibly harboring him. In sum, 25 detainees provided information on Abu Ahmad al-Kuwaiti, his al-Qa'ida membership, and his historic role as a courier for Bin Ladin. Nine of the 25 were held in non-CIA custody. Of the 16 held in CIA custody, all but three had given information after being subjected to enhanced interrogation techniques (EITs), although of the 13 only two (KSM and Abu Zubaydah) had been waterboarded. Even so, KSM gave false information about Abu Ahmad, as did Abu Faraj, who received lesser EITs. Ironically, the falsity of the information was itself important in establishing Abu Ahmad's significance.[392]

(TS// ███████████ //NF) The Study asserts that information acquired in 2002 ███████

was the "tip-off to Abu Ahmad al-Kuwaiti, but this information sat unnoticed in a CIA database for five years. [393] It was multiple detainee reports about a Bin Ladin courier with the alias Abu Ahmad al-Kuwaiti that triggered a search that uncovered the old information.[394] This is another example of the Study's use of hindsight to criticize the CIA for not recognizing the significance of previously collected, but not fully-understood, intelligence information. It is also an attempt to use this ████████████ ██████████████████████████ information to categorize the subsequently collected detainee information as being "otherwise obtainable." Under the Study's flawed analytical methodology, information in that category cannot be used as evidence of the effectiveness of the CIA's Detention and Interrogation Program. We are not similarly constrained.

(TS//████████████████████████//NF) The Study – benefiting from the ability to search a database compiled of only information relevant to its specific task (something intelligence analysts are not able to do) with the advantage of hindsight to understand which names are now important – asserts that prior to receiving information from CIA detainees, the CIA had other critical reporting on the courier. The Study cites Abu Ahmad's phone number and e-mail address, a body of intelligence reporting linking him to KSM's operational planning, and reporting on Abu Ahmad's age, physical appearance, and family – including information the CIA would later cite as pivotal in identifying his true name.[395]

(TS//██████████████████████//NF) While it is true that the CIA was conducting technical intelligence collection linked to Abu Ahmad al-Kuwaiti in 2002, CIA fact-checking confirmed that this information was meaningless because: (1) it did not link Abu Ahmad to Bin Ladin; (2) Abu Ahmad had stopped using the phone number and e-mail address in 2002; and (3) Abu Ahmad was not linked to that email address in any of his subsequent correspondence.[396] According to the CIA,

> [t]hat intelligence was insufficient to distinguish Abu Ahmad from many other Bin Ladin associates until additional information from detainees put it into context and allowed us to better understand his true role and potential in the hunt for Bin Ladin.[397]

Further review of CIA records confirmed that the phone number at issue was an Inmarsat number associated with "Mukhtar" and "Ahmad 'al-Kuwahadi."[398] According to Adam Robinson, the author of *Bin Laden Behind the Mask of the Terrorist*, "[a]fter a long period of use of the Inmarsat system, Osama learned that this system is open to interception, both for covert observation and possibly for homing in on the signal.... After he became aware of this, he used the system only periodically for calling his mother."[399] If this claim about Bin Ladin's belief is accurate and al-Qa'ida leadership believed that phones were vulnerable, it may explain why this particular phone number was abandoned by KSM and Abu Ahmad.

~~(TS//~~ ████████████████████ ~~//NF)~~ The information providing Kuwaiti's physical description and family details was critical to ultimately identifying al-Kuwaiti's true name, but not until years later – 2007 to be exact – after detainee reporting provided enough information about the courier that a search of old records illuminated key information in that reporting. The CIA Center for the Study of Intelligence said such information was "an unnoticed needle in the haystack on an unending plain of haystacks" until that time.[400] One of the lead CIA analysts called similar information that later turned out to be important "meaningless" until years later when detainee reporting illuminated its importance.[401] Thus, this information really only became critical to the CIA after detainee reporting provided enough information about the courier that a search of old records illuminated key information in that reporting.

Study Claim:

> (TS// ███████████████ //NF) "[T]he most accurate information on Abu Ahmad al-Kuwaiti obtained from a CIA detainee [Hassan Ghul] was provided by a CIA detainee who had not yet been subjected to the CIA's enhanced interrogation techniques."[402]

Fact:

> (TS// ███████████████ //NF) Detainees who provided useful and accurate information on Abu Ahmadal-Kuwaiti and Bin Ladin had undergone enhanced interrogation prior to providing the information. For example, Hassan Ghul provided more specificity about Abu Ahmad after being transferred from COBALT and receiving enhanced interrogation techniques.

(U) The Study disputes statements from current and former CIA officials that information from detainees in CIA's enhanced interrogation program provided valuable information on Abu Ahmad al-Kuwaiti. For example, then-CIA Director Leon Panetta told ABC News in May 2011, soon after the Bin Ladin raid, that enhanced interrogation techniques were used to extract information that led to the mission's success.[403] Former Director Hayden said in an interview that "the original lead information – and frankly it was incomplete identity information on the couriers –

began with information from CIA detainees at the black sites."[404] Both of these statements are accurate.

(TS// ████████████████████ //NF) While numerous detainees at CIA black sites provided information on Abu Ahmad al-Kuwaiti, as noted above, two detainees, Hassan Ghul and Ammar al-Baluchi, in particular were cited by the lead CIA analyst as leading her to search old intelligence files.[405] Ammar aJ-Baluchi, who appears to be the first detainee to mention Abu Ahmad al-Kuwaiti's role as a Bin Ladin courier and a possible connection with Abu Faraj al-Libi, provided this information at a CIA black site during a period of enhanced interrogation.[406]

(TS// ████████████████████ //NF) The second detainee, Hassan Ghul, is described in the Study as providing the "best" and "most accurate" information on the courier. While we are not sure it was the "best" or "most accurate" information, a CIA report on the Bin Ladin raid described Ghul's information as a "milestone in the long analytic targeting trek that led to Bin Ladin."[407] Clearly it was important. According the CIA,

> Gul, while in CIA custody – before undergoing
> enhanced techniques – speculated that Abu Ahmad
> could be one of three people with Bin Ladin and
> speculated that Abu Ahmad may have handled Bin
> Ladin's needs, including sending messages to I'iis
> gatekeeper, Abu Faraj al-Libi.[408]

Additional CIA fact-checking explained that Ghul offered more details about Abu Ahmad's role after being transferred from COBALT and receiving enhanced interrogation. Specifically, the CIA stated:

> After undergoing enhanced techniques, Gul stated that
> Abu Ahmad specifically passed a letter from Bin Ladin
> to Abu Faraj in late 2003 and that Abu Ahmad had
> "disappeared" from Karachi, Pakistan, in 2002. This
> information was not only more concrete and less
> speculative, it also corroborated information from
> Ammar that Khalid Shaykh Muhammad (KSM) was
> lying when he claimed Abu Ahmad left al-Qa'ida in
> 2002.

Ghul stated that while he had "no proof," he believed that Abu Faraj was in contact with Abu Ahmad and that Abu Ahmad might act as an intermediary contact between Abu Faraj and Bin Ladin. Ghul said that this belief "made sense" since Abu Ahmad had disappeared and Ghul had heard that Abu Ahmad was in contact with Abu Faraj.[410] Months later, Ghul also told his interrogators that he knew Abu Ahmad was close to Bin Ladin, which was another reason he suggested that Abu Ahmad had direct contact with Bin Ladin as one of his couriers.[411]

~~(TS//~~ ███████████████ ~~//NF)~~ CIA documents make clear that when detainees like Abu Zubaydah, KSM, and Abu Faraj al-Libi – who had undergone enhanced interrogation and were otherwise cooperative – denied knowing Abu Ahmad al-Kuwaiti or suggested that he had "retired," it was a clear sign to CIA analysts that these detainees had something to hide, and it further confirmed other detainee information that had tipped them off about the true importance of Abu Ahmad al-Kuwaiti.[412]

Δ

Endnotes

[387] SSCI and SASC Transcript, Briefing on Operation Neptune's Spear, May 4, 2011, pp. 53-54 (DTS 2011-2049) (CIA Director Panetta stated, "I want to be able to get back to you with specifics... But clearly the tipoff on the couriers came from those [detainee] interviews."); Scott Hennen radio interview of former CIA Director Michael Hayden, May 3, 2011 (Former Director Hayden stated, "What we got, the original lead information – and frankly it was incomplete identity information on the couriers – began with information from CIA detainees at the black sites").

[388] SSCI Study, Executive Summary, December 3, 2014, p. 389.

[389] SSCI Transcript, Briefing on the Operation That Killed Usama Bin Ladin, May 2, 2011, pp. 7 and 39 (DTS 2011-1941).

[390] CIA Intelligence Assessment, Al-Qa'ida Watch, Probable Identification of Suspected Bin Ladin Facilitator Abu Ahmad al-Kuwaiti, November 23, 2007, p. 2.

[391] CIA Intelligence Assessment, Al-Qa'ida Watch, Probable Identification of Suspected Bin Ladin Facilitator Abu Ahmad al-Kuwaiti, November 23, 2007, p. 2.

[392] CIA Center for the Study of Intelligence, Lessons from the Hunt for Usama Bin Ladin, September 2012, p. 14 (DTS 2012-3826).

[393] CIA Center for the Study of Intelligence, Lessons from the Hunt for Usama Bin Ladin, September 2012, p. 9 (DTS 2012-3826).

[394] SSCI Transcript, Briefing on Operation Neptune's Spear Targeting Usama Bin Ladin, May 4, 2011 pp 13-14, 47-49, and 53-54 (DTS 2011-2049).

[395] SSCI Study, Executive Summary, December 3, 2014, p. 385.

[396] CIA Study Response, Case Studies (TAB C), June 27, 2013, p. 40.

[397] CIA Study Response, Case Studies (TAB C), June 27, 2013, p. 38; CIA Study Response, Comments (TAB A), June 27, 2013, p. 14.

[398] CIA, ALEC ███████████████████ -

[399] Adam Robinson, *Bin Laden Behind the Mask of the Terrorist*, Arcade Publishing. Inc., New York, 2002, p. 247. [http://www.amazon.com/dp/142235427X]

[400] CIA Center for the Study of Intelligence, Lessons from the Hunt for Usama Bin Ladin, September 2012 p 9 (DTS 2012-3826).

[401] CIA Center for the Study of Intelligence, Lessons from the Hunt for Usama Bin Ladin, September 2012, p 9 (DTS 2012-3826).

[402] SSCI Study, Executive Summary, December 3, 2014, p. 379.

[403] Interview with CIA Director Leon Panetta, Brian Williams, ABC News, May 3, 2011.

[404] Interview with former CIA Director Michael Hayden, Scott Hennen Show, May 3, 2011.

[405] CIA Intelligence Assessment, Al-Qa'ida Watch, Probable Identification of Suspected Bin Ladin Facilitator Abu Ahmad al-Kuwaiti, November 23. 2007, p. 2.

[406] CIA, WASHINGTON DC ███████████ - ███████████ Ammar al-Baluchi attempted to recant his earlier description of Abu Ahmad as a Bin Ladin courier. CIA, DIRECTOR ███████████

[407] CIA Center for the Study of Intelligence, Lessons from the Hunt for Usama Bin Ladin, dated September 2012, p. 9 (DTS 2012-3826).

[408] CIA Study Response, Case Studies (TAB C), June 27, 2013, p. 38 (citing CIA, DIRECTOR ███████ - ███████████ .

[409] CIA Study Response, Case Studies (TAB C), June 27, 2013, p. 38 (citing CIA, ███████ - ███████████ .

[410] CIA, ███████████ - ███████████

[411] CIA, DIRECTOR ███████████ - ███████████

[412] CIA, DIRECTOR ███████████ - ███████████ CIA Center for the Study of Intelligence, Lessons from the Hunt for Usama Bin Ladin, dated September 2012, pp. 9-10 (DTS 2012-3826); CIA Intelligence Assessment, Al-Qa'ida Watch, Probable Identification of Suspected Bin Ladin Facilitator Abu Ahmad al-Kuwaiti, November 23, 2007, p. 2.

(U) Conclusion 6 (CIA Impeded Congressional Oversight)

(TS// ███████████████ //NF) Conclusion 6 states: "[t]he CIA has actively avoided or impeded congressional oversight of the program."[413] In reality, the overall pattern of engagement with the Congress on this issue shows that the CIA attempted to keep the Congress informed of its activities. From 2002 to 2008, the CIA claims to have provided more than 35 briefings to SSCI members and staff, more than 30 similar briefings to HPSCI members and staff, and more than 20 congressional notifications.[414] For some of these briefings, there are no transcripts[415], likely because they were limited to the Chairman and Vice Chairman/Ranking Member of the congressional intelligence committees. Because the Study did not interview the participants in these restricted briefings, it is impossible to document how much information the CIA provided to Committee leadership during those briefings. Often, the Study's own examples contradict the assertion that the CIA tried to avoid its overseers' scrutiny. For example, the Study notes that the CIA reacted to Vice Chairman Rockefeller's suspicion about the agency's honesty by planning a detailed briefing on the Program for him.[416]

(U) Timing of the CIA's Briefings on Enhanced Interrogation Techniques

Study Claim:

~~(TS//~~ ███████████████ ~~//NF)~~ "The CIA did not brief the Senate Intelligence Committee leadership on the CIA's enhanced interrogation techniques until September 2002, after the techniques had been approved and used."[417]

Fact:

~~(TS//~~ ███████████████ ~~//NF)~~ The CIA provided information to the Committee in hearings, briefings, and notifications beginning shortly after the signing of the Memorandum of Notification (MON) on September 17, 2001.

~~(TS//~~ ███████████████ ~~//NF)~~ Conclusion 6 opens with the statement that the CIA did not brief the Senate Intelligence Committee leadership on the CIA's enhanced interrogation techniques until after the techniques had been approved and used, setting the tone for a narrative that the CIA actively and systematically concealed information from the Congress. In reality, the CIA began discussing concerns about interrogation with the Committee even prior to the creation of the Program. The Study's review of the CIA's representations to Congress cites CIA hearing testimony from November 7, 2001, discussing the uncertainty in the boundaries on interrogation techniques.[418] The Study also cites additional discussions between staff and CIA lawyers in February 2002.[419]

(TS// ▓▓▓▓▓▓▓▓▓▓▓▓▓▓▓▓▓▓ //NF) The Study seems to fault the CIA for not briefing the Committee leadership until after the enhanced interrogation techniques had been approved and used. The CIA briefed HPSCI leadership on September 4, 2002. SSCI leadership received the same briefing on September 27, 2002.[420] The Study does not include information on when the CIA offered briefings to Congress or how long it took to schedule them. Briefing Committee leadership in the month after beginning a new activity does not constitute actively avoiding or impeding congressional oversight.

(U) Access to Documents

Study Claim:

(TS// ▓▓▓▓▓▓▓▓▓▓▓▓▓▓▓▓▓▓ //NF) "The CIA subsequently resisted efforts by then-Vice Chairman John D. Rockefeller, IV, to investigate the program, including by refusing in 2006 to provide requested documents."[421]

Fact:

(TS// ▓▓▓▓▓▓▓▓▓▓▓▓▓▓▓▓▓▓ //NF) The CIA provided access to the documents requested.

(TS// ▓▓▓▓▓▓▓▓▓▓▓▓▓▓▓▓▓▓ //NF) The Study asserts that the CIA refused to provide requested documents. However, this misrepresents both the Vice Chairman's document request and the Intelligence Community's response. As noted in the Study, on January 5, 2006, the Director of National Intelligence's Chief of Staff wrote a letter to Vice Chairman Rockefeller which denied an earlier request for full Committee access to over 100 documents related to the Inspector General's May 2004 Special Review. [422] However, this denial of "full Committee access," did not mean that the documents were not made available to the CIA's congressional overseers. In fact, the Chief of Staff s letter stated, "Consistent with the provisions of the National Security Act of 1947, the White House has directed that specific information related to aspects of the detention and interrogation program be provided only to the SSCI leadership and staff directors."[423] The letter concluded by advising Vice Chairman Rockefeller that the documents "remain available for review by SSCI leadership and staff directors at any time through arrangements with CIA's Office of Congressional Affairs."[424]

(U) Breadth of Congressional Access

Study Claim:

(TS// ▮▮▮▮▮▮▮▮▮▮▮▮▮▮▮▮ //NF) The CIA impeded congressional oversight by restricting access to information about the Program from members of the Committee beyond the Chairman and Vice Chairman.[425]

Fact:

(TS// ▮▮▮▮▮▮▮▮▮▮▮▮▮▮▮▮ //NF) The CIA's limitation of access to sensitive covert action information is a long-standing practice codified in

Section 503 of the National Security Act of 1947, as amended.

(TS// ▮▮▮▮▮▮▮▮▮▮▮▮▮▮▮▮ //NF) The Study notes numerous times that the CIA refused to provide information on its Detention and Interrogation Program to Committee members and staff.[426] The underlying assertion is that the CIA's restriction of access to the Chairman and Vice Chairman somehow constituted an attempt to avoid or impede congressional oversight of the Program. This is simply untrue. According to section 503(c)(2) of the National Security Act of 1947, as amended:

> If the president determines that it is essential to limit access to the finding to meet extraordinary circumstances affecting vital interests of the United States, the finding may be reported to the chairmen and ranking minority members of the congressional intelligence committees, the Speaker and minority leader of the House of Representatives, the majority and minority leaders of the Senate, and such other member or members of the congressional leadership as may be included by the President.

The CIA's decision to limit the briefing of this particularly sensitive covert action program to the Chairman and Vice Chairman was in keeping with customary practice and complied with the law. The Committee has conducted oversight of other sensitive covert action programs under similar access limitations and continues to do so at this time.

(TS// ▮▮▮▮▮▮▮▮▮▮▮▮▮▮▮▮ //NF) The Study notes that the CIA briefed a number of additional senators who were not on the Select Committee on Intelligence.[427] As cited above, the law allows the President discretion to provide senators with information about covert action programs at his discretion, without regard to Committee membership. Moreover, providing a briefing to inform key senators working on legislation relevant to the CIA's program is inconsistent with the narrative that the CIA sought to avoid congressional scrutiny.

Δ

Endnotes

[413] SSCI Study, Findings and Conclusions, December 3, 2014, p. 5.

[414] CIA Study Response, Conclusions (TAB B), June 27, 2013, p. 35.

[415] SSCI Study, Executive Summary, December 3, 2014, p. 441.

[416] SSCI Study, Executive Summary, December 3, 2014, p. 441.

[417] SSCI Study, Findings and Conclusions, December 3, 2014, p. 5.

[418] SSCI Study, Executive Summary, December 3, 2014, p. 437 n.2447. *See also* SSCI Transcript, Briefing on Covert Action, November 7, 2001, p. 56 (DTS 2002-0611).

[419] SSCI Study, Executive Summary, December 3, 2014, p. 437. *See also* Email from: Christopher Ford, SSCI Staff, to: █████ Cleared SSCI staff; subject: Meeting yesterday with CIA lawyers on ███████████████████, date: February 26, 2002 (DTS 2002-0925).

[420] CIA Study Response, Conclusions (TAB B), June 27, 2013, p. 36.

[421] SSCI Study, Findings and Conclusions, December 3, 2014, pp. 5-6.

[422] SSCI Study, Executive Summary, December 3, 2014, p. 442.

[423] Letter from David Shedd to Andy Johnson, January 5, 2006 (DTS 2006-0373).

[424] Letter trom David Shedd to Andy Johnson, January 5, 2006 (DTS 2006-0373).

[425] SSCI Study, Findings and Conclusions, December 3, 2014, p. 6.

[426] SSCI Study, Executive Summary, December 3, 2014, pp. 439-441.

[427] SSCI Study, Executive Summary, December 3, 2014, p. 443.

(U) Conclusion 7 (CIA Impeded White House Oversight)

(U) Conclusion 7 states, "[t]he CIA impeded effective White House oversight and decision-making."[428] It is important to place this serious allegation within its proper context – the CIA's Detention and Interrogation Program was conducted as a covert action.[429] Covert action is the sole responsibility of the White House, a principle enshrined in law since the National Security Act of 1947. [430] The President, working with his National Security Staff, approves and oversees all covert action programs. The congressional intelligence committees also conduct ongoing oversight of all covert actions and receive quarterly covert action briefings. Given this extensive covert action oversight regime, this conclusion seems to imply falsely that the CIA was operating a rogue intelligence operation designed to "impede" the White House. We reject this unfounded implication and it appears the CIA has rejected it as well:

> While we were able to find points in the preceding themes with which to both agree and disagree, the *Study* seems to most seriously diverge from the facts and, indeed, from simple plausibility in its characterizations of the manner in which CIA dealt with others with regard to the RDl program. The *Study* would have the reader believe that CIA 'actively' avoided and interfered with oversight by the Executive Branch and Congress... [and] withheld information from the President....

We would observe that, to accomplish this, there would have had to have been a years-long conspiracy among CIA leaders at all levels, supported by a large number of analysts and other line officers. This conspiracy would have had to include three former CIA Directors....

We cannot vouch for every individual statement that was made over the years of the program, and we acknowledge that some of those statements were wrong. But the image portrayed in the *Study* of an organization that – on an institutional scale – intentionally misled and routinely resisted oversight from the White House, the Congress, the Department of Justice, and its own OIG simply does not comport with the record....

[The] CIA did not, as the *Study* alleges, intentionally misrepresent to anyone the overall value of the intelligence acquired, the number of detainees, the propensity of detainees to withhold and fabricate, or other aspects of the program.[431]

Our analysis of the documentary record demonstrates that most of the CIA's representations about the Detention and Interrogation Program were accurate.

(U) Executive Branch Oversight

Study Claim:

~~(TS//~~ ████████████████████████ ~~//NF)~~
"According to CIA records, no CIA officer, up to and including CIA Directors George Tenet and Porter

Goss, briefed the President on the specific CIA enhanced interrogation techniques before April 2006. By that time, 38 of the 39 detainees identified as having been subjected to the CIA's enhanced interrogation techniques had already been subjected to the techniques."[432]

Fact:

(U) CIA records are contradictory and incomplete regarding when the President was briefed, but President Bush himself says he was briefed in 2002, before any techniques were used.[433]

~~(TS//~~ ████████████████ ~~//NF)~~ The Study finds that the CIA "impeded" executive branch oversight, not just by withholding information about the Program, but by providing inaccurate information about its operation and effectiveness. Beginning with the premise that the CIA did not obtain approval from the President or the National Security Council prior to using enhanced interrogation techniques on Abu Zubaydah, the Study identifies records that cast some doubt on whether the President was briefed before April 2006.[434] However, CIA records are inconsistent on this point.

~~(TS//~~ ████████████████ ~~//NF)~~ One chronology of the approvals obtained for the CIA program, dated April 2008, lists a meeting held on August 1, 2002, between the President and the Deputy Director of the CIA concerning the "Next Phase of the Abu Zubaydah Interrogation," which strongly suggests that the President had been briefed on the interrogation. Another undated chronology, however, notes that, according to a July 31, 2002, memorandum, the National Security Council communicated to the CIA that the President would not be briefed.[435] An Inspector General interview with former DCI Tenet also suggests that he did not brief the President on enhanced interrogation techniques (EITs). Tenet said "he had never spoken to the President regarding EITs, nor was he aware of whether the President had been briefed by his staff.[436] An interview of the former Director or his staff, or a review of Director Tenet's e-mail communications and those of his staff, might also have helped clarify this point.

(U) Since no interviews were conducted and since – as we learned during the course of our review of the Study material – the majority never requested e-mail communications from Director Tenet or other senior CIA leaders, such a clarification was impossible. In fact, as noted earlier, we learned that the majority did not request the e-mail communications of *any* senior CIA leaders who likely would have discussed the Program with the President – not Director Tenet, Director Goss, Deputy Director McLaughlin, Director of Operations Pavitt, Director of Operations Kappes, Director of the Counterterrorism Center Bob Grenier, and many others. Because of this gap in emails from critical participants, the majority's document review is incomplete. In the absence of interviews and with the gap in documents, the Study's reliance on the CIA records it did review, therefore, is simply not definitive on whether the President was briefed on the use of interrogation techniques on Zubaydah. Yet the Study interprets the absence of clarity on this point as confirmation that the CIA must have withheld information from the President.

(U) There is at least one person, however, who disputes this narrative and says that the President was briefed and approved the use of enhanced techniques on Zubaydah – President George W. Bush. In his book, *Decision Points,* the President has a different recollection than Director Tenet. The President recalls being told that Abu Zubaydah was withholding information; that "CIA experts drew up a list of interrogation techniques that differed from those Zubaydah had successfully resisted;" and that "Department of Justice and CIA lawyers conducted a careful legal review."[437] He describes looking at the list of techniques, including watetboarding, and approving their use, while directing the CIA not to use two of them that he "felt went too far, even if they were legal."[438] President Bush also confirms that he approved the use of enhanced interrogation techniques, including the waterboard, on KSM.[439] So while the Study assumes the President did not give his approval prior to the use of enhanced techniques on Abu Zubaydah because the majority cannot find CIA records that unequivocally say when and how it happened, the President's own words set the record straight.[440]

(TS// ███████████████████ //NF) Regardless, even if it were true that the President had not been briefed by the CIA, we find it odd that the Study would assign blame for "withholding information" to the CIA, when the Study itself acknowledges the role of officials outside the CIA in making determinations about what should be briefed to policymakers. For example, the Study correctly notes that the description of the waterboard was removed from the 2002 Deputy DCI (DDCI) talking points for the meeting with the President, but its account of why this change was made is misleading.[441] In describing an e-mail regarding the planned briefing, the Study states that "per an agreement between DCI Tenet and White House Counsel Gonzales, the briefing would include no 'further details about the interrogation techniques than those in the (revised) talking points.'"[442] In reality, the e-mail says that the "WH asks that DDCI brief POTUS tomorrow at 0800 meeting without any further details about the interrogation techniques than those in the talking points."[443] Thus, it was at the request of the White House – not the CIA – that only a broad description of the nature of the techniques would be provided; specifically, that the "techniques incorporate mild physical pressure, while others may place Abu Zubaydah in fear for his life" and they "include an intense physical and psychological stressor used by the U.S. Navy in its interrogation resistance training for the Navy SEALS."[444]

(U) Accuracy of Information Provided

Study Claim:

(TS// ▮▮▮▮▮▮▮▮▮▮▮▮▮▮▮▮▮ //NF) "The information provided connecting the CIA's detention and interrogation program directly to [the "Dirty Bomb" Plot/Tall Buildings Plot, the Karachi Plots, Heathrow and Canary Wharf Plot, and the Identification/Capture of Iyman Faris] was, to a great extent, inaccurate."[445]

Fact:

> (U) The information provided to the White House attributing the arrests of these terrorists and the thwarting of these plots to the CIA's Detention and Interrogation Program was accurate.

(S//NF) The Study accuses the CIA of providing inaccurate information to the White House and the National Security Council Principals about the Program and its effectiveness. Pivotal to this allegation is a July 29, 2003, briefing that the CIA Director and General Counsel had with executive branch officials, including the Vice President, the National Security Advisor, the White House Counsel, and the Attorney General. According to the six-page memorandum for the record prepared by the CIA General Counsel on August 5, 2003, the purpose of the meeting was to "discuss current, past and future CIA policies and practices concerning the interrogation of certain detainees held by CIA."[446]

(TS// ▓▓▓▓▓▓▓▓▓▓▓▓▓▓▓▓▓ //NF) The Study notes that the memorandum provided four of the eight "most frequently cited examples from 2002-2009" as evidence of the effectiveness of CIA's interrogation program, including: "the 'dirty bomb' plot/tall buildings plot (also referenced as the Capture of Jose Padilla), the Karachi Plots, the Heathrow and Canary Wharf Plot, and the Identification/Capture of Iyman Faris."[447] While the Study asserts, "the information provided connecting the CIA's detention and interrogation program directly to the above disruptions and captures was, to a great extent, inaccurate," we found that the examples provided were, in fact, accurate.[448]

Δ

Endnotes

[428] SSCI Study, Findings and Conclusions, December 3, 2014, p. 6.

[429] *See* SSCI Study, Executive Summary, December 3, 2014, p. 11. "On September 17, 2001, six days after the terrorist attacks of September 11, 2001, President George W. Bush signed a covert action MON to authorize the Director of Central Intelligence (DCI) to '*undertake operations, designed to capture and detain* persons who pose a continuing, serious threat of violence or death to U.S. persons and interests or who are planning terrorist activities.'" (emphasis added).

[430] In 1974, the Hughes-Ryan amendment to the Foreign Assistance Act of 1961 created the requirement for presidential "Findings" for covert action. The Intelligence Oversight Acts of 1980 and

1988 amended the Finding process, and the Intelligence Oversight Act of 1991 replaced Hughes-Ryan with the current Finding process. *See* William Daugherty, *Executive Secrets: Covert Action and the Presidency*, The University Press of Kentucky 2004 pp. 92-98. [http://www.amazon.com/dp/B0078XFPO8]

[431] CIA Study Response, Comments (TAB A), June 27, 2013, pp. 15-16 (emphasis in original).

[432] SSCI Study, Findings and Conclusions, December 3, 2014, p. 6.

[433] George W. Bush, *Decision Points*, Broadway Paperbacks, New York,2010, p. 169. [http://www.amazon.com/dp/B003F3PK5Y/]

[434] *See, e.g.*, SSCI Study, Findings and Conclusions, December 3, 2014, p. 18 n.17, SSCI Study, Executive Summary, December 3, 2014, pp. 38-40.

[435] Chronology of Renditions, Detainees and Interrogations Program and Interrogation Approvals: 2001-2008, undated; *see also* April 3, 2014, SSCI Study, Executive Summary, December 3, 2014, p. 40, n.179.

[436] Office of the General Counsel, Comments on the Inspector General, Special Review, Counterterrorism Detention and Interrogation Activities (September 2001-October 2003), May 7, 2004 (DTS 2004-2710). [http://media.washingtonpost.com/wp-srv/nation/documents/cia_oig_report.pdf]

[437] Bush, p. 169. [see 433]

[438] Bush. p. 169. [see 433]

[439] Bush, p. 170, ("George Tenet asked if he had permission to use enhanced interrogation techniques, including waterboarding, on Khalid Sheikh Mohammed. I thought about my meeting with Danny

Pearl's widow, who was pregnant with his son when he was murdered. I thought about the 2,973 people stolen from their families by al Qaeda on 9/11. And I thought about my duty to protect the country from another act of terror. 'Damn right,' I said"). [http://www.amazon.com/dp/B003F3PK5Y/]

[440] The CIA Study response also made reference to President Bush's autobiography, noting that "he discussed the program, including the use of enhanced techniques, with then [DCI] Tenet in 2002, prior to the application of the techniques on Abu Zubaydah, and personally approved the techniques." CIA Study Response, Conclusions, p. 6. The Study chooses to rebut President Bush's recollections of these events by stating, "A memoir by former Acting CIA General Counsel John Rizzo disputes the President's autobiographical account." SSCI Study, Findings and Conclusions, December 3, 2014, p. 18, n.17. Again, further clarification of these events was hampered by the lack of witness interviews.

[441] SSCI Study, Executive Summary, December 3, 2014, p. 38.

[442] SSCI Study, Volume I, March 31, 2014, p. 135.

[443] CIA, E-mail to DDCI, dated July 31, 2002, Briefing of POTUS tomorrow (1 Aug) re AZ interrogation.

[444] DDCI Talking Points for Meeting with the President, 31 July 2001 (sic).

[445] SSCI Study, April 1, 2014, Volume II, p. 446.

[446] CIA General Counsel Memorandum for the Record, August 5, 2003, Review of Interrogation Program on 29 July 2003.

[447] SSCI Study, Volume II, April 1, 2014, p. 446.

[448] *See supra*, The Thwarting of the Dirty Bomb /
Tall Buildings Plot and the Capture of Jose Padilla,
pp. 150-155; The Thwarting of the Karachi Plots,
pp. 181-183; The Heathrow and Canary Wharf Plots,
pp. 188-192; and The Arrest and Prosecution of Iyman
Faris, pp. 215-221.

(U) Conclusion 8 (CIA Impeded National Security Missions of Executive Branch Agencies)

(U) Conclusion 8 states, "[t]he CIA's operation and management of the program complicated, and in some cases impeded, the national security missions of other Executive Branch agencies.[449]

~~(TS//~~ ████████████████ ~~//NF)~~ The standard by which the Study claims the CIA "impeded" national security missions of other executive branch agencies is based entirely on subjective standards that are never defined in the text. Equally problematic are statements that the CIA blocked or denied requests for information from other executive branch agencies. By inference this implies the President and the National Security Council did not control access to the covert action program. However, the September 17, 2001, Memorandum of Notification authorizing the detainee program, states: "Approval of the Principals shall be sought in advance whenever feasible with respect to such operations...."[450] As noted in the CIA response to the Study, "the National Security Council established the parameters for when and how CIA could engage on the program with other executive branch agencies."[451] The CIA was not responsible nor did it have control over the sharing or dissemination of information to other executive branch agencies or members of the Principals Committee itself. That responsibility rested solely with the White House.

(U) Access to the Covert Action Program

Study Claim:

~~(TS//~~ ███████████████████ ~~//NF)~~ "The CIA blocked State Department leadership from access to information crucial to foreign policy decision-making and diplomatic activities."[452]

Fact:

~~(TS//~~ ███████████████ ~~//NF)~~ The National Security Staff controlled access to the covert action program and there is no evidence that the CIA refused to brief State Department leadership when directed.

~~(TS//~~ ███████████████ ~~//NF)~~ The Study does not provide any evidence that the CIA deliberately impeded, obstructed or blocked the State Department from obtaining information about the Program inconsistent with directions from the White House or the National Security Council. In fact, the Study acknowledges that CIA officers were in close and constant contact with their State Department counterparts where detention facilities were located and among senior leadership to include the Secretary of State and the U.S. Deputy Secretary of State. For example, leading to the establishment of a facility in Country ███████, the Study notes that the chief of station (COS) was coordinating activities with the ambassador. Because the Program was highly compartmented, the ambassador was directed by the National Security Council not to discuss with his immediate superior at headquarters

283

due to the highly compartmented nature of the covert action. Instead, the COS, sent feedback from the ambassador through CIA channels, to the NSC, whereby the Deputy Secretary of State with the knowledge of the Secretary, would discuss any issues or concerns with the ambassador in country.[453] While the process was less direct, the security precautions to protect sensitive information did not impede the national security mission of the State Department.

(U) CIA Denied FBI Requests

Study Claim:

(TS// ███████████████████ //NF) "The CIA denied specific requests from FBI Director Robert Mueller, III, for FBI access to CIA detainees that the FBI believed was necessary to understand CIA detainee reporting on threats to the U.S. Homeland."[454]

Fact:

(TS// ███████████████████ //NF) While the FBI's participation in the interrogation of detainees was self-proscribed, the Bureau was still able to submit requirements to the CIA and received reports on interrogations.

(TS// ███████████████ //NF) This Study claim appears to focus on FBI access to KSM in 2003 after FBI Director Mueller read an interrogation report that vaguely referenced possible threats to New York, Washington, DC, Chicago, Dallas, and SanFrancisco.[455] However, the Study acknowledges the FBI's fear that the use of enhanced techniques activity would place FBI agents at future legal risk if they participated in interrogations.[456] Recognizing the need for FBI access to detainees, both agencies finalized a memorandum of understanding in the fall of 2003 that detailed how FBI ████████████████████████ ████████████████████████████████████ ███████████████████ agents would be provided access to detainees ███████████████████████ ███████████████████████[457]

(U) The ODNI was Provided with Inaccurate and Incomplete Information

Study Claim:

(TS// ████████████████ //NF) "The ODNI was provided with inaccurate and incomplete information about the program, preventing the ODNI from effectively carrying out its statutory responsibility to serve as the principal advisor to the President on intelligence matters."[458]

Fact:

(TS// ████████████████ //NF) The Study incorrectly claims that inaccurate information was provided to the Office of the Director of National Intelligence.

(U) The updated Study treats this claim differently than it did in the version that was adopted by the Committee during the 112th Congress. The original Study sought to dispute claims regarding the use of enhanced interrogation techniques and disruption of several plots. However, the updated Study drops the direct reference to coercive measures and instead focuses on the Detention and Interrogation Program in general.[459] The 2006 press release from the Office of Director of National Intelligence[460] does not reference the use of enhanced interrogation techniques, but states unequivocally: "The detention of terrorists disrupts – at least temporarily – the plots they were involved in." To claim that the detention and interrogation of terrorists did not yield intelligence of value is simply not credible.

Δ

Endnotes

[449] SSCI Study, Findings and Conclusions, December 3, 2014, p. 7.

[450] DTS 2002-0371, p. 3.

[451] CIA Study Response, Comments (TAB A), June 27, 2013, p. 11.

[452] SSCI Study, Findings and Conclusions, December 3, 2014, p. 7.

[453]

[454] SSCI Study, Findings and Conclusions, December 3, 2014, p. 7.

[455] SSCI Study, Volume I, March 31, 2014, p. 414.

[456] Email from: James Pavitt; to: ███████████████; subject: Re: Mueller's Interest in FBI Access to KSM; Date: April 24, 2003, 2:35 PM.

[457] SSCI Study, Volume I, March 31, 2014, p. 413.

[458] SSCI Study, Findings and Conclusions, December 3, 2014, p. 8.

[459] SSCI Study, Findings and Conclusions, December 3, 2014, p. 8.

[460] ODNI Press Release, September 6, 2006, "Information on the High Value Terrorist Detainee Program."
[http://www.dni.gov/files/documents/Newsroom/Press%20Releases/2006%20Press%20Releases/-TheHighValueDetaineeProgram.pdf]

(U) Conclusion 5 (CIA Provided Inaccurate Information to the Department of Justice)

(U) Conclusion 5 states, "[t]he CIA repeatedly provided inaccurate information to the Department of Justice, impeding a proper legal analysis of the CIA's detention and Interrogation Program."[461] Our analysis of the claims used in support of this conclusion revealed that many of the Study's claims were themselves inaccurate or otherwise without merit.

(U) "Novel" Use of the Necessity Defense

Study Claim:

> ~~(TS//~~ █████████████████ ~~//NF)~~ "CIA attorneys stated that 'a novel application of using the necessity defense' could be used 'to avoid prosecution of U.S. officials who tortured to obtain information that saved many lives.'"[462]

Fact:

> ~~(TS//~~ █████████████████ ~~//NF)~~ The draft CIA Office of General Counsel (OGC) legal appendix cited by the report contained a cursory discussion of the necessity defense that did not support the use of such defense in the context of the CIA's Detention and Interrogation Program.[463]

(U) This particular claim appears to be a remnant from

what had been "Conclusion 2" in the original version of the Study approved by the SSCI during the 112th Congress. Our original minority views were very critical of the claims made in support of the "necessity defense" conclusion. We were pleased to see that the original "Conclusion 2" was dropped from the conclusions in the updated version of the Study; however, we are disappointed to see this factually and legally incorrect claim repeated here in support of a conclusion alleging that the CIA provided inaccurate information to the Department of Justice.

(U) This claim advances the faulty proposition that a "novel application" of the necessity defense could be used by participants in the CIA's Detention and Interrogation Program to avoid criminal liability. On its face, this claim leaves the reader with the false impression that CIA attorneys endorsed the possible use of the "necessity" defense in the context of the CIA's Detention and Interrogation Program, when, in fact, the draft legal appendix cited by the Study[464] actually reached the *opposite* conclusion

(TS// ██████████████████ //NF) Contrary to the Study's claim, the legal analysis provided in the cited draft legal appendix *did not* support the use of the necessity defense in the context of the CIA's program. The Study achieved this erroneous result by modifying the following original quote that it cherry picked from the legal analysis: "It would, therefore, be a novel application of the necessity defense to avoid prosecution of U.S. officials who tortured to obtain information that saved many lives...."[466] Specifically, the Study modified this quote by separating

289

portions of the text and inserting its own factually misleading text, which was not supported by the legal analysis, to achieve the following result: *"CIA attorneys stated that* a novel application of the necessity defense *could he used* to avoid prosecution of U.S. officials who tortured to obtain information that saved lives."[467] Fortunately, this erroneously doctored quotation only appears once in the Study – in this Conclusion.

(TS// ███████████████████ //NF) The Study does, however, cite the original "novel application" quotation in at least 12 different places in its updated report to support its incorrect assertion that CIA attorneys viewed necessity "as a defense" or as a "potential legal defense."[468] While this quotation is technically accurate, it is consistently removed from its context within the legal analysis to create the false impression that the defense of necessity might have been available to CIA employees engaged in interrogation activities. The legal appendix clearly conceded that since "U.S. courts have not yet considered the necessity defense in the context of torture/murder/assault cases... [i]t would, therefore, be a novel application of the necessity defense to avoid prosecution...."[469] When the "novel application" quote is placed back into its proper original context, it becomes clear that the legal analysis *did not* conclude that the necessity defense could be used to avoid prosecution. The use of the word "novel" in this context clearly suggests the drafting attorney viewed the approach as problematic.[470]

(TS// ███████████████████ //NF) The Study's Executive Summary contains a section entitled, "The

Origins of CIA Representations Regarding the Effectiveness of the CIA's Enhanced Interrogation Techniques As Having 'Saved Lives,' 'Thwarted Plots' and 'Captured Terrorists.'"[471] In that section, the Study cites to the "novel application" of the necessity defense contained in the draft legal appendix. This "Origins" section, when combined with the erroneous necessity defense claim made here, appears to have been designed to guide the reader into falsely inferring that the CIA represented that the enhanced interrogation techniques were necessary to acquire "otherwise unavailable" intelligence that "saved lives" because of the draft legal appendix's discussion of the necessity defense.

(U) There are a number of problems with this false inference. If this inference is based simply on the fact that the CIA's representations were made *after* the circulation of the draft legal appendix's discussion of the necessity defense, then the claim is little more than a classic example of *"post hoc"* erroneous reasoning. Simply put, just because the CIA represented that the Program saved lives does not mean that such representations were caused by the draft legal appendix.

~~(TS//~~ ███████████ ~~//NF)~~ It seems unlikely that the single appearance of the phrase "saved many lives" in the context of the draft legal appendix's discussion of the necessity defense was the reason behind the use of singular terminology in subsequent accounts of the Program. Aside from the false inference made in the "Origins" section, there is no evidence to support this leap of logic.

(TS// ~~[redacted]~~ //NF) Moreover, the draft legal appendix concluded that the necessity defense did not apply in the context of the CIA's Detention and Interrogation Program. Therefore, this false inference – that the CIA's representations regarding the "otherwise unavailable intelligence" that "saved lives" were the result of efforts to preserve the necessity defense – does not make sense because the draft legal appendix had already concluded that the necessity defense raised in the context of a torture prosecution was unlikely to succeed in a U.S. court.

(U) In this conclusion, the Study appears to buttress its argument about the applicability of the necessity defense in the context of the CIA's Detention and Interrogation Program by noting that OLC included a discussion of the "necessity defense" in its August 1, 2002, memorandum to the White House.[472] That memorandum opinion stated: *"under the current circumstances, necessity or self-defense **may** justify* interrogation methods that might violate" the criminal prohibition against torture.[473] Not surprisingly, this August 1, 2002, memorandum opinion was withdrawn in June 2004 and formally superseded in its entirety on December 30, 2004. Specifically, the superseding memorandum stated, "Because the discussion in that memorandum concerning the President's Commander-in-Chief power and *the potential defenses to liability was – and remains – unnecessary, it has been eliminated from the analysis that follows."*[474] Although the Study acknowledges this subsequent withdrawal of the necessity defense analysis in a footnote,[475] it suggests that OLC included its discussion

292

of the necessity defense at the request of the CIA.[476]

(U) The August 1, 2002, memorandum opinion, however, did finally conclude with the somewhat more definitive statement: "even if an interrogation method might violate [the criminal prohibition against torture], necessity or self-defense could provide justifications that would eliminate any criminal liability."[477] Regardless, the Study's apparent reliance upon this *withdrawn* OLC opinion is misplaced, because it actually seems to undermine its conclusion that the CIA provided inaccurate information to the Department of Justice. Assuming for the sake of argument that the CIA provided OLC with a copy of its legal analysis on the necessity defense – which seems highly unlikely – the CIA legal opinion was correct about necessity being a "novel" application, while the OLC opinion reached a different result by concluding incorrectly that the defense of necessity would eliminate criminal liability.

(U) Accuracy of Claims about Abu Zubaydah

Study Claim:

(TS// ███████████████████ //NF) The OLC "relied on inaccurate CIA representations about Abu Zubaydah's status in al-Qa'ida and the interrogation team's 'certain[ty]' that Abu Zubaydah was withholding information about planned terrorist attacks."[478]

(TS// ███████████████████ //NF) The CIA assessment that Abu Zubaydah was the "third or fourth man" in al-Qa'ida was "based on single-source reporting that was recanted prior to the August 1, 2002, OLC memorandum."[479]

(TS// ███████████████████ //NF) The CIA later concluded that Abu Zubaydah was not a member of al-Qa'ida."[480]

Fact:

(TS// ███████████████████ //NF) The information relied upon by the Study to criticize the CIA's representations about Abu Zubaydah withholding of information about planned terrorists attacks neglected to include important statements from within that same intelligence cable, which supported those representations by the CIA.

(TS// ███████████████████ //NF) The CIA was in possession of multiple threads of intelligence supporting Abu Zubaydah's prominent role in al-Qa'ida. The ███████████████████

████████████████████████████████████
████████████████████████████████████
████████████████████████████████████

294

██████████████████████████████████. The level
of detail that the detainee had previously provided
dbout Abu Zubaydah undermined his later attempts to
retract his earlier admissions about his involvement in
future terrorist attacks ███████████████ and his
denials about meeting with Abu Zubaydah.

~~(TS//~~ ██████████████████ ~~//NF)~~ The
Study's incredible assertion that the "CIA later
concluded that Abu Zubaydah was not a member of al-
Qa'ida" is factually incorrect.

~~(TS//~~ ██████████████████ ~~//NF)~~ On August 1,
2002, the OLC provided the CIA with a memorandum on its
legal analysis of the application of enhanced interrogation
techniques to Abu Zubaydah. The Study asserts that
"[m]uch of the information provided by the CIA to the
OLC, however, was unsupported by CIA records."[481]
While the CIA acknowledges that it should have kept OLC
better informed and up-to-date, the Agency found no
evidence that any information was known to be false when
it was provided to OLC.[482]

~~(TS//~~ ██████████████████ ~~//NF)~~ The Study claims
that the CIA's unsupported representations to OLC
included the characterization of Abu Zubaydah as
withholding critical threat information.[483] The Study cites
an email from the CIA's interrogation team that included
the sentence: "[o]ur assumption is the objective of this
operation [the interrogation of Abu Zubaydah] is to achieve
a high degree of confidence that [Abu Zubaydah] is not
holding back actionable information concerning threats to
the United States beyond that which [Abu Zubaydah] has

already provided."[484] However, this carefully chosen text omits critical statements from later in the same cable: "[t]here is information and analysis to indicate that subject has information on terrorist threats to the United States" and "[h]e is an incredibly strong-willed individual which is why he has resisted this long."[485]

~~(TS//~~ ███████████████ ~~//NF)~~ The Study argues that the CIA provided inaccurate information to OLC which was subsequently included in the OLC legal guidance contained in its August 1, 2002, memorandum.[486] Specifically, the Study argues that the CIA information about Abu Zubaydah's status in al-Qa'ida was inaccurate because the representation that Abu Zubaydah was the "third or fourth man" in al-Qa'ida was based on single source reporting of a ███████████████████ ████████████████ who had recanted prior to the issuance of the memorandum, and unbelievably, *"[t]he CIA later concluded that Abu Zubaydah was not a member of al-Qa'ida."*[487] Our review of the underlying documents revealed that both of these Study assertions were wrong.

~~(TS//~~ ███████████████ ~~//NF)~~ The Study criticizes the CIA representation that Abu Zubaydah was the "third or fourth man" in al-Qa'ida was based on a single source who had recanted prior to the drafting of the August 1, 2002, OLC memorandum.[488] The CIA counters this criticism by stating that the Agency had:

> multiple threads of reporting indicating that Zubaydah
> was a dangerous terrorist, close associate of senior al
> Qa'ida leaders, and was aware of critical logistical and

operational details of the organization, whether or not
he held formal rank in al-Qa'ida. Analysts did not alter
their fundamental assessment of Zubaydah's
intelligence value as a result of anything said or later
recanted by the single source.[489]

███████████████████████

██████████████████who had admitted that he was
sent by Abu Zubaydah to conduct terrorist operations
████████████, including an attack on a U.S. embassy.
[490] ████████████had also reported to interrogators
that Abu Zubaydah was considered the "third or fourth
ranking individual after Bin Ladin."[491] He provided the
following additional information that Abu Zubaydah: (1)
was considered the financial officer; (2) handled the
"fraudulent" operations; (3) was considered to be
responsible for the Gulf networks; and (4) was considered
to be experienced in military affairs.[492]
████████████████also admitted to meeting with Abu
Zubaydah at least twice.[493] An intelligence cable indicates
that "as of 2 October 2001, [████████████had retracted his
previous admissions... to carry out a terrorist attack against
the U.S. embassy...."[494] ████████████████
were certain, however, that despite ████████████████
retraction of his admissions concerning a plot against a U.S.
embassy, he was involved in terrorist planning activity
against unknown targets. They also assessed that
████████████████had not been previously aware of
the September 11, 2001, terrorist attacks by al-Qa'ida when
he made his earlier admissions related to Abu Zubaydah.
[495]

(TS// █████████████████ //NF)

297

████████████████████████further "denied that he ever met [Abu Zubaydah]" and "also denied any affiliation" with al-Qa'ida.[496] Given the level of detail ████████████████████ provided about Abu Zubaydah, including Abu Zubaydah's rank within al-Qa'ida, his denials of meeting with Abu Zubaydah do not ring true. Moreover, Abu Zubaydah himself admitted to at least one meeting with ████████████████ which undermines the ████████████████ denials about such meetings.[497] Based on this information, we are not so quick to dismiss the validity of ████████████████████original assessments of Abu Zubaydah's stature within al-Qa'ida, especially since the timing of his recantation ████████████████████

██

██

████████████████.

(TS// ████████████████████ //NF) The Study cites to a finished intelligence product entitled, *Countering Misconceptions About Training Camps in Afghanistan, 1990-2001*, as support for its stunning claim that Abu Zubaydah was not a member of al-Qa'ida. In a text box, this intelligence product makes the following assertions:

> A common misperception in outside articles is that Khaldan camp was run by al-Qa'ida. Pre-9/11 September 2001 reporting miscast Abu Zubaydah as a "senior al-Qa'ida lieutenant," which led to the inference that the Khaldan camp he was administering was tied to Usama Bin Ladin.... Al-Qa'ida rejected Abu Zubaydah's request *in 1993* to join the group and that Khaldan was not overseen by Bin Ladin's organization. [498]

At best, this text supports the rather useless assertion that in August 2006, a CIA intelligence product stated that *Abu Zubaydah was not a member of al-Qa'ida in 1993* – not the Study's erroneous claim that the CIA later concluded in 2006 that "Abu Zubaydah was not a member of al-Qa'ida." This misrepresentation of the actual text is another example of poor analytical tradecraft by the Study. As previously noted, there were multiple threads of intelligence demonstrating Abu Zubaydah's leadership role in al-Qa'ida prior to September 11, 2001.[499] Moreover, by the Study's own count, the interrogations of Abu Zubaydah resulted in 766 sole-source disseminated intelligence reports.[500] There should be absolutely no doubt in the Study that Abu Zubaydah was a senior and very-well informed member of al-Qa'ida.

(U) Breadth of Application of Enhanced Interrogation Techniques

Study Claim:

(TS// ████████████ //NF) "[T]he CIA applied its enhanced interrogation techniques to numerous other CIA detainees without seeking additional formal legal advice from the OLC."[501]

Fact:

(TS// ████████████ //NF) The CIA appropriately applied the legal principles of the August 1, 2002, OLC memorandum to other CIA detainees.

299

(TS// ████████████ //NF)   The   Study
authors appear to misunderstand the role of the OLC. The
OLC does not exercise line management responsibility for
CIA organizations, nor is it responsible for day-to-day legal
advice to the agency. The OLC does provide legal analysis
on specific questions of law applicable to a defined set of
facts. The CIA then applies the OLC's guidance to similar
scenarios under the guidance of its own legal counsel. The
fact that the CIA felt comfortable enough with OLC's
August 1, 2002, legal opinion to apply the same legal
principles to other detainees does not constitute an
impediment to DOJ's legal analysis of the Program. In fact,
the Attorney General later expressed the view that "the
legal principles reflected in DOJ's specific original advice
could appropriately be extended to allow use of the same
approved techniques (under the same conditions and
subject to the same safeguards) to other individuals besides
the subject of DOJ's specific original advice."[502]

(U) Detainees' Importance Overstated

Study Claim:

(TS// ███████████████████ //NF) The CIA made inaccurate representations to DOJ that Janat Gul and Ahmed Khalfan Ghailani were high-value al Qaeda operatives with knowledge of a pre-election plot against the United States when seeking legal guidance on whether the use of four additional interrogation techniques might violate U.S. law or treaty obligations. [503]

(TS// ███████████████████ //NF) "[T]he threat of a terrorist attack to precede the November 2004 U.S. election was found to be based on a CIA source whose information was questioned by senior CTC officials at the time and who admitted to fabricating the information after a ███████████ in ███████ October 2004."[504]

Fact:

(TS// ███████████████████ //NF) Contrary to the Study's claim, the CIA believed the representations to be true at the time it made them to the OLC. The CIA did not learn that some of these representations had been fabricated by a sensitive CIA source until months *after* OLC had approved the use of enhanced interrogation techniques against Janat Gul and Ahmed Khalfan Ghailani.

(TS// ███████████████████ //NF) The email relied upon by the Study does not support the proposition that senior CTC officials questioned the veracity of the sensitive CIA source. Also, while the source did admit to fabricating information about a meeting that never occurred, the Study does not acknowledge that the Chief of Base believed that the source was "generally truthful" about his discussions on the pre-election threat, despite ███████████ ███████████████████████████████████ result on that issue.

(TS// ███████████████████ //NF) The Study notes that the August 26, 2004, OLC letter advising that the use of four particular interrogation techniques on Janat Gul outside of the United States would not violate U.S. law or treaty obligations was based on the understanding that Janat Gul is a "high-value al Qaeda operative who is believed to possess information concerning an imminent terrorist threat to the United States."[505] The Study also notes that the September 6, 2004, OLC letter advising that the use of twelve particular interrogation techniques outside of the United States on Ahmed Khalfan Ghailani would not violate U.S. law or treaty obligations was based on the understanding that "Ghailani is an al-Qa'ida operative who 'is believed to be involved in the operational planning of an al-Qa'ida attack or attacks to take place in the United states prior to the November elections.'"[506] With the benefit of faulty hindsight, the Study claims that these representations were inaccurate.[507]

(TS// ███████████████████ //NF) This claim gives the false impression that the CIA intentionally withheld information from OLC about known fabrications from a questionable source. The truth is that the sensitive CIA source did not recant some of the underlying threat information that was contained in the CIA representations until October ███ and ███, 2004, *40 days after the issuance of the OLC letter for Gul and 29 days after the issuance of OLC letter for Ghailani.* Thus, the CIA made its August and September representations to OLC in good faith, believing them to be accurate.

~~(TS//~~ ███████████████ ~~//NF)~~ Moreover, the authorities cited by the Study do not fully support its claim that the CIA source's representations about the pre-election threat were inaccurate.[508] Specifically, the cited email does not question the credibility of the sources who provided the threat information in March 2004; and the cable reporting the fabrication by one of these sources in October 2004 clearly indicates that some of the source's pre-election threat information was considered to be "generally truthful."

~~(TS//~~ ███████████████ ~~//NF)~~ As the subject of the email implies – "Re: could AQ be testing ASSET Y and [source name REDACTED]?" – the concerns raised were not about the credibility of the sources, but more about the possibility that al-Qa'ida might be using this threat information to test the sources who had provided the pre-election threat information. The email raising the concern specifically states, "this is not to say that either ASSET Y or [source name REDACTED] are wrong or that the AQ statement below[509] is anything more than dis-information."[510] The reply email stated that it was possible the sources were just hearing the same rumors, but recollected that when al-Qa'ida put out similar rumors in the summer of 2001, those turned out to be true.[511] These emails do not support any inference about early suspicions of the source's credibility nor do they dismiss the legitimacy of the threat information provided by the sources.

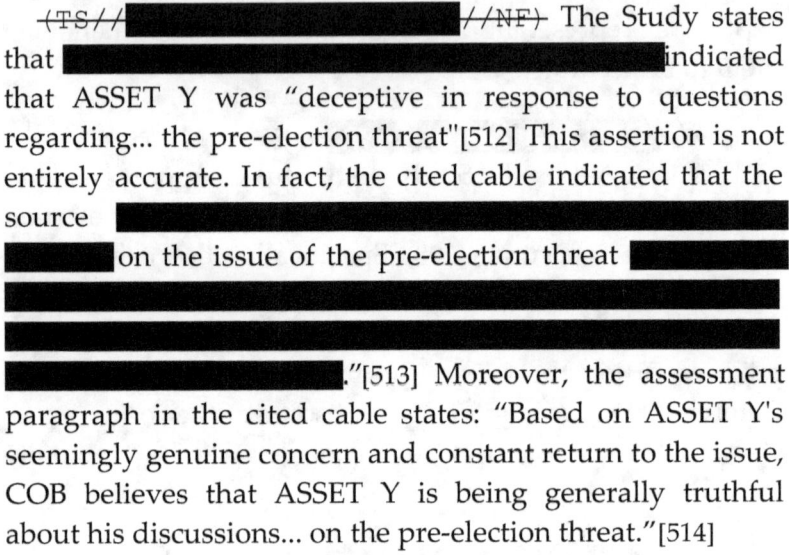

(TS// ████████████████ //NF) The Study states that ██████████████████████████████ indicated that ASSET Y was "deceptive in response to questions regarding... the pre-election threat"[512] This assertion is not entirely accurate. In fact, the cited cable indicated that the source ████████████████████████████████ ████████ on the issue of the pre-election threat ██████ ██████████████████████████████████████ ██████████████████████████████████████ ████████████████████."[513] Moreover, the assessment paragraph in the cited cable states: "Based on ASSET Y's seemingly genuine concern and constant return to the issue, COB believes that ASSET Y is being generally truthful about his discussions... on the pre-election threat."[514]

(U) Effectiveness of the Program

Study Claim:

(TS// ████████████████ //NF) The CIA's "Representations of 'effectiveness' were almost entirely inaccurate and mirrored other inaccurate information provided to the White House, Congress, and the CIA inspector general."[515]

Fact:

(TS// ████████████████ //NF) The CIA's Detention and Interrogation Program, to include the use of enhanced interrogation techniques, was effective and yielded valuable intelligence. The Study's exaggerated and absolute claims about inaccurate "effectiveness" representations by the CIA have been largely discredited by these minority views and the CIA's June 27, 2013, response to the Study.

(TS// ███████████████ //NF) In our view, the CIA's June 27, 2013, response to the Study identified significant problems with the original Study approved by the SSCI during the 112th Congress. Their response also fairly addressed the Study's many allegations of inaccurate representations in the context of the effectiveness of the Detention and Interrogation Program. For the most part, we found that the CIA acknowledged those representations that were made in error or could have benefitted from the inclusion of additional clarification.

(TS// ███████████████ //NF) As previously discussed, our own review of the documentary record in response to these serious allegations against the CIA found that many of the Study's claims of alleged misrepresentations were themselves inaccurate. As a reminder of these inaccurate Study claims, we provide the following sampling of our findings related to the CIA's effectiveness representations: (1) "There is considerable evidence that the information Abu Zubaydah provided identifying KSM as 'Mukhtar' and the mastermind of 9/11 was significant to CIA analysts, operators, and FBI interrogators";[516] (2) "CIA records clearly indicate that sleep deprivation played a significant role in Abu Zubaydah's identification of Jose Padilla as an al-Qa'ida operative tasked to carry out an attack against the United

States";[517] (3) "Abu Zubaydah provided information about how he would go about locating Hassan Ghul and other al-Qa'ida associates in Karachi. This information caused ████████████████████Pakistani authorities to intensify their efforts and helped lead them to capture Ramzi bin al-Shibh and other al-Qa'ida associates during the Karachi safe house raids conducted on September 10-11, 2002";[518] (4) "Information produced through detainee interrogation was pivotal to the retention of a key CIA asset whose cooperation led directly to the capture of KSM";[519] (5) "CIA documents show that key intelligence collected through the CIA's Detention and Interrogation Program, including information obtained after the use of enhanced interrogation techniques, played a major role in disrupting the Karachi hotels bombing plot";[520] (6) "The CIA interrogation program played a key role in disrupting the Heathrow and Canary Wharf plotting";[521] (7) "CIA documents show that the interrogation of KSM and al-Qa'ida operative Zubair, during and after the use of enhanced interrogation techniques on both individuals, played a key role in the capture of Hambali";[522] (8) "The CIA interrogation program played a key role in disrupting the "Second Wave" plot and led to the capture of the 17-member al-Ghuraba group";[523] (9) "CIA, FBI, and Department of Justice documents show that information obtained from detainees in CIA custody was important to identifying Ja'far al-Tayyar";[524] (10) "KSM provided valuable intelligence that helped to clarify Saleh al-Marri's role in al Qa'ida operations";[525] (11) "CIA, FBI, and Department of Justice documents show that information obtained from KSM after he was waterboarded led directly to Faris's arrest and was key in his prosecution";[526] (12) "Information obtained from detainee reporting, particularly KSM, provided otherwise unavailable intelligence that led to the identification of Saifullah Paracha as an al-Qa'ida operative involved in a potential plot, which spurred FBI action against him and his son, Uzhair";[527] (13) "Representations about the thwarting of an attack against Camp Lemonier in Djibouti, specifically President Bush's 2006 comments that 'Terrorists held in CIA custody have also provided information that helped stop a planned strike on U.S. Marines at Camp Lemonier in Djibouti,' were accurate and have been mischaracterized by the Study"; [528] and (14) "CIA documents show that detainee information served as the "tip-off and played a significant role in leading CIA analysts to the courier Abu Ahmad al-Kuwaiti. While there was other information in CIA databases about al-Kuwaiti, this information was not recognized as important by analysts until after detainees provided information on him."[529]

(U) Use of Constant Light, White Noise, and Shaving of Detainees

Study Claim:

(TS// ███████████████ //NF) CIA assertions to the OLC that loud music and white noise, constant light, and 24-hour shackling were all for security purposes were inaccurate.[530]

Fact:

(TS// ███████████████ //NF) The CIA disclosed to OLC that these confinement conditions were both for security and for other purposes.

(TS// ███████████████ //NF) The Study asserts that the CIA inaccurately represented its purpose for confining detainees in conditions including loud music, white noise, constant light, 24-hour shackling, and shaving of the head and face.[531] The CIA's response asserts that this characterization takes the CIA's representations out of context. The Agency claimed that such conditions were necessary for security, not that the mechanisms served no other purpose. The Agency noted that in responding to a draft OLC opinion, the CIA tried to correct the misunderstanding, noting that "these conditions are also used for other valid reasons, such as to create an environment conducive to transitioning captured and resistant terrorist to detainees participating in debriefings."[532]

Δ

Endnotes

[461] SSCI Study, Findings and Conclusions, December 3, 2014, p. 4.

[462] SSCI Study, Findings and Conclusions, December 3, 2014. p. 5.

[463] *See* CIA Office of General Counsel draft Legal Appendix: Paragraph 5 – Hostile Interrogations: Legal Considerations for CIA Officers, November 26, 2001, pp. 5-6 (CIA, Draft Appendix on Necessity Defense). This document is attached as Appendix IV, *see infra*, p. IV-1.

[464] SSCI Study, Findings and Conclusions, December 3, 2014, p. 5, n.13.

[465] *See* CIA, CIA Draft Appendix on Necessity Defense.

[466] CIA, CIA Draft Appendix on Necessity Defense, p. 6. *See also* SSCI Study, Executive Summary, December 3, 2014, p. 179 (the Study provides an accurate quotation of this text).

[467] SSCI Study, Findings and Conclusions, December 3, 2014, p. 5 (Erroneous text indicated by italics).

[468] *See* SSCI Study. Executive Summary, December 3, 2014. pp. 19 and 179; SSCI Study, Volume I, March 31, 2014, pp. 55, 220, 255, 262 n.1700, and 283 n.1854; SSCI Study, Volume II, April 1, 2014, pp. 28, 316, and 1753; and SSCI Study, Volume III, March 31, 2014, pp. 1179 and 1723 n.10679.

[469] CIA, Draft Appendix on Necessity Defense, p. 6.

[470] The CIA confirmed that the use of "novel" in

the context of this document meant "tenuous" or "untested," because U.S. courts had not accepted such an argument. *See,* CIA Study Response, Comments, p. 7 and CIA Study Response, Conclusions, pp. 4-5.

[471] SSCI Study, Executive Summary, December 3, 2014, p. 179.

[472] SSCI Study, Findings and Conclusions, December 3, 2014, p. 5 (citing DOJ, Memorandum from Jay S. Bybee, Assistant Attorney General, Office of Legal Counsel, DOJ, to Alberto R. Gonzales, Counsel to the President, re: Standards of Conduct for Interrogation, August 1, 2002).
[http://www.justice.gov/olc/docs/memo-gonzales-aug2002.pdf]

[473] DOJ, Memorandum from Jay S. Bybee, Assistant Attorney General, Office of Legal Counsel, DOJ, to Alberto R. Gonzales, Counsel to the President, re: Standards of Conduct for Interrogation, August 1, 2002, p. 46 (emphasis added).
[http://www.justice.gov/olc/docs/memo-gonzales-aug2002.pdf]

[474] DOJ, Memorandum from Daniel Levin, Acting Assistant Attorney General, Office of Legal Counsel, to James B. Comey, Deputy Attorney General, Re: Legal Standards Applicable under 18 U.S.C. §§ 2340-2340A, December 30, 2004, p. 2.

[475] SSCI Study, Executive Summary, December 3, 2014, p. 181, n.1069.

[476] *See* SSCI Study, Executive Summary, December 3, 2014, p. 181.

[477] SSCI Study, Executive Summary, December 3, 2014, p. 180, n.1065 (citing DOJ, Memorandum from Jay S. Bybee, Assistant Attorney General, Office of

Legal Counsel, DOJ, to Alberto R. Gonzales, Counsel to the President, re: Standards of Conduct for Interrogation, August 1, 2002, p. 46). [http://www.justice.gov/olc/docs/memo-gonzales-aug2002.pdf]

[478] [SSCI Study, Findings and Conclusions, December 3, 2014, p. 5.

[479] SSCI Study, Executive Summary, December 3, 2014, p. 410.

[480] SSCI Study, Executive Summary, December 3, 2014, p. 410.

[481] SSCI Study, Executive Summary, December 3, 2014, p. 410.

[482] CIA Study Response, Conclusions (TAB B), June 27, 2013, p. 32.

[483] SSCI Study, Executive Summary, December 3, 2014, p. 411.

[484] CIA, [REDACTED] 73208, July 23, 2003, p. 3; Email from: CIA staff officer; to: [REDACTED], [REDACTED], █████████████; subject: Addendum from ██████████, [REDACTED] 73208 (231043Z JUL 02); date: July 23, 2004, at 07:56:49 PM. *See also* email from: [REDACTED]; to: [REDACTED]; subject: Re: Grayson SWIGERT and Hammond DUNBAR; date; August 8, 21, 2002, at 10:21 PM.

[485] CIA, [REDACTED] 73208, July 23, 2003, p. 3; Email from: CIA staff officer; to: [REDACTED], [REDACTED], █████████████; subject: Addendum from ██████████, [REDACTED] 73208 (231043Z JUL 02); date: July 23, 2004, at 07:56 PM. *See also* Email from; [REDACTED]; to: [REDACTED]; subject: Re: Grayson SWIGERT and Hammond DUNBAR; date: August 8, 21, 2002, at 10:21 PM.

[486] SSCI Study, Executive Summary, December 3, 2014, p. 410.

[487] SSCI Study, Executive Summary, December 3, 2014, p. 410 (emphasis added).

[488] SSCI Study, Executive Summary, December 3, 2014, p. 410.

[489] *See* CIA Study Response, Conclusions (TAB B), June 27, 2013, p. 32.

[490] CIA, ALEC ██████████

[491] CIA, CIA ██████████

[492] CIA, CIA ██████████

[493] CIA, CIA ██████████

[494] CIA, CIA ██████████ . *See also* CIA, ALEC ██████████ .

[495] *See* CIA, CIA ██████████

[496] *See* CIA, CIA ██████████

[497] CIA, ALEC ██████████ CIA, ALEC ██████████ Abu Zubaydah and ██████████ accounts differ as to the location of this meeting(s).

[498] CIA, *Countering Misconceptions About Training Camps in Afghanistan, 1990-2001*, August 16, 2006, p. 2

(emphasis added).

[499] *See* CIA Study Response, Conclusions (TAB B), June 27, 2013, p. 32.

[500] SSCI Study, Volume III, March 31, 2014, pp. 282-283.

[501] SSCI Study, Executive Summary, December 3, 2014, p. 411.

[502] *See* Memorandum from Jack Goldsmith III, Assistant Attorney General, Office of Legal Counsel, Department of Justice, to John Helgerson, Inspector General, Central Intelligence Agency, June 18, 2004, Addendum, p. 2 (DTS 2004-2730).

[503] *See* SSCI Study, Executive Summary, December 3, 2014, pp. 417-418.

[504] SSCI Study, Executive Summary, December 3, 2014, p. 417.

[505] DOJ, Letter from Dan Levin, Acting Assistant Attorney General, to John A. Rizzo, Acting General Counsel, August 26, 2004, p. 1; SSCI Study, Executive Summary, December 3, 2014, p. 417.

[506] DOJ, Letter from Dan Levin, Acting Assistant Attorney General, to John A. Rizzo, Acting General Counsel, September 6, 2004. p. 1; SSCI Study, Executive Summary, December 3. 2014, p. 417-418.

[507] SSCI Study, Executive Summary, December 3, 2014, p. 417.

[508] *See* SSCI Study, Executive Summary, December 3, 2014, p. 417.

[509] The referenced statement was issued by al-Qa'ida on March 17, 2004, and asserted that al-Qa'ida would not operate any large-scale operation prior to the

election.

[510] Email from: ███████████████ ; to: ███████████████████████████████ , [REDACTED], ███████████████████████████████ ; subject: could AQ be testing ASSET Y ███ and [source name REDACTED]?; date: March ███, 2004, at 06:55 AM; Email from: ███████████████ ; to: ███████████████████████████ ; cc: ███████████████████ , [REDACTED], ███████████ ; subject: Re: could AQ be testing [the source] and ██████████████████ ?; date: March ███, 2004, at 7:52:32 AM, p. 1 (footnote added).

[511] Email from ████████████████████████████ to ████████████████████████████ - ██████ REDACTED ██████████████████████████████ ; subject: could AQ be testing [ASSET Y] and [source name REDACTED]?; ███ date: March ███, 2004, at 06:55 AM; Email from ████ ████████████████████████████████████ [REDACTED], ██████████ ; subject: Re: AQ be testing [the source] and ████████████ ; date: March ███, 2004, at 7:52:32 AM, p. 1 (footnote added). This email confirms that the sensitive source who subsequently admitted to fabricating information was not the only source providing information related to a possible pre-election terrorist threat. ████████ ██ .

[512] SSCI Study, Executive Summary, December 3, 2014, p. 348.

[513] CIA, CIA CABLE 1411. ██████████████ 2004.

p. 4.

[514] CIA, CIA CABLE 1411. ███████████ 2004.
p. 5.

[515] SSCI Study, Executive Summary, December 3, 2014, p. 426.

[516] *See supra*, pp. 140-144.

[517] *See supra*, pp. 150-155.

[518] *See supra*, pp. 159-166.

[519] *See supra*, pp. 171-178.

[520] *See supra*, pp. 181-183.

[521] *See supra*, pp. 188-192.

[522] *See supra*, pp. 194-199.

[523] *See supra*, pp. 203-208.

[524] *See supra*, pp. 210-211.

[525] *See supra*, pp. 213-215.

[526] *See supra*, pp. 215-221.

[527] *See supra*, pp. 223-228.

[528] *See supra*, pp. 239-242.

[529] *See supra*, pp. 253-260.

[530] SSCI Study, Executive Summary, December 3, 2014, pp. 428-429.

[531] SSCI Study, Executive Summary, December 3, 2014, pp. 428-429.

[532] CIA Study Response, Conclusions (TAB B), June 27, 2013, p. 34.

(U) Conclusion 9 (CIA Impeded Oversight by CIA Office of Inspector General)

(U) Conclusion 9 states, "[t]he CIA impeded oversight by the CIA's Office of Inspector General."[533] This allegation is among the most serious charges the Study levels against the CIA. As such, the Study should back up this charge with clear and convincing evidence. In our opinion it not only fails in that effort, but the Study itself is replete with examples that lead to the opposite conclusion – that the CIA did not significantly impede oversight by the CIA Office of the Inspector General (OIG).

(U) The law requires the CIA Inspector General to certify that "the Inspector General has had full and direct access to all information relevant to the performance of his function."[534] If the CIA OIG had been impeded in its oversight related to the CIA's Detention and Interrogation Program, it would have had to report that it was unable to make the required certification with respect to its oversight ofthis program. Yet, during the timeframe of the Program, the Inspector General certified in everyone of its semiannual reports that it had "full and direct access to all CIA information relevant to the performance of its oversight duties."[535] The law also requires the Inspector General to *immediately* report to the congressional intelligence committees if the Inspector General is "unable to obtain significant documentary information in the course of an investigation, inspection or audit...."[536] Again, we are not aware of any such report being made to the SSCI

316

during the relevant time period. We do know, however, that John Helgerson, the CIA Inspector General, testified before SSCI prior to the commencement of the SSCI's review of the CIA Detention and Interrogation Program in February 2007 and did not complain of access to Agency information."[537] Instead, he said that, during 2006, the IG took a comprehensive look at the operations of the CIA's Counterterrorism Center and conducted a separate, comprehensive audit of detention facilities. General Helgerson also testified,

> [W]e look carefully at *all* cases of alleged abuse of detainees. The first paper of this kind that came to the Committee was in October 2003, not long after these programs had begun, when we looked at allegations of unauthorized interrogation techniques used at one of our facilities. It proved that indeed unauthorized techniques had been used. I'm happy to say that the processes worked properly. An Accountability Board was held. The individuals were in fact disciplined. The system worked as it should.

> On this subject, Mr. Chairman, I cannot but underscore that we also look at a fair number of cases where, at the end of the day, we find that we cannot find that there was substance to the allegation that came to our attention. We, of course, make careful record of these investigations because we think it important that you and others know that we investigate all allegations, some of which are borne out, some of which are not.[538]

Thus, the allegation made by this conclusion is attacking the credibility and integrity of both the CIA OIG and the CIA. Issues of credibility and integrity can rarely be resolved by resorting to a documentary record alone. They are best resolved by personally interviewing and assessing the performance of relevant witnesses, which, with some limited exceptions, was not done during the course of this Study. The absence of evidence relating to these statutory reporting requirements is a strong indicator the CIA OIG was not impeded in its oversight of the CIA's Detention and Interrogation Program.

(U) Another possible indicator of impeded oversight would be evidence that the CIA OIG was blocked from conducting or completing its desired reviews of the program. If such oversight had been impeded, we would expect to see few, if any, completed investigations, reviews, or audits of the Program. Instead, it appears that the opposite took place. The Study itself acknowledges the existence of at least 29 OIG investigations on detainee-related issues, including 23 that were open or had been completed in 2005.[539] We would also expect to see indications in completed OIG reports that the investigation was hampered by limited access to documents, personnel, or site locations necessary for completing such investigations. Again, according to the OIG's own reports, we found evidence that the OIG had extensive access to documents, personnel, and locations. For example, in its May 2004 Special Review of the RDI program, the CIA OIG reported that it was provided more than 38,000 pages of documents and conducted more than 100 interviews, including with the DCI, the Deputy Director of the CIA, the Executive Director, the General Counsel, and the Deputy Director of Operations. The OIG made site visits to two interrogation facilities ███████████████████████████████ ██████████████████████ and reviewed 92 videotapes of the interrogation of Abu Zubaydah. The CIA IG's 2006 Audit is another good example of extensive access to documents, personnel, and locations. During this audit, the OIG not only conducted interviews of current and former officials responsible for CIA-controlled detention facilities, but it also reviewed operational cable traffic in extremely restricted access databases, reports, other Agency documents, policies, standard operating procedures, and guidelines pertaining to the detention program. The OIG also had access to the facilities and officials responsible for managing and operating three detention sites. The OIG was able to review documentation on site, observe detainees through closed-circuit television or one-way mirrors, and the IG even observed the transfer of a detainee aboard a transport aircraft. They even reviewed the medical and operational files maintained on each detainee in those locations.[540]

(U) The Study's case in support of this conclusion seems to rest mainly upon the following four observations: (I) the CIA did not inform the CIA OIG of the existence of the Program until November 2002; (2) some CIA employees provided the OIG with some inaccurate information about the Program; (3) CIA Director Goss directed the Inspector General in 2005 not to initiate planned review of the Program until the reviews already underway were completed; and (4) Director Hayden ordered a review of the OIG itself in 2007.[541] Our examination of these observations supports our conclusion that the CIA OIG was not impeded in its oversight of the CIA's Detention and Interrogation Program.

(U) The Study seems to fault the CIA for not briefing the CIA Inspector General on the existence of the Detention and Interrogation Program until November 2002, but does not really pursue why this fact alone was a problem or how it actually "impeded" the CIA OIG. Acting under the authority of the President's September 17, 2001, Memorandum of Notification, the CIA initiated the Program in late-March, 2002, when the first detainee was taken into its custody.[542] The CIA's Detention and Interrogation Program was part of a highly classified and compartmented covert action program. As the Program was being implemented, the CIA sought legal guidance from the Department of Justice and began briefing the White House. [543] Congressional access to details about the Program was restricted to leadership of the congressional intelligence committees during that same timeframe.[544] The CIA Inspector General was notified in November about the Program's existence in November 2002, because of the need for an OIG investigation into the death of a detainee who had been in the custody of the CIA.[545] At that point, the OIG had a clear "need to know" about the Program. We see nothing sinister in these events.

(U) The second "impeding" observation concerned the fact that CIA personnel provided the OIG with inaccurate information on the operation and management of the Detention and Interrogation Program, which was subsequently not corrected by the CIA and was included in the OIG's final report. The CIA has acknowledged in two cases that it made "mistakes that caused the IG to incorrectly describe in its 2004 *Special Review* the precise role that information acquired from KSM played in the detention of two terrorists involved in plots against targets in the [United States]."[546] The inclusion of erroneous information in an oversight report is disappointing, but absolute precision in matters such as these is rarely obtainable. Overall, these errors did not fundamentally alter the overall representations the CIA made about the RDI program to the OIG and policy makers.

(U) The Study's third observation about CIA Director Goss contains an error. It states that in 2005, "CIA Director Goss directed the Inspector General not to initiate planned reviews of the CIA Detention and Interrogation Program until reviews already underway were completed."[547] In fact, Director Goss did not "direct," but rather asked that a newly proposed review by the OIG be rescheduled until a mutually agreed-upon date. We find that the actual text from Director Goss's request provides sufficient justification against any allegation of "impeding" OIG oversight with the respect to the timing of the proposed OIG review. The memorandum states;

> Given its mission, CTC unquestionably must be subjected to rigorous independent oversight. This, in fact, has been the case, as evidenced by the 20 or so ongoing, incomplete OIG reviews directed at the Center. I am increasingly concerned about the cumulative impact of the OIG's work on CTC's performance. As I have said in previous correspondence to you, I believe it makes sense to complete existing reviews, particularly resource-

> intensive investigations such as those now impacting
> CTC, before opening new ones. As CIA continues to
> wage battle in the Global War on Terrorism, I *ask* that
> you reschedule these aspects of the new CTC review
> until a mutually agreeable time in the future.[548]

(U) The final observation in support of this "impeding" conclusion was that CIA Director Michael Hayden ordered a review of the OIG itself in 2007. The law governing the CIA OIG states, "The Inspector General shall report directly to and be under the general supervision of the Director."[549] Director Hayden's request for this review stemmed from a disagreement between the Office of the General Counsel (OGC) and the OIG over a legal interpretation related to the CIA's Detention and Interrogation Program. Director Hayden tasked Special Counselor Robert Deitz to assess how OGC and OIG interacted on legal issues. He also subsequently tasked Deitz with reviewing complaints of alleged OIG bias and unfair treatment of CIA officers as part of this review. On October 24, 2007, Deitz and his review team made an oral presentation to the Inspector General and his senior staff. They presented a number of recommendations regarding modifications to the OIG's procedures and practices, a number of which were adopted by the Inspector General. Director Hayden subsequently sent a message to the CIA workforce, stating that the Inspector General had "chosen to take a number of steps to heighten the efficiency, assure the quality, and increase the transparency of the investigative process." Director Hayden's message listed the agreed-upon recommendations.[550] Rather than impeding the CIA OIG's oversight, it appears that Director Hayden's order resulted in agreed-upon improvements to that office.

(U) We find that these observations, whether considered individually or in combination, do not support the conclusion that the CIA improperly impeded oversight of the CIA's Detention and Interrogation Program by the CIA OIG.

Δ

Endnotes

[533] SSCI Study, Findings and Conclusions, December 3, 2014, p. 8.

[534] 50 U.S.C. 3517(d)(1)(D).

[535] *See* CIA OIG, Semi-Annual Report to the Director, Central Intelligence Agency, July-December 2006, p. 5 (DTS 2007-0669); CIA OIG, Semi-Annual Report to the Director, Central Intelligence Agency, January-June 2006. p. 5 (DTS 2006-3195); CIA OIG, Semi-Annual Report to the Director, Central Intelligence Agency, July-December 2005, p. 5 (DTS 2006-0678); CIA OIG, Semi-Annual Report to the Director, Central Intelligence Agency, January-June 2005, p. 5 (DTS 2005-3140); CIA OIG, Semi-Annual Report to the Director of Central Intelligence, January-June 2004, p. 5 (DTS 2004-3307); and CIA OIG, Semi-Annual Report to the Director of Central Intelligence, January-June 2003, p. 5 (DTS 2003-3327); CIA Study Response, Comments (TAB A), June 27, 2013, pp. 4-6; and 10; and CIA Study Response, Conclusions (TAB B), June 27, 2013, pp. 7-9.

[536] 50 U.S.C. 3517(d)(3)(E).

[537] *See* SSCI Transcript, Hearing on the Central Intelligence Agency Rendition Program, February 14, 2007,p. 24 (DTS 2007-1337).

[538] SSCI Transcript, Hearing on the Central Intelligence Agency Rendition Program, February 14, 2007, p. 25 (DTS 2007-1337) (emphasis added).

[539] SSCI Study, Volume I, March 31, 2014, p. 899 n.6257. The CIA asserts that the "OIG conducted nearly 60 investigations" related to the CIA's Detention and Interrogation Program and that the OIG found the initial allegations in 50 of these investigations to be unsubstantiated or did not make findings warranting an accountability review. Of the remaining 10 investigations, one resulted in a felony conviction, one resulted in the termination of a contractor and the revocation of his security clearances, and six led to Agency accountability reviews. CIA Study Response, Conclusions (TAB B), June 27, 2013, p. 7.

[540] CIA OIG, CIA-controlled Detention Facilities Operated Under the 17 September 2001 Memorandum of Notification, July 14, 2006, APPENDIX A, pp. 1-2 (DTS 2006-2793).

[541] SSCI Study, Findings and Conclusions, April 3. 2014. p. 8. [[This factual error and misrepresentation of events was corrected in the December 3, 2014, version of the Findings and Conclusions by editing the text to read, "In 2005, CIA Director Goss requested in writing that the inspector general not initiate further reviews of the CIA's Detention and Interrogation Program until review already underway were completed." (emphasis added). *Compare* SSCI Study, Findings and Conclusions, April 3, 2014, p. 8 *with* SSCI Study, Findings and Conclusions, December 3, 2014, p. 8.]]

[542] *See* CIA, ALEC ███████████████████
███████████████████

[543] *See* CIA OIG, Special Review: Counterterrorism Detention and Interrogation Activities. (September 2001-October 2003), May 7, 2004, p. 4 (DTS 2004-2710). [http://media.washingtonpost.com/wp-srv/nation/documents/cia_oig_report.pdf]

[544] The CIA briefed HPSCI leadership on September 4, 2002, shortly after the August recess. SSCI leadership was briefed on the Program on September 27, 2002. *See* CIA Study Response, Conclusions, June 27, 2013, p. 36.

[545] CIA OIG, Special Review: Counterterrorism Detention and Interrogation Activities, (September 2001– October 2003), May 7, 2004, p. 52 (DTS 2004-2710). [http://media.washingtonpost.com/wp-srv/nation/-documents/cia_oig_report.pdf]

[546] CIA Study Response, Conclusions (TAB B), June 27, 2013, p. 22 (emphasis in original).

[547] SSCI Study, Findings and Conclusions, April 3. 2014. p. 8 (emphasis added). [[This factual error and misrepresentation of events was corrected in the December 3, 2014, version of the Findings and Conclusions by editing the text to read, "In 2005, CIA Director Goss requested in writing that the inspector general not initiate further reviews of the CIA's Detention and Interrogation Program until review already underway were completed." (emphasis added). *Compare* SSCI Study, Findings and Conclusions, April 3, 2014, p. 8 *with* SSCI Study, Findings and Conclusions, December 3, 2014, p. 8.]]

[548] CIA, Memorandum from Porter J. Goss, Director, Central Intelligence Agency to CIA Inspector General, re: New IG Work Impacting the Counter

Terrorism Center July 21, 2005 (emphasis added). In this same memorandum, Director Goss did exercise his statutory authority to direct the Inspector General to stand down from talking directly with high-value detainees until he received a compelling explanation. Ibid., p. 1. *See* 50 U.S.C. 403q. A few days later, a compromise was reached that permitted the audit of the CIA black sites with the agreement that no high value detainees would be interviewed by the OIG during the audit. *See* July 28, 2005, 08:54 AM, email from [REDACTED], DCI/OIG/Audit Staff/Operations Division to: [REDACTED] cc:

[REDACTED], [REDACTED], [REDACTED], [REDACTED], Robert Grenier, , [REDACTED], John P. Mudd, [REDACTED], [REDACTED], CIA attorney, CIA attorney, [REDACTED], [REDACTED] Re: Request for TDY Support; CIA OIG, CIA-controlled Detention Facilities Operated Under the 17 September 2001 Memorandum of Notification, July 14, 2006, Appendix A, p. 3 (DTS 2006-2793). Director Goss's lawful exercise of his statutory authority cannot be labeled as "impeding" oversight, especially here, where a reasonable accommodation was reached within a matter of days.

[549] 50 U.S.C. 403q.

[550] *See* Letter from DCIA Michael Hayden to Senator John D. Rockefeller, January 29, 2008 (DTS 2012-0606).

(U) Conclusion 10 (The CIA Released Classified Information on EITs to the Media)

(U) Conclusion 10 asserts, "[t]he CIA coordinated the release of classified information to the media, including inaccurate information concerning the effectiveness of the CIA's enhanced interrogation techniques."[551] This conclusion insinuates that there was something improper about the manner in which the CIA managed the process by which information about the Detention and Interrogation Program was disclosed to the media. It also repeats one of its main faulty claims – that the CIA released inaccurate information about the Program's effectiveness. Our examination of the record revealed that the CIA's disclosures were authorized and that the CIA's representations about the Program were largely accurate.

Study Claim:

> (TS// ███████████████ //NF) "The CIA's Office of Public Affairs and senior CIA officials coordinated to share classified information on the CIA's Detention and Interrogation Program to select members of the media to counter public criticism, shape public opinion, and avoid potential congressional action to restrict the CIA's detention and interrogation authorities and budget. These disclosures occurred when the program was a classified covert action program and before the CIA had briefed the full Committee membership on the program."[552]

Fact:

> (U) The National Security Council Policy Coordinating Committee designated the CIA as "the lead" on the "Public Diplomacy issue regarding detainees."

(U) The Study seems to confuse the difference between an authorized disclosure of classified information and the unauthorized "leak" of that same information. Despite acknowledging that the "National Security Council Principals Committee discussed a public campaign for the CIA's Detention and Interrogation Program,[553] the Study tries to cast the authorized disclosures as a "media campaign" that must be "done cleverly,"[554] and dwells on CIA officers providing information on the Program to journalists.[555] Specifically, on April 15, 2005, the National Security Council (NSC) Policy Coordinating Committee (PCC) determined that the CIA would have "the lead" on the "Public Diplomacy issue regarding detainees."[556] Once the PCC designated CIA as "the lead" on this matter, the CIA was authorized to make determinations on what information related to this highly classified covert action could be disclosed to the public on a case-by-case basis, without having to return to the White House for subsequent approvals.

(U) The White House did, however, retain its authority with respect to protecting sources and methods in the context of keeping the congressional intelligence fully and currently informed of this particular covert action. It is within the President's discretion to determine which members of Congress, beyond the "gang of eight," are briefed on sensitive covert action programs. There is no requirement for the White House to brief the full Committee as a prerequisite to the declassification or disclosure of information to the media.

(U) The Study acknowledges the White House's guiding influence on opening aspects of the Program to public scrutiny[557] in a section entitled, "NSC Principals Agree to Public Campaign Defending the CIA Detention and Interrogation Program."[558] In a subsequent section, referring to another "media plan," the Study states, "In the fall of 2005, the CIA expanded on its draft public briefing document. One draft, dated November 8, 2005, was specifically intended for National Security Advisor Stephen Hadley, who had requested it."[559] Later, "[t]hroughout the summer of 2006, the CIA assisted the White House in preparing the public roll-out of the program, culminating in President Bush's September 6, 2006 speech describing specific intelligence obtained from CIA detainees."[560] The Study cites no examples of the White House objecting to CIA activities that followed from these discussions.

(U) The Study is correct that, "The CIA's Office of Public Affairs and senior CIA officials coordinated to share classified information on the CIA's Detention and Interrogation Program to select members of the media."[561] That is the function of the Office of Public Affairs (OPA), which is the CIA office primarily responsible for dealing with the routine daily inquiries from the media. The CIA response to the Study indicates that the "vast majority of CIA's engagement with the media on the program was the result of queries from reporters seeking Agency comment on information they had obtained *elsewhere*.[562] The Study made no effort to review established procedures at OPA. The OPA's guidelines and practices include coordinating any information with "senior CIA officials," in order to mitigate or limit the disclosure of classified information. The OPA responds to media requests in a variety of ways that range from "no comment," to, in some cases, working with the media to provide context and improve the accuracy of stories that do not damage the CIA's equities.

(U) The Study cites a few select examples of media inquiries that resulted in stories about the Detention and Interrogation Program. The Study does not make clear, in most cases, who initiated these requests, nor does the Study make clear in what way their selected examples represent the body of media exchanges that OPA had with the media during the period of the Program. Interviews with OPA personnel would have rendered some clarity on these questions.

(U) The Study quotes, inconclusively, emails with various CTA counsels on how to handle the protection of covert action equities against public revelations[563] and chat sessions between officers in CTC who were tasked to prepare and review talking points for an appearance by senior CTA officials on NBC Dateline with Tom Brokaw. Their exchanges include comments on the rhetorical context of the possible media discussion, ("we either get out and sell, or we get hammered... we either put out our story or get eaten, there is no middle ground").[564] As noted in the CIA response to the Study, "the informal comments of any one CIA officer do not constitute Agency policy with regard

330

to media interactions."[565] One officer's speculation in a chat session about the risks of the Congress' reaction to unfavorable media coverage does not support the conclusion that the CIA shaped its public affairs strategy as a means to avoid congressional action. Moreover, the CIA refuted the suggestion that this chat session exchange related to the disclosure of classified information by stating that the NBC Dateline broadcast for which the officers were preparing, "contained no public disclosures of classified CIA, information; indeed, *the RDI program was not discussed.*"[566]

Study Claim:

(TS// ███████████████ //NF) "Much of the information the CIA provided to the media on the operation of the CIA's Detention and Interrogation Program and the effectiveness of its enhanced interrogation techniques was inaccurate and was similar to the inaccurate information provided by the CIA to the Congress, the Department of Justice, and the White House."[567]

Fact:

(TS// ███████████████ //NF) The CIA's Detention and Interrogation Program, to include the use of enhanced interrogation techniques, was effective and yielded valuable intelligence. The Study's exaggerated and absolute claims about inaccurate "effectiveness" representations by the CIA have been largely discredited by these minority views and the CIA's June 27, 2013, response to the Study.

(TS// ███████████████ //NF) As previously

discussed, our own review of the documentary record in response to the Study's serious allegations against the CIA found that many of these claims of alleged misrepresentations were themselves inaccurate. The Study's flawed analytical methodology cannot suppress the reality that the CIA's Detention and Interrogation Program set up an effective cycle of events whereby al-Qa'ida terrorists were removed from the battlefield, which had a disruptive effect on their current terrorist activities and often permitted the Intelligence Community to collect additional intelligence, which, in turn, often led back to the capture of more terrorists. We found, with a few limited exceptions, that the CIA generally did a good job in explaining the Program's accomplishments to policymakers. We will not repeat the listing of our specific effectiveness findings here. [568]

Δ

Endnotes

[551] SSCI Study, Findings and Conclusions, December 3, 2014, p. 8.

[552] SSCI Study, Findings and Conclusions, December 3, 2014, p. 8.

[553] SSCI Study, Executive Summary, December 3, 2014, p. 403.

[554] SSCI Study, Vol. II, April 1, 2014, pp. 1521-1522.

[555] SSCI Study, Executive Summary, December 3, 2014, pp. 403-404.

[556] Email from: ███████████ to: CIA attorney; subject: Brokaw interview: Take one; date: April 15, 2005, at

1:00 PM.

[557] DECISION PAPER: Background for 10 March Principals Committee Meeting on Long-Term Disposition of Selected High Value Detainees, March 4, 2005. *See also* email from: ███████████████████ to Robert L. Grenier; cc: John P. Mudd, ███████████████, [REDACTED], ███████████████████; subject: DCI Briefing Material/Talking points for upcoming PC; date: 3/01/05 11:33 AM. SSCI Study, Volume II, April 1, 2004, pp. 1508-54.

[558] SSCI Study, Volume II, April I, 2014, p. 1521.

[559] SSCI Study, Volume II, April 1, 2014, p. 1528.

[560] SSCI Study, Volume II, April 1, 2014, p. 1535.

[561] SSCI Study, Findings and Conclusions, December 3, 2014, p. 8.

[562] CIA Study Response, Conclusions (TAB B), June 27, 2013, p. 39 (emphasis in original).

[563] SSCI Study, Executive Summary, December 3, 2014, p. 403-405.

[564] CIA, Sametime communication, between John P. Mudd and ███████████████████ dated April 13, 2005, from 19:23:50 to 19:56:05.

[565] CIA Study Response, Conclusions (TAB B), June 27, 2013, p. 40.

[566] CIA Study Response, Conclusions (TAB B), June 27, 2013, p. 40 (emphasis in original).

[567] CIA Study Response, Conclusions (TAB B), June 27, 2013, p. 9.

[568] That list may be found in the discussion of Conclusion 5 under the *Effectiveness of the Program* heading, *supra*, pp. 304-307.

(U) CONCLUSION

(U) The Study concludes that the CIA was unprepared to initiate a program of indefinite, clandestine detention using coercive interrogation techniques, something we found obvious, as no element of our government was immediately prepared to deal with the aftermath of what had happened on September 11, 2001. In reviewing the information the CIA provided for the Study, however, we were in awe of what the men and women of the CIA accomplished in their efforts to prevent another attack. The rendition, detention, and interrogation program they created, of which enhanced interrogation was only a small part, enabled a stream of collection and intelligence validation that was unprecedented. The most important capability this program provided had nothing to do with enhanced interrogation – it was the ability to hold and question terrorists, who, if released, would certainly return to the fight, but whose guilt would be difficult to establish in a criminal proceeding without compromising sensitive sources and methods. The CIA called the detention program a "crucial pillar of US counterterrorism efforts, aiding intelligence and law enforcement operations to capture additional terrorists, helping to thwart terrorist plots, and advancing our analysis of the al-Qa'ida target."[569] We agree. We have no doubt that the CIA's detention program saved lives and played a vital role in weakening al-Qa'ida while the Program was in operation. When asked about the value of detainee information and whether he missed the intelligence from it, one senior CIA operator told members, "I miss it every day."[570] We understand why.

Δ

Endnotes

[569] *Detainee Reporting Pivotal for the War Against al-Qa'ida*, June 1, 2005, p. i. [http://documents.nytimes.com/c-i-a-reports-on-interrogation-methods#p=245]

[570] ███████████Chambliss, ███████████████████ conversation between SSCI members and CIA officers, ███████████████████████.

Δ

(U) APPENDIX I; CIA, Countering Misconceptions About Training Camps in Afghanistan, 1990-2001, August 16, 2006

16 August 2006

Countering Misconceptions About Training Camps in Afghanistan, 1990-2001 ▮▮▮▮

- Arab mujahidin took courses in explosives, electronics, and document falsification in private residences in Kabul where instructors charged fees of between $50 and $100 per month.

- A Moroccan guesthouse in Kabul provided target reconnaissance training primarily to Moroccans.

- One trainee received informal training on the placement, extraction,and camouflage of antitank and antipersonnel mines while on the frontlines in Bagram ▮▮▮▮

The degree of al-Qa'ida involvement in the Afghanistan training scene during the 1990s is often overstated. Al-Qa'ida had only a peripheral role in training during the middle part of the decade when Bin Ladin and most of his group were located in Sudan. From 1993 to 1997, al-Faruq was used to train Tajiks with only a few al-Qa'ida members assisting. Al-Qa'ida reportedly was "in control of al-Faruq" again in 1997.

- Some of the camps have been misidentified as being run by al-Qa'da, including Khaldan and Abu Khabab al-Masri's poisons-related facilities at

337

Derunta and Kargha.

- Recent reporting suggests that the degree to which al-Qa'ida financed non-al-Qa'ida camps may have been exaggerated. For example, a senior al-Qa'ida leader reportedly said that he did not know of al-Qa'ida providing any money, material, or trainers to non-al-Qa'da camps. ███████████

By the late 1990s, al-Qa'ida – with the assistance of the Taliban – sought to gain hegemony over training in Afghanistan, but the group never controlled all the camps.

Khaldan Not Affiliated With Al-Qa'ida ███████████

A common misperception in outside articles is that Khaldan camp was run by al-Qa'ida. Pre-11 September 2001 reporting miscast Abu Zubaydah as a "senior al-Qa'ida lieutenant," which led to the inference that the Khaldan camp he was administering was tied to Usama Bin Ladin.

- The group's flagship camp, al-Faruq, reportedly was created in the late 1980s so that Bin Ladin's new organization could have a training infrastructure independent of Abdullah Azzam's Maktab al-Khidamat, the nongovernmental organization that supported Khaldan.

- Al-Qa'ida rejected Abu Zubaydah's request in 1993 to join the group and that Khaldan was not overseen by Bin Ladin's organization.

- There were relations between the al-Qa'ida camps and Khaldan. Trainees, particularly Saudis, who had finished basic training at Khaldan were referred to al-Qa'ida camps for advanced courses, and Khaldan staff observed al-Qa'ida training. The two groups, however, did not exchange trainers.

████████████████

- An al-Qa'ida facilitator reportedly said that in 1998 Bin Ladin began to pressure other Arabs to close their facilities because he wanted all the recruits sent to al-Qa'ida.

- Ibn al-Shaykh al-Libi initially foiled attempts to shut down Khaldan, but by April 2000 the camp had closed.

- The Libyan Islamic Fighting Group and Abu Mus'ab al-Suri were able to bribe or convince Taliban officials to allow them to continue operating their camps despite al-Qa'ida's pressure on the Taliban to close them. ████████████████

Δ

(U) APPENDIX II: CIA, Briefing Notes on the Value of Detainee Reporting, August 2005

Briefing Notes on the Value of Detainee Reporting

August 2005

I'm glad to speak to you today about the results we have seen from high and mid value detainee reporting, which since 9/11 has become a crucial pillar of US counterterrorism efforts. To get a sense for the importance of this reporting to CIA's overall collection effort, let me share some statistics with you:

- Since we began the program in March 2002, detainees have produced over 6,000 disseminated intelligence reports.

- Approximately half of CTC's disseminated intelligence reporting in 2004 on al-Qa'ida came from CIA-held detainees.

- For both warning and operational purposes, detainee reporting is disseminated broadly among US intelligence and law enforcement entities ███████████████████████████████ ███████████████████████ (S//NF)

For today's briefing, I'm going to highlight five key areas in which detainee reporting has played a critical role: aiding intelligence and law enforcement operations to capture additional terrorists, helping to thwart terrorist plots, advancing our analysis of the al-Qa'ida target, illuminating other collection, and validating sources. (S//NF)

Capturing Other Terrorists

Detainees have given us a wealth of useful targeting information on al-Qa'ida members and associates. Detainees have played some role – from identification of photos to providing initial lead and in depth targeting information – in nearly every capture of al-Qa'ida members and associates since 2002, including ███████████ ███████████████ detentions we assess as "key" because the individuals captured represented a significant threat to the United States or were playing leading roles in assisting al-Qa'ida.

I have handed you graphics that tell the story of two such cases:

Unraveling Hambali's network. In March 2003, al-Qa'ida operations chief Khalid Shaykh Muhammad (KSM) provided information about an al-Qa'ida operative, Majid Khan, whom he was aware had recently been captured. KSM – possibly believing the detained operative was "talking" – admitted to having tasked Majid with delivering a large sum of money to individuals working for another senior al-Qa'ida associate.

- In an example of how information from one detainee can be used in debriefing another detainee in a "building block" process, Khan – confronted with KSM's information about the money – acknowledged that he delivered the money to an operative named "Zubair" and provided Zubair's physical description and contact number. Based on that information, Zubair was captured in June 2003.

- During debriefings, Zubair revealed that he worked directly for Jemaah Istamlyah (JI) leader and al-Qa'ida's South Asia representative Hambaii. Zubair provided information ███████████████████████

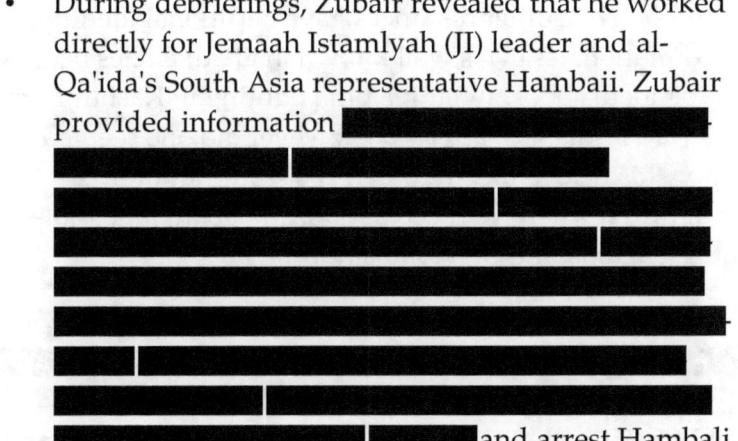

████████████████ and arrest Hambali.

- Next, KSM – when explicitly queried on the issue – identified Hambali's brother, 'Abd al-Hadi, as a prospective successor to Hambali. Information from multiple detainees, including KSM, narrowed down 'Abd al-Hadi's location and enabled his capture

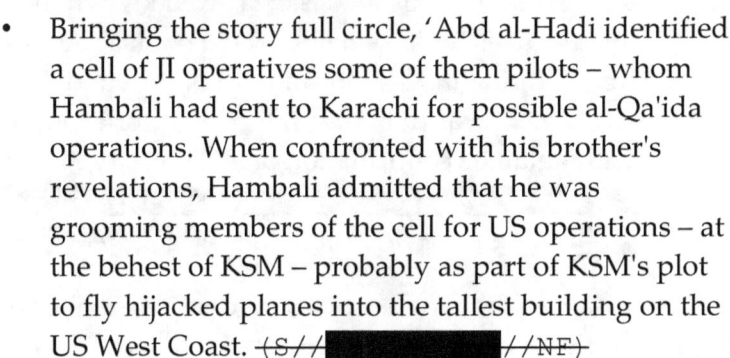

- Bringing the story full circle, 'Abd al-Hadi identified a cell of JI operatives some of them pilots – whom Hambali had sent to Karachi for possible al-Qa'ida operations. When confronted with his brother's revelations, Hambali admitted that he was grooming members of the cell for US operations – at the behest of KSM – probably as part of KSM's plot to fly hijacked planes into the tallest building on the US West Coast. ~~(S//~~███████~~//NF)~~

The Arrest of Dhiren Barot (aka Issa al-Hindi). KSM also provided the first lead to an operative known as "Issa al-Hindi," while other detainees gave additional identifying information. Issa was well known in jihadi circles because he penned a book about his time fighting in Kashmir under his "al-Hindi" *nom de guerre*; however, no one seemed to know his true name. In March 2004, our hunt for Issa intensified when we receive reporting about a possible attack against the US Homeland.

KSM positively identified the photo as Issa al-Hindi, and we were able to identify through a new search mechanism a separate individual who had traveled to the United States with Issa prior to 9/11.

- Issa and his former traveling companion – who were arrested in 2004 – appear to have been involved in plots in the UK. Moreover, in early 2004, Issa had briefed US targeting packages to al-Qa'ida senior leadership in Pakistan. Issa was well known in jihadi circles because he penned a book about his time fighting in Kashmir under his "al-Hindi" *nom de guerre*; it was only through police work coupled with detainee confirmation on his identity, that ▮▮▮- ▮▮▮▮▮▮▮▮▮▮▮▮▮▮▮▮▮▮▮▮▮▮▮▮▮▮- ▮▮ were able to find him. ~~(S//~~ ▮▮▮▮ ~~/NF~~

In addition to these two prominent cases, a number of other significant captures have resulted thanks to detainee reporting. It is important to highlight that a number of these cases involve law enforcement's use of our detainee reporting:

- *Arrest of key al-Qa'ida facilitator* ███████████ ███ ████████████████████. In debriefings, KSM in March 2003 noted that he had created and used a specified e-mail account to communicate with senior ████████████████ █████████ ████████████████████████████████ ███████████████████████. CIA then determined that KSM had been using this account actively in ongoing operational planning for an ████████threat, which KSM confirmed. Analysis of ████████████████e-mails after KSM's detention led to his being located and arrested on ███████████ ████2003.

- *Identifying the "other" shoe bomber.* Leads provided by KSM in November 2003 led directly to the arrest of shoe bomber Richard Reid's one-time partner Sajid Badat in the UK. KSM had volunteered the existence of Badat – whom he knew as "Issa al-Pakistani" – as the operative who was slated to launch a simultaneous shoe bomb attack with Richard Reid in December 2001.

- *Jose Padilla.* After his capture in March 2002, Abu Zubaydah provided infornnation leading to the identification of alleged al-Qa'ida operative Jose Padilla. Arrested by the FBI in 2002 as he arrived at O'Hare Airport in Chicago, he was transferred to military custody in Charleston, South Carolina, where he is currently being held. The FBI began participating in the military debriefings in March 2003, after KSM reported Padilla might know the true name of a US-bound al-Qa'ida operative known at the time only as Jafar al-Tayyar. Padilla confirmed Jafar's true name as Adnan El Shukrijumah.

- *Iyman Faris.* Soon after his arrest, KSM described an Ohio-based truck driver whom the FBI identified as Iyman Faris, already under suspicion for his contacts with al-Qa'ida operative Majid Khan. FBI and CIA shared intelligence from interviews of KSM, Khan, and Faris on a near real-time basis and quickly ascertained that Faris had met and accepted operational taskings from KSM on several occasions. Faris is currently serving a 20-year sentence for conspiracy and material support to a terrorist organization. (TS// █████████████ //NF █████

Bringing new targets to light. A variety of detainee reporting has provided our initial information about individuals having links to al-Qa'ida and has given us insight into individuals about whom we had reporting but whose al-Qa'ida involvement was unclear. For example, detainees in mid-2003 helped us build a list of ███████████ ████████████████████ individuals – many of whom we had never heard of before – that al-Qa'ida deemed suitable for Western operations. We have shared this list broadly within the US intelligence and law enforcement communities,

██
██

███████████████████████████

- Jafar al-Tayyar first came ito FBI's attention when
  Abu Zubaydah named him as one of the most likely
  individuals to be used by al-Qa'ida for operations in
  the United States or Europe. Jafar was further
  described by detainees, whose description of Jafar's
  family in the United States was key to uncovering
  Jafar's true name. An FBI investigation identified
  Gulshair El Shukrijumah, leader of a mosque in
  Hollywood, Florida, as having a son named Adnan
  who matched the biographical and physical
  descriptions given by the detainees. A "Be On The
  Lookout" notice has been issued for Adnan El
  Shukrijumah.

- Most recently, for example, Abu Faraj al-Libi has
  revealed that an operative we were only vaguely
  aware of was actually sent to ██████████████ in
  2004 to lay the groundwork for al-Qa'ida attacks
  there ██████████████████████████

  ████████████████████████████████████
  ████████████████████████████████████-
  ████████████████████████

  (S// ██████████████ //NF)

Revealing Plots, Potential Targets (S//NF)

One of the fall-outs of detaining these additional
terrorists has been the unearthing and at least temporary
thwarting of a number of al-Qa'ida operations in the United

States and overseas.

Possible Nuclear Threat to the United States, In some of the most groundbreaking information on al-Qa'ida collected in 2004, detainee Sharif al-Masri provided at least 11 intelligence reports on nuclear and biological issues related to al-Qa'ida and may have revealed a new nuclear threat to the US Homeland associated with al-Qa'ida's key explosives expert Abu 'Abd al-Rahman al-Muhajir.

- Sharif's debriefings indicated that he was aware of recent and possibly ongoing efforts to move an unspecified nuclear "bomb" into the United States, possibly via Mexico, through his discussion in February 2004 with Muhajir. This reporting confirmed and fleshed out ██████████████ ████████ reporting from 2004 about a plan to move people into the US through Mexico. The nuclear aspects to the threat, however, were new and confirmed al-Qa'ida's continuing interest in WMD. ~~(TS//~~██████████~~//NF)~~

Heathrow Airport plot. Shortly after his capture in March 2003, KSM divulged limited information about his plot to use commercial airliners to attack Heathrow Airport and other targets in the United Kingdom; he discussed this plot probably because he believed that key Heathrow plotter Ramzi bin al-Shibh, who had been detained six months previously, had already revealed the information.

- Debriefers used KSM's and Bin al-Shibh's reporting to confront Khallad and Ammar al-Baluchi, who were caught two months after KSM. Khallad admitted to having been involved in the plot and revealed that he directed group leader Hazim al-Sha'ir to begin locating pilots who could hijack planes and crash them into the airport. Khallad said he and operative Abu Talha al-Pakistani considered ███████████████ countries as possible launch sites for the hijacking attempts and that they narrowed the options to ███████████████

███████████████████████████ ████████

██████████████████

- Khallad's statements provided leverage in debriefings of KSM. KSM fleshed out the status of the operation, including identifying an additional target in the United Kingdom, Canary Wharf. (S//NF)

Revealing the Karachi plots. When confronted with information provided by al-Qa'ida senior facilitator Ammar al-Baluchi, Khallad admitted during debriefings that al-Qa'ida was planning to attack the US Consulate in Karachi, Westerners at the Karachi Airport, and Western housing areas. (S//NF)

Aiding Our Understanding Of Al-Qaida (S//NF)

The capture and debriefing of detainees has transformed our understanding of al-Qa'ida and affiliated terrorist groups, providing increased avenues for sophisticated analysis. Prior to the capture of Abu Zubaydah in March 2002, we had large gaps in knowledge of al-Qa'ida's organizational structure, key members and associates, intentions and capabilities, possible targets for the next attack, and its presence around the globe.

- Within months of his arrest, Abu Zubaydah provided details about al-Qa'ida's organizational structure, key operatives, and modus operandi. It also was Abu Zubaydah, early in his detention, who identified KSM as the mastermind of 9/11. ~~(S//~~ █████ ~~//NF)~~

In the years since 9/11, successive detainees have helped us gauge our progress in the fight against al-Qa'ida by providing updated information on the changing structure and health of the organization.

Hassan Ghul. After his early 2004 capture, Hassan Ghul provided considerable intelligence on al-Qa'ida's senior operatives in Waziristan and elsewhere in the tribal regions of Pakistan. We had fragmentary information ████████ ██ ████████████████████████████████████ identifying the Shkai valley as a safehaven for al-Qa'ida and associated mujahidin before Ghul's capture; however, Ghufs reporting brought instant credibility to all this disparate reporting and added minute details to what had previously been a murky, nascent picture. Ghul helped us assess that this valley, as of December 2003, was not just one haven for al-Qa'ida in Waziristan, but the home base for al-Qa'ida in the area and one that al-Qa'ida was reluctant to abandon.

- ████████████████████████ Ghul – a key al-

Qa'ida facilitator – pointed out the location in the Shkai valley, Waziristan, Pakistan of safehouses of specific al-Qa'ida senior leaders, ███████ ▪

███████████████████ ███████████
████████████████████████████ █████▪
███████████████████████████████
████▌
████████████▌
██████████████▌
███████████████████████████████▌
███████████████████████████████▌ ▪
██████████████████████████████▪
████████████████▌
███████████████████████████████▌
██████████████████████

███████▌ Although we had a body of reporting from clandestine and other sources indicating that senior al-Qa'ida targets were congregating in the Shkai valley in 2004, Ghul's confirmation and critical narrative helped counterterrorism officiers ██████
███████████████████████████████
███████████████████████████
██████████████████████████
████████████████████████▪

• Ghul also provided our first knowledge of Pakistan operatives trained ███████████████████████
███████████████████████████████
███████████████████████████
███████▌Ghul then supplied detailed insight into

the nature of their training, the al-Qa'ida operatives involved in their grooming, and the location of ███████ facllities in Shkai where the operatives trained. ███████ learned later through debriefings of Abu Talha al-Pakistani – who helped recruit the Pakistanis – that one of the operatives, ███████ ███████ was attempting to apply for a US student visa ███████ ███████. ~~(S~~ ███████ ~~NF)~~

Sharif al-Masri. Sharif al-Masri also provided invaluable insights in over 150 disseminated reports that have aided our analysis of al-Qa'ida's current organization, the personalities of its key members, and al-Qa'ida's decision-making process. ~~(TS//~~ ███████ ~~//NF)~~

Various operatives discuss capabilities, including CBRN. Detained al-Qa'ida technical experts – some of whom had very focused roles in the organization – have provided unique insight into the origins of the group's efforts to develop weapons and the technical limitations of key al-Qa'ida personnel – in particular, detainees have helped to clarify al-Qa'ida's CBRN program.

- Abu Zubaydah and senior al-Qa'ida military trainer Ibn al-Shaykh identified ███████ - ███████ – who had been associated with poison training – as the individual who conducted experiments with mustard on rabbits and dogs.

- KSM's reporting advanced our understanding of al-Qa'ida's interest in developing a nuclear weapons program, and also revealed important information about al-Qa'ida's program to produce anthrax. He apparently calculated incorrectly that we had this information already, qiven that one of the three – Yazid Sufaat – had been in foreign custody

████████████████████████████████████

███████████████████████████████.

- After being confronted with KSM's reporting, Yazid eventually admitted his principal role in the anthrax program and provided fragmentary information on

████████████████████████████████████
████████████████████████████████████
████████████████████████████████████
████████████████████████████████████
████████████████████████████████████
████████████████████████████████████
█████████████████████████████████

⟨S████████████████████//NF⟩

Illuminating Other Collection ⟨S//NF⟩

Detainee reporting has allowed us to confirm reporting from clandestine and other sources, and makes sense of fragmentary information. ███████████████████████

████████████████████████████████████
████████████████████████████████████
████████████████████████████████████
████████████████████████████████████
████████████████████████████████████
████████████████████████████████████

- As noted earlier, Abu Faraj – along with other detainees – has begun to flesh out threat reporting received ███████████████████ ████████during 2004, including tasking to send operatives to the US via Mexico and hopes to mount an attack prior to the 2004 US Presidential elections. While we are still in the early stages of exploiting the full extent of Abu Faraj's knowledge on Homeland threats, information he and others have provided has confirmed that efforts were underway to mount an attack in the US Homeland beginning in late 2003. ████████████████████

▬▬▬▬▬▬▬▬▬▬▬▬▬▬
▬▬▬▬▬▬▬▬▬▬▬▬▬▬
▬▬▬▬▬▬▬▬▬▬▬▬▬▬
▬▬▬▬▬▬▬▬▬▬▬▬▬▬
▬▬▬▬▬▬▬▬▬▬▬▬▬▬
▬▬▬▬▬▬▬▬▬▬▬▬▬▬
▬▬▬▬▬▬▬▬▬▬▬▬▬▬

- Hassan Ghul's disc containing a message from Zarqawi for Bin Ladin about Zarqawi's plan in Iraq coupled with Ghul's own reporting brought the burgeoning relationship between Zarqawi and al-Qa'ida into clear focus for the first time since the US entry into Iraq. ~~(S~~ ▬▬▬▬ ~~//NF)~~

▬▬▬▬▬▬▬▬▬▬▬▬▬▬
▬▬▬▬▬▬▬▬▬▬▬▬▬▬
▬▬▬▬▬▬▬▬▬▬▬▬▬▬
▬▬▬▬▬▬▬▬▬▬▬▬▬▬
▬▬▬▬▬▬▬▬▬▬▬▬▬▬
▬▬▬▬▬▬▬▬▬▬▬▬▬▬
▬▬▬▬▬▬▬▬▬▬▬▬▬▬
▬▬▬▬▬▬▬▬▬▬▬▬▬▬
▬▬▬▬▬▬▬▬▬▬▬▬▬▬

Detainees have been particularly useful in sorting out the large volumes of documents and computer data seized in raids. Such information potentially can be used in legal proceedings, as physical evidence, ▬▬▬▬▬▬▬
▬▬▬▬▬▬▬▬▬▬▬▬▬▬

355

████████████████████████████████████.It also can be used in confronting detainees to get them to talk about topics they would otherwise not reveal.

- For example, lists of names found on Mustafa al-Hawsawi's computer seized in March 2003 represented al-Qa'ida members who were to receive money. Debriefers questioned detainees extensively on these names to determine who they were and how important they were to the organization. This information helped us to better understand al-Qa'ida's revenues and expenditures, particularly in Pakistan, and money that was available to families.

- The same computer had a list of e-mail addresses for individuals KSM helped deploy abroad that he hoped would execute operations; most of these names were unknown to us, and we used this information in debriefings of KSM and other detainees to unravel KSM's plots. (S// ████████████████ //NF)

Helping To Validate Other Sources (S//NF)

Detainee information is a key tool for validating clandestine sources who may have reported false information. In one case, the detainee's information proved to be the accurate story, and the clandestine source was confronted and subsequently admitted to embellishing or fabricating some or all the details in his report.

- Pakistan-based facilitator Janat Gul's most

significant reporting helped us validate a CIA asset who was providing information about the 2004 pre-election threat. The asset claimed that Gul had arranged a meeting between himself and al-Qa'ida's chief of finance, Shaykh Sa'id, a claim that Gul vehemently denied.

- Gul's reporting was later matched with information obtained from Sharif al-Masri and Abu Talha, captured after Gul. With this reporting in hand, CIA ███████████████████████ the asset, who subsequently admitted to fabricating his reporting about the meeting. ~~(S//~~ ███████████████ ~~//NF)~~

In other instances, detainee information has been useful in identifying clandestine assets who are providing good reporting. For example, Hassan Ghul's reporting on Shkai helped us validate several assets ██████████████ who also told us that al-Qa'ida members had found safe-haven at this location.

- Sometimes one detainee validates reporting from others. Sharif corroborated information from ████████████████████who were involved in facilitating the movement of al-Qalda personnel, money, and messages into and out of ███████.For example, █████████████████████ ██████indicated that ███████████████████ ████████████████████████████████ ████████████████████████████████ ██████████████was the link between al-Qa'ida and ████████████████████████████████-

357

████████ and Sharif corroborated that fact when he noted that ███████████████████████ was the "go-between" for al-Qa'ida and ███████. ~~(S//~~ ██████████████ ~~//NF)~~

Challenges of Detainee Reporting ~~(S//NF)~~

I don't want to leave you with the impression that we do not assess detainee reporting with the same critical eye that we would other sources of intelligence. Detainees' information must be corroborated using multiple sources of intelligence; uncorroborated information from detainees must be regarded with some degree of suspicion. A detainee is more likely to budge if the debriefer, using information from another source, can demonstrate that the detainee possesses knowledge of the particular subject.

- This tendency to reveal information when cornered with facts is one of the reasons we view unilateral custody as so critical. Not only are we certain of the exact questions being asked and answers being given, ██████████████████████

   ██████████████████████████████

   ██████████████████████████████

   ██████████████████████████████

   ████████████████████████████

   ██████████████████████████████

   ██████████ ~~(S//~~ ██████████████ ~~//NF)~~

Δ

(U) APPENDIX III

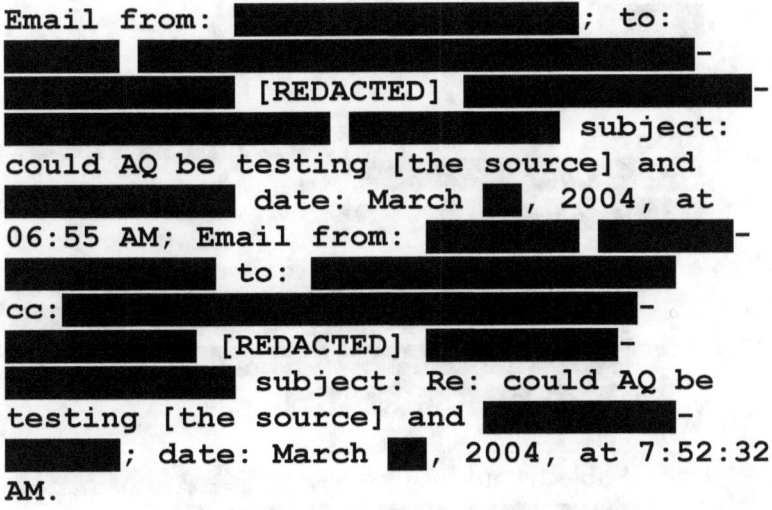

Email from: [REDACTED] ; to:
[REDACTED] -
[REDACTED] -
[REDACTED] subject:
could AQ be testing [the source] and
[REDACTED] date: March ■, 2004, at
06:55 AM; Email from: [REDACTED] -
[REDACTED] to: [REDACTED]
cc: [REDACTED] -
[REDACTED] -
[REDACTED] subject: Re: could AQ be
testing [the source] and [REDACTED] -
[REDACTED] ; date: March ■, 2004, at 7:52:32
AM.

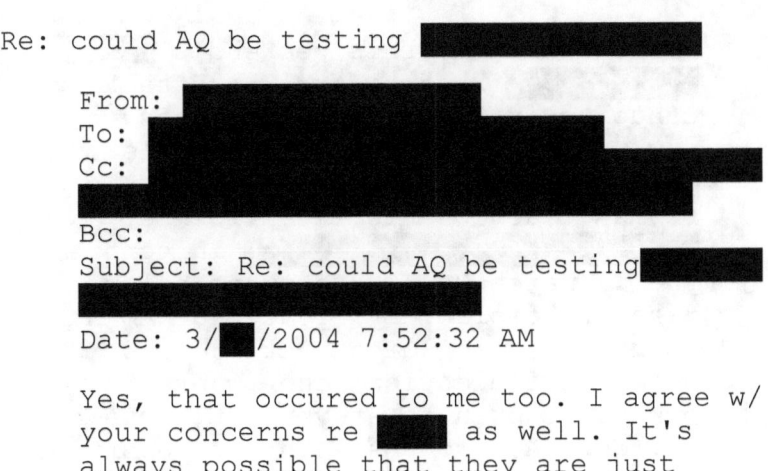

Re: could AQ be testing [REDACTED]

From: [REDACTED]
To: [REDACTED]
Cc: [REDACTED]
Bcc:
Subject: Re: could AQ be testing [REDACTED]

Date: 3/■/2004 7:52:32 AM

Yes, that occured to me too. I agree w/
your concerns re ■ as well. It's
always possible that they are just

hearing the same "rumint" as well.
however, when ███████████ █ ███████████ ▬
███████████████. So I just don't know. But
again, I've been a bit concerned about
██████ too....

Original Text of ████████████████████████
                              -- CTC/UBL --
████████████ 03/██/04 06:55 AM

To: ████████████████████████████████████
██
██
██████████████████████████

cc:
Subject: could AQ be testing ██████████████
████████████████████████████

I was struck by this weekend's ████████ ▬
████████████ reporting re an attack on
conus to influence the elections on
nov. 04. both reported vague "plans",
████████████████████████████ worthless in
terms of actionable intelligence,
████████████████████████████████ in contrast,
the 17 march 04 AQ statement below
makes it explicitly cleac that AQ has
no/no intention of attacking conus
before the election; they want
president bush to stay right whece he
is. Now, AQ knows all threat reporting

causes panic in Washington and that it leaks soon after it is received -- as will the reports from 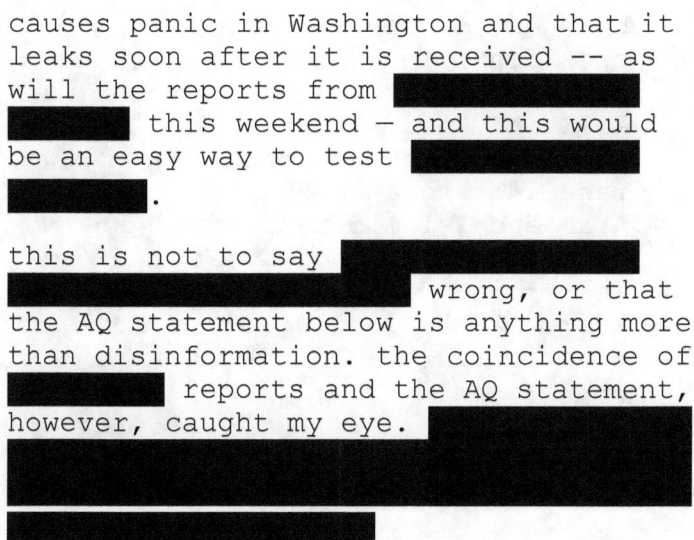 this weekend — and this would be an easy way to test ▮▮▮▮▮▮▮▮.

this is not to say ▮▮▮▮▮▮▮▮▮▮▮▮▮▮▮▮▮ wrong, or that the AQ statement below is anything more than disinformation. the coincidence of ▮▮▮▮▮▮ reports and the AQ statement, however, caught my eye. ▮▮▮▮▮

A word to the idiot Bush[0]

We know you live the worst days of your life in fear of the brigades of death that ruined your life. We tell you we are all keen that you do not lose the forthcoming elections. We are aware that any large-scale operation will destroy your government but we do not want this to happen. We will not find a person dumber[0] than you. You adopt force rather than wisdom and shrewdness. Yes, your stupidity and religious fanaticism is what we want because our nation will not wake up from its sleep unless an enemy emerges that lies in wait for the nation. Actually, there is no difference

between you and [Democratic
presidential candidate John] Kerry.
Kerry will take our nation unawares and
kill it. Kerry and the Democrats
possess enough deception to give a
face-lift to atheism and convince the
Arab and Islamic nation to support it
in the name of modernization.
Therefore, we are very keen that you,
criminal Bush(0), will win the upcoming
elections.

Δ

(U) APPENDIX IV: CIA, Office of General Counsel draft Legal Appendix: Paragraph 5 – Hostile Interrogations: Legal Considerations for CIA Officers, November 26, 2002

D-R-A-F-T
26 November 2001 @ 1600

Hostile Interrogations: Legal Considerations for CIA Officers

1. U.S. federal law makes it a crime for a U.S. citizen to torture someone both at home and abroad, even when directed to do so by superiors.

A. 18 U.S.C. §12340 – 2340B implements the United Nations Convention Against Torture and Other Cruel, Inhumane, or Degrading Treatment or Punishment, and incorporates verbatim the definition of "torture" from that treaty; namely, the Convention defines torture as "an act committed by a person acting under color of law specifically intended to inflict severe physical or mental pain or suffering," where "severe mental suffering" is further defined as "the prolonged mental harm resuiting from" either causing or threatening infliction of severe physical pain; the administration or threat of administration of mind-altering drugs; the threat of imminent death; or threatening to do the above to someone else.

B. Use of necessity as a defense to prosecution in a U.S. court

1. Israel's Supreme Court has recognized that government officials who are prosecuted for torture may use the affirmative defense of necessity – i.e., "for the purpose of saving the life, liberty, body or property, of either himself or his fellow person, from substantial danger of serious harm, imminent from the particular state of things (circumstances), at the requisite timing, and absent alternative means for avoiding the harm."[3] That is, a government officer can avoid criminal prosecution if the torture was necessary to prevent a danger "certain to materialize" and when no other means of preventing the harm are available.

2. The ruling, however, specifically notes that although necessity can be used as a *post factum* defense, it cannot serve as a source of positive, *ab initio* authority for the systemic (even if rare) use of torture as a valid interrogation tool.

3. The U.S. Code does not contain a statutory necessity defense provision, but U.S. common law has recognized an analogous doctrine:

• **State v. Marley**. 509 P.2d 1095, 1097 (1973); Defendants were charged with criminal trespass on the property of Honeywell Corporation in Honolulu. They argued that they were seeking to stop the Vietnam War and raised as one of their defenses the "necessity defense." The court stated:

The "necessity defense" exonerates persons who commit a crime under the pressure of circumstances if the harm that would have resulted from compliance with the law would have significantly exceeded the harm actually resulting from the defendant's breach of the law. Successful use of the "necessiity defense" requires (a) that there is no third and legal alternative available, (b) that the harm to be prevented be imminent, and (c) that a direct, causal relationship be reasonable anticipated to exist between defendant's action and the avoidance of harm.

Although the Marley court decided the necessity defense was not available to these particular defendants, the standard they set out is the norm.

• In **United States v. Seward**, 687 F.2d 1270, 1275 (10th Cir. 1982) (en banc), *cert. denied*, 459 U.S. 1147 (1983), the court held that a defendant may successfully use a defense of necessity to excuse otherwise illegal acts if (1) there is no legal alternative to violating the law, (2) the harm to be prevented is imminent, and (3) a direct, causal relationship is reasonable anticipated to exist between defendant's action and the avoidance of harm. Under the defense of necessity, "one principle remains constant: if there was a reasonable, legal alternative to violating the law, 'a chance both to refuse to do the criminal act and also to avoid the threatened harm,' the defense will fail," *Id*, at 1276, quoting **United States v. Bailey**, 444 U.S. 394 (1980). In proving that there were no legal alternatives available to assist him, a defendant must show he was "confronted with... a crisis which did not permit a selection from among several solutions, some of which did not involve criminal acts." *Id*.

• See also **United States v. Contento-Pachon**. 723 F.2d 691, 695 n.2 (9th Cir. 1984) (defense of necessity available when person faced with a choice of two evils and must decide whether to commit a crime or an alternative act that constitutes a greater evil); **United States v. Nolan**. 700 F.2d 479 ,484 (9th Cir.) (the necessity defense requires a showing that the defendant acted to prevent an imminent harm which no available options could similarly prevent).

• **In sum:** U.S. courts have not yet considered the necessity defense in the context of torture/murder/assault cases, primarily because in cases where one or two individuals were hurt out of necessity, this was treated as a *self-defense* analysis. *See* Tab 2, *supra*. It would, therefore, be a novel application of the necessity defense to avoid prosecution of U.S. officials who tortured to obtain information that saved many lives; however, if we follow the Israeli example, CIA could argue that the torture was necessary to prevent imminent, significant, physical harm to persons, where there is no other available means to prevent the harm.

[3] H.C. 5100/94, 4054/95, 6536/95, 5188/96, 7563/97, 7628/97, 1043/99.

D-R-A-F-T 26 November 2001 @ 1600

Δ

ADDITIONAL MINORITY VIEWS OF SENATOR COBURN, VICE CHAIRMAN CHAMBLISS, SENATORS BURR, RISCH, COATS, AND RUBIO

Δ

ADDITIONAL VIEWS BY SENATOR TOM COBURN, MD, VICE CHAIRMAN CHAMBLISS, SENATORS BURR, RISCH, COATS, AND RUBIO

(U) As parts of the Senate Select Committee on Intelligence (SSCI) "Committee Study of the Interrogation and Detention Program" (hereafter, the "Study") become declassified, it is our hope that, in addition to these and the other Minority views, the Central Intelligence Agency (CIA) response of June, 2013 also be declassified. Interested and objective readers will be able to balance these various views as they make their own assessments of the flaws, errors, initiatives and value of the CIA's detention and interrogation program conducted and terminated in the previous decade.

~~(S//NF)~~ For those who hold already set views, they may or may not be surprised that the CIA agreed with a number of the Study's findings, at least in part, although the CIA disagreed, in substance, with the core assertions of the Study: that the interrogation program provided little valuable intelligence and that the CIA misrepresented the program to the White House, other executive agencies, the Congress and the public (through the media).

(U) As stated in the Minority views and the CIA response, so only briefly reiterated here, the methodology for the Study was inherently flawed. A SSCI investigation of this depth and importance requires that, in addition to a

369

document review, interviews with participants and managers be conducted. This standard approach was included in the terms of reference that established the Study in March, 2009. For a recent and relevant example, the SSCI's investigation into the intelligence failures regarding weapons of mass destruction in Iraq, "U.S. Intelligence Community's Prewar Intelligence Assessments on Iraq," (July, 2004), was based on Committee interviews with more than 200 intelligence community (IC) officers, including analysts and senior officials, in addition to a review of tens of thousands of documents. Some of those individuals were interviewed up to 4 times, as Committee staff worked to reconcile the complex documentary record with the perspectives of those involved in the analytic production. (That report, when published, was supported unanimously by the Committee, 15-0. This is significant in that properly performed reviews tend to gain bipartisan approval.)

(COMMITTEE SENSITIVE) In addition, no Committee hearings were conducted with members of the IC once the Study was initiated in 2009 until it was first voted out of Committee in 2012. In sum, a massive (but still incomplete) outlay of documents was reviewed in isolation (outside of Committee spaces). without the benefit of interpretation or perspective provided by the actual participants in the program.

(COMMITTEE SENSITIVE) Perhaps if such interviews had occurred, the authors of the Study would have had better exposure to the analytic processes that underpin a global collection program that sought, in response to die attacks of 9/11, to assemble an analytic picture of a poorly understood global terrorism network, al-Qa'ida. Thousands of analysts worked with the reports that were derived from the interrogations (most of which were conducted without the use of enhanced interrogation procedures) and thousands of analytic products were generated to build an understanding of the terror organization that attacked us on September 11, 2001. To read the Committee Study, the reader could conclude that majority of those analysts did not properly understand their profession and their products were flawed. That conclusion would be false.

(U) A fundamental fact is missing from the point of departure for the Study: For any nation to respond to an attack by an insurgency, terrorist organization or armed group, the primary source of human intelligence will be detainee reporting. The CIA's program, improvised in its early stages because the CIA had no established protocols to draw on, sought to build the capacity to gather this intelligence by creating a global information network where the intelligence gained from interrogations around the world could be assessed, corroborated and challenged by analysts working in real-time to better develop an intelligence picture of a very real threat whose dimensions and direction were unknown to us.

(U) How detainee reporting is collected – through what protocols of interrogation – is the challenge that every nation, and, in particular, nations bound by the rule of law, must answer. This fundamental question is not addressed in the Study.

(U) Instead, the most adamant supporters of the Study

have declared that the effect of this Study will be that the abuses they assess occurred will never happen again. This is an odd conclusion, in that the CIA's interrogation program was ended in the last decade, and President Obama's Executive Orders put in place measures and procedures that clearly indicate the program would not be reconstituted. If the point of the Study was to end something the supporters of the Study wanted to terminate, the objective was achieved before the Study began.

(U) But if the point of the Study is to ensure that abuses assessed by the supporters of the Study never occur again, the Study made no contribution to ensuring this because it failed to offer recommendations for lawful interrogation protocols for the collection of detainee intelligence in the future. Even more striking than the fact that the Study was completed without conducting interviews is the complete absence of any recommendations, recommendations that could provide meaningful guideposts for the future.

(U) There is a cycle that can be observed in democracies fighting armed groups and relying upon detainee intelligence gained from interrogation. It is a cycle that has occurred in democracies throughout the last century and, in fact, throughout American history.[1] An episode of national security crisis is responded to with urgency and frenzy, and the detention cycle begins. The early stage of the cycle is usually when the instances of brutality may occur. Over time, interrogation protocols are reconciled with the rule of law (and practicality, as brutality does not guarantee good intelligence). A consideration of American, British and Israeli history – to cite three examples of democratic societies – provides examples of this cycle in each country.

~~(S//NF)~~ That this cycle can repeat reflects an apparent weakness in democracies, including our own, in their inability to process and retain "lessons learned." We have certainly seen this elsewhere in the national security sphere – how our various national security institutions have "forgotten," for example, counterinsurgency theory, public diplomacy, and covert influence practices.

(U) This Study has many flaws, articulated in the other Minority views and the CIA response. To that we would add is the failure to extract "lessons learned," in the form of recommendations that provide insights into which interrogation techniques work in gathering foreign intelligence and are consistent with rule-of-law principles. This knowledge, were it to be captured and held in doctrine, would provide the tools for this nation as it continues to face threats from terrorist organization or other armed group overseas. Only in this way could the intent of "never again" be in fact ensured.

(U) The Study provided no such recommendations for the future. Instead it is a partisan prosecutor's brief against history. It is a 6,000 page exercise in the rhetorical trope of synecdoche, where a part – in this case, the most egregious abuses, such as waterboarding – is substituted for the whole – in this case, the entire CIA detention and interrogation program, most of which did not rely on enhanced interrogation techniques and most of which provided the intelligence picture of al-Qai'da in the first decade of the

21st century. We caution any reader of the Study against ever concluding that the threats of today and tomorrow can be addressed without the value of detainee intelligence that provided this picture of al-Qa'ida that allows us to prevail against it in the second decade of the 21st century.

[1] Dr. Coburn is grateful to have had access to *United States Detention Policy in Counter-terrorism and Counterinsurgency Operations: 2001 to 2011*, particularly chapter 1, "Detention in US History from 1775 to 2000," Dr. Ahmed Qureshi, unpublished thesis submitted for the Degree of Philosophy (PhD), Kings College, University of London, 2013.

Δ

SENATORS RISCH, COATS, AND RUBIO ADDITIONAL VIEWS

Δ

ADDITIONAL MINORITY VIEWS OF SENATORS RISCH, COATS, AND RUBIO

(U) As the only two members of both the Senate Foreign Relations Committee and the Senate Select Committee on Intelligence (SSCI), and as a former U.S. Ambassador to Germany, we maintain a unique perspective on declassification of the Study as it pertains to U.S. foreign policy and the security of U.S. embassies and consulates overseas. That perspective was further informed by the Department of State's intelligence chief, who warned the SSCI in 2013 that declassification could endanger U.S. personnel and jeopardize U.S. relations with other countries. This warning was particularly significant following the Benghazi terrorist attacks, which serve as a fresh reminder of the enormous risk facing U.S. embassies and consulates overseas. As a result, we voted against declassification of the Study.

U.S. Foreign Policy Considerations

(TS// ███████████████████ //NF) On June 10, 2013, the SSCI received a classified letter from Assistant Secretary of State Philip Goldberg regarding the potential declassification of the Study. The letter raised two "significant State Department equities" pertaining to foreign policy concerns and the security of diplomatic facilities. With respect to foreign policy concerns, the letter states:

If the report is declassified or disclosed without appropriate preparation or precautions, it could negatively impact foreign relations with multiple U.S. allies and partners who have participated in or have had nationals involved in the detention and interrogation program. Even with some country names redacted, context and publicly available information make it possible to identify some specific countries and facilities. Many of these countries cooperated with the United States on this program based on the understanding that their involvement would not be publicly disclosed. Publicly acknowledging their roles at this stage would have significant implications for our bilateral relationships and future cooperation on a variety of national security priorities, and could impact our relationships with countries even beyond those involved in the program. Should the report be declassified or released in any form, the Department would request notice well in advance to allow for coordination with our embassies and foreign counterparts.

These concerns were not limited to the U.S. Department of State. Multiple diplomatic envoys posted in Washington raised similar concerns with us individually.

Diplomatic Security

(TS// ▓▓▓▓▓▓▓▓▓▓▓▓▓▓▓ //NF) With respect to the security of diplomatic facilities, the letter states: "With heightened threats and ongoing instability in the Middle East, North Africa, and elsewhere, the release of this report has the potential to provoke additional demonstrations against U.S. interests and to increase targeting of U.S. missions and U.S. citizens around the globe." In the days leading up to the SSCI vote to declassify the Study, the Minority also contacted the White House to obtain their views on this issue. The Minority learned that at the time of the vote to declassify the Study, the Executive Branch was already developing security upgrades at various diplomatic facilities to coincide with the expected release of the Study. This fact was confirmed in a letter the SSCI received on April 18, 2014, from White House Counsel Kathryn Ruemmler. This letter stated: "Prior to the release of any information related to the former RDI program, the Administration will also need to take a series of security steps to prepare our personnel and facilities overseas."

Conclusion

(U) While we generally support efforts to provide the American public with as much information as possible, our experiences and the stark warnings provided by the Department of State, the White House, and foreign diplomats serving in Washington made a compelling case to keep this material classified. We hope and pray the declassification process does not jeopardize the safety and security of the men and women who serve our country overseas or U.S. foreign policy. Ultimately, we could not take the risk to vote to declassify the Study, especially given our shared concerns for the utility of the underlying process and report.

Δ Δ Δ